Patent Strategy

Patent Strategy
The Manager's Guide to Profiting from Patent Portfolios

Anthony L. Miele

JOHN WILEY & SONS, INC.
New York • Chichester • Weinheim • Brisbane • Singapore • Toronto

Intellectual Property Series

Early-Stage Technologies: Risk Management, Valuation, and Pricing
by Richard Razgaitis

How to License Technology
by Robert C. Megantz

Intellectual Property Infringement Damages: A Litigation Support Handbook, Second Edition
by Russell L. Parr

Intellectual Property: Licensing and Joint Venture Profit Strategies, Second Edition
by Gordon V. Smith and Russell L. Parr

Licensing Intellectual Property: Legal, Business, and Market Dynamics
by John W. Schlicher

Intellectual Property in the Global Marketplace: Commercial Exploitation and Country-by-Country Profiles, Second Edition
by Melvin Simensky, Lanning G. Bryer, and Neil Wilkof

Profiting from Intellectual Capital: Extracting Value from Innovation
by Patrick H. Sullivan

Technology Licensing: Corporate Strategies for Maximizing Value
by Russell L. Parr and Patrick H. Sullivan

Trademark Valuation
by Gordon V. Smith

Valuation of Intellectual Property and Intangible Assets, Third Edition
by Gordon V. Smith and Russell L. Parr

Value-Driven Intellectual Capital: How to Convert Intangible Corporate Assets into Market Value
by Patrick H. Sullivan

This publication is designed to provide accurate and authoritative information in regard to the subject matter covered. It is sold with the understanding that the publisher is not engaged in rendering legal, accounting, or other professional services. If legal advice or other expert assistance is required, the services of a competent professional person should be sought.

Library of Congress Cataloging-in-Publication Data:

Miele, Anthony L.
    Patent strategy : the manager's guide to profiting from patent portfolios / Anthony L. Miele.
        p. cm.
    Includes index.
    ISBN 0-471-39075-5 (cloth : alk. paper)
    1. Patent practice—United States. 2. Patent suits—United States.
  3. Patents—United States. 4. Industrial property—United States—Management.
  5. Industrial management—United States. I. Title.

KF3120 .M54 2001
346.7304'86—dc12

                             00-068541

Printed in the United States of America.

10 9 8 7 6 5 4 3 2 1

To Adriana, Anthony, Rafael, and Nancy

to my parents

and to

Ann Miele, Louis Miele, Ruby Thomas,
and Henry Thomas

Contents

Acknowledgments

I extend thanks to my family. I also must thank all those colleagues who have helped me in one way or another on this book, including (and I fear I may miss someone—please forgive me) Bruce Bernstein, George Sirilla, Glenn Perry, Dale Lazar, Lynn Eccleston, Paul White, Kim Sacre, Violet White, Jordan Weinstein, Jamie, Sandra Felder, Danielle Avolio, Paul Gennari, Paul White, Christina Patrick, and Jack Barufka. The investment of many defines achievement.

Foreword

By George M. Sirilla

We are living in an age of exploding technology—computers; software; ultra-high speed optical communication networks for the internet, telecommunications, and cable television; human, animal, and plant genetics; machine vision; pharmaceutical "miracle" drugs; business method patents; and so forth—an age where increased emphasis has been placed on securing, protecting, and enforcing intellectual property rights in such technology.

Running parallel with this technological explosion, and to a great degree enhancing and contributing to it, is an explosion in our patent system that began in the 1980s when Congress created a special court of appeals, the Federal Circuit Court of Appeals, as the sole and exclusive appellate court to hear *all* the appeals in patent infringement cases in this country. Prior to that time, appeals from United States District Courts in patent infringement cases were taken to the circuit court of appeals for the geographical region that included the district court in question. For example, an appeal from a patent infringement lawsuit in the United States District Court for the Southern District of New York would have to be taken to the Second Circuit Court of Appeals, also sitting in New York.

There were 11 such circuits, and their decisions on various points of patent law were not always consistent from circuit to circuit. Also, it was difficult to sustain patents in litigation at that time and even more difficult (and exceedingly rare) to secure a high damage award. The Federal Circuit Court of Appeals has changed all that. Now patents are upheld in litigation more often than not, and eight- and nine-figure damage and/or settlement awards are not uncommon in patent cases. It might be noted that prior to the formation of the Federal Circuit Court of Appeals, there were only a few reported decisions where the patent damage award exceeded one million dollars.

Let us consider for a moment how damage awards in patent cases have changed since the establishment of the Federal Circuit Court of Appeals. One of the first cases at that time involved patent rights on doxycycline, and its damage award of 56 million dollars was hailed in the media as the largest damage award ever secured in patent litigation. Later, in a patent case on an oil well drilling tool, the damage award was 200 million dollars. That was followed by a damage award for over 100 million dollars on patent rights covering so called soft-casts for broken bones. Then, there was the *Polaroid vs. Kodak* case on instant photography that wound up with Polaroid securing a 900 million dollar damage award as well as a 94 million dollar damage award for infringement of a patent on automatic camera focusing. In the office furniture industry, there was a damage aware of 211 million dollars in a patent infringement lawsuit involving electrified space-dividing office panels.

Those are only a few of the cases that have appeared in reported decisions involving large damage awards. There have also been media reports of nine-figure settlements in patent litigation in the last 10 years. For example, Texas Instruments was reported to have secured over 600 million dollars in settlement of litigation over its patent rights on DRAMs, and Proctor and Gamble was reported to have received 125 million dollars in settlement of litigation over its patent on soft batch chocolate chip cookies.

Notably, most of the highest patent damage awards result from litigation between head-to-head competitors in a particular industry where valuable market share was at stake. For that reason, not only must business managers today be mindful of the importance of identifying and patenting useful inventions developed in their own companies, but they must also be alert to patents issuing to their competitors.

Anthony Miele's book provides the kind of well-organized and easily digested strategic information that every technology company manager should know and needs to know about patents—from avoiding patent liability to profiting from patents. His work provides useful and clear insights into the procedures and strategies for securing optimum patent protection, here and abroad, for your company's innovations. It also provides a sound and accurate explanation of the risks, uncertainties, costs, and benefits of licensing, litigation, and settlement of patent disputes.

At the end of the book, there is a chapter summarizing important provisions of the recently enacted American Inventors Protection Act of 1999. You will also find a number of appendices containing sample patents, including business method patents, and lists identifying patent lawsuits brought, as well as patents sought, in the last decade involving computer-related technology.

All in all, this well-conceived and thorough work should prove to be a useful reference for all those managers of tomorrow's technology companies.

Patent Strategy

CHAPTER 1

Patents in Context— Incorporating Patents into Your Business

1.1 THE IMPORTANCE OF PATENTS

Patents and patent strategies are playing a bigger role in such information age technologies as biotechnology and life sciences, telecommunications, the internet, and computers. These technologies are on the cutting edge, entering all facets of everyday life, from food and medicine, to video conferencing using the internet, to making travel arrangements on the web. The new services and products being offered require technologies from previously segregated markets. The distinctions between these markets are blurring, with many companies utilizing technologies now residing in a "common market." As a result, competition among businesses is changing.

In order to compete, companies are acquiring interests in other companies having the expertise needed to enter new markets, while others, even former competitors, are partnering with each other. In this setting, businesses are using patents as a weapon to hinder competitors from encroaching upon their developed technology, and as a shield to deter others from forcing them out of their own market. Businesses are also using patents to increase their balance sheets, to realize certain tax advantages, or to justify higher valuations, (e.g., allowing them to charge investors (or acquirers) higher share prices or helping convince an underwriter to increase the starting price per share when taking the company public.) Patents are also used to better a business' position in deals such as strategic alliances and value added reseller (VAR) and original equipment manufacturer (OEM) agreements. However, when a business manages its patent rights poorly, valuable rights may be forfeited to the public domain, or worse— to a competitor who can now either charge the business a toll for its use of key technologies or force the business out of its own market.

Depending upon how a business deals with patents, they can have a positive or negative impact on the business' general efforts. Some have benefited

1

enormously from the patent system. IBM's patent and intellectual property licensing efforts generate more than a billion dollars in revenue annually. Nicholas Donofrio, IBM's senior vice president and group executive of corporate technology and manufacturing, credits IBM's patent portfolio with a role in the successful generation of more than $30 billion worth of OEM agreements signed by IBM's Technology Group in 1999. Recently acquired companies like WebTV and Amati Communications each commanded substantial purchase prices, rumored to be due in large part to their substantial patent portfolios. Priceline.com capitalized on the patent system by patenting its reverse auction technology. However, a lack of attention to patents have caused companies problems. For example, in 1993, Eastman Kodak terminated one of its imaging technology subsidiaries after Wang Laboratories, Inc. brought a patent infringement suit against the subsidiary.

Middle and upper level managers need a basic understanding of the patent process and its laws and strategies from a business-goal perspective so they can recognize the significance of patents in relation to their business efforts, and can employ proper patent management to complement those efforts. This knowledge will be important when management and executives make patent-related decisions such as whether a patent infringement study must be performed; whether the budget for patent matters should be changed; whether to license certain patent technology; and whether to sue a competitor for patent infringement.

Decisions about patents will involve executives even at the highest levels. Patents are frequently worth millions or tens of millions of dollars (sometimes even hundreds of millions), and can be highly pertinent to key partner relationships the business may enter into. They can affect the bottom line, the balance sheet, and the value of the company as a whole. Even more critical, in the off chance key patents are owned by a competitor, markets commanding a substantial portion of the business' total annual revenues could be in jeopardy.

Businesses that provide information-age technological products or services derive profits from their use of technologies. A local telephone company may assemble a telephone network platform to provide services such as call-waiting, call-forwarding, and voice mail. A computer and communications equipment manufacturer may develop and manufacture computers and communications hardware for use in the telephone network platform. A software publisher may develop database software for managing a database to be accessed by the telephone network platform.

In each of these instances, technology is a critical part of the product or service the business offers to its customers, and the unimpeded availability of key technologies can be imperative to the success of the business. Businesses that own patents covering key technologies are therefore at an advantage, while those that do not own such patents are at a disadvantage.

1.2 MARKET PRESERVATION

A properly executed patent plan can preserve a company's existence in the market. For example, DVD consortium members obtaining patents are able to stay in the DVD market; their patent portfolio offsets patent royalties required by competitors so that the royalties do not become cost prohibitive. As another example, patents covering the activities of competitors serve as a deterrent to those competitors enjoining the company from using its own technology and from participating in its markets.

1.3 SHAREHOLDER VALUE

Patents can be used to command royalties, and are assets which could affect the valuation of the company. Thus, patents can complement exit strategies such as initial public offerings, mergers, and acquisitions. Patents defined in terms of their relevance to the business can serve as a substantial factor in the valuation of the business. Similarly, acquired companies have commanded substantially larger purchase prices when the company has a successful strategically executed patent program. Large companies have acquired ownership interests in companies, in part because of their patent portfolio.

Patents can indirectly contribute to shareholder value by preserving a business and deterring others from suing the company. Patents can have an impact on, and sometimes directly affect, the bottom line in terms of profits and revenues. This will affect the earnings in a given quarter or year, and thus the perceived value of the company.

1.4 DEALS

If proper patent strategies are employed, substantial deals can be negotiated with more ease and closed quicker, with less argument as to intellectual property interests. The existence of a patent filing before contract negotiations begin clears up any ambiguity as to whether ownership of a particular technology would be transferred to the customer as part of the contract, or whether that technology was already owned by the company before the contract was entered into. In the case of trade secret technology, a company which has a patent pending can more freely disclose its technology to prospective customers, thus flexing its muscles without fear of losing its protection, whereas, if the company's only protection is its trade secret rights, it will have to get a nondisclosure agreement signed before showing its product to a prospective customer. Many customers, small and large, will not sign nondisclosure agreements. Even if they do, the secrecy obligation they agree to may last for only a limited time, perhaps one to three years. Agreements negotiated for longer periods of time tend to get undercut with hard-to-recognize language providing loopholes and booby traps. Even with a good nondisclosure agreement, there is no guarantee that employees of both companies will protect the information.

For example, a fictitious company called Capital Software receives a request for proposal (RFP) from a leading telecommunications company. The RFP asks for certain types of information, poses a list of questions, and requires that all information requested be supplied and that all questions be answered. The RFP also requires that all information provided in the response not be deemed confidential or proprietary. This creates tension between Capital Software's legal department and its sales department. Sales wants to remove all obstacles to making the sale, while Legal remains concerned that the information provided will no longer be the property of the company. Even if Capital Software responds to the RFP, it faces a risk that a competitor will be awarded the contract, while Capital Software has divulged trade secret information to the telecommunications company. Patents can provide companies like Capitol Software with an added safeguard. Even if Capital Software discloses valuable information, it can rely on its patent rights to protect against third parties using the technology without its permission.

1.5 THE NATURE OF PATENT RIGHTS

Patent rights are like options. Any company that develops its own ideas automatically acquires, with no additional effort, for a limited time, patent rights (i.e., the option to file for and obtain a patent covering such ideas). To exercise the option (secure the patent rights), a patent application must be timely filed. Bad patent management habits can cause the option to be needlessly forfeited. The ability to obtain a patent could be diminished or negated completely.

1.6 PATENTS AT THE MANAGEMENT LEVEL

Several business objectives are common to most businesses. They strive to generate sustained profits and, where possible, to increase those profits. Businesses must successfully manage their cash flow. It is also critical that they meet revenue goals, and generate perceived shareholder value. Other common objectives include achieving a sustained growth in revenues, maintaining good morale among company personnel, maximizing the quality of the company's products and services, and achieving a positive public image.

It is difficult to devise and implement a plan to achieve these and other objectives. Steps will need to be defined, clarified, and scheduled, and their success needs to be measured. When the objectives are long-range, they are more vague, and the plans needed to achieve them are typically more complex and less predictable. Planning for an accomplishment in five years is less certain, while short-range plans dealing with the immediate year will be more comprehensive and specific.

Patents are long-range objectives, and are thus difficult to incorporate into the planning process. It takes two to four years to obtain a patent. It is difficult to speculate on the importance a given patent application will have four or even 10 years into the future, especially when patents are easily misunderstood and the yet-to-be obtained patent is still an unknown quantity.

However, a well-developed and implemented patent plan is within the reach of most businesses. Many businesses implement patent plans which allow them to produce assets and business tools that can create value. Meanwhile, the effort and cash needed to earn their patent rights (including research and development and related efforts and costs) have already been spent. As many companies have demonstrated, patent efforts need not divert the attention of management away from priorities like sales revenues goals, cash management, earnings, and shareholder value. Nor do patents need to hinder core efforts supporting the business, such as sales, finance, product development, and marketing.

When properly pursued, patents can have a strategic or even a tactical relevance to core business efforts, and should complement and augment other areas. The key is to incorporate good intellectual property habits into the business' culture. Just as the doors are locked at night to prevent theft, routine steps can be taken to protect and preserve the interests of the company in its information and technology.

Managers tend to pay more attention to the areas into which their superiors inquire most. Thus, for example, a sales manager may give attention to achieving sales revenue goals at the expense of training the sales team. A prolonged neglect of sales training can, of course, adversely affect sales—by, for example, causing a decline in morale and an inefficient use of resources towards sales efforts.

Similarly, R&D efforts may take priority at the expense of obtaining, with patents, ownership rights in the developed techniques and products. However, the value of the expended efforts to develop such techniques and products is diminished if the company's use of such techniques and products can be brought into question where others may freely use the same with less or no R&D costs.

Managers in technology-driven businesses will not knowingly produce products while forfeiting the right to use the developments or forfeiting a proprietary interest in the same. Nonetheless, their focus is on producing a product, as it should be. The basic precautions they take regarding intellectual property rights, if further honed, would go a long way toward maximizing the value of the R&D efforts invested.

Before a business can improve its intellectual property habits, it will encounter a transition barrier. Just as with the introduction of any new process or system (e.g., consider the logistical difficulties associated with switching all of the business' computers to a new word processing package), there will be a barrier to entry. Without the support and mandate from the top, initial investment will not become quickly, fully, and properly part of the company's habits. The same goes for patent management. At companies like AT&T, Lucent, IBM, and Texas Instruments, just about everyone has a part in protecting the business' patent rights. For example, IBM regularly patents its developments. When it does not patent a particular technology, it publishes to reduce the risk others will patent the same development and thereby bar IBM from using its own developed technology.

The introduction of such a "lock the door" culture requires the involvement of the executive team managers and technical personnel alike. An incentive plan is usually put in place to motivate engineers and developers (1) to record their developments on a regular basis, thereby producing evidence of their developments, and (2) to submit disclosures of them for patenting or publishing as may be appropriate.

Middle and upper-level managers now have an increasing need to recognize the significance of patents in relation to the business, and to incorporate a patent strategy in short-term internal business planning and in long-term corporate strategic planning. Those already executing a patent policy can benefit from improving their current understanding of patents and the range of opportunities they present. Promoting an understanding of patents among business executives will improve the communication between executives and patent counsel. A goal of this book is to bridge the communication gap that may exist between the decision makers in a business and patent attorneys.

While important patent issues are presented to the reader, there is no absolute advice as to how a particular business should address a patent problem when it arises. The way a business handles each patent situation can, and should, vary, depending upon many factors, including the size of the business, the business' financial situation, public opinion, and the mission and philosophy of the business. Accordingly, it is always critical to carefully evaluate with patent counsel the legal effects a proposed course of action could have. Moreover, any action or inaction will have its own set of risks, which will need to be weighed against the benefits.

1.7 PATENTS DESCRIBED, IN COMPARISON TO OTHER TYPES OF INTELLECTUAL PROPERTY

Patents can be distinguished from other types of property in some respects yet are similar in others. Property rights give an owner some type of dominion or control over something. In many respects, property rights serve as an incentive for the owner to invest in, or add value to, something. For example, real property rights may give an owner dominion over land. Because the owner retains control over the land, the owner may invest time and effort to improve the land and then reap the rewards of that time and effort.

Intellectual property rights provide people with dominion over ideas or information embodied in a form worthy of protection. Some of the types of intellectual property rights are trademarks, trade secrets, copyrights, and patents. Trademarks (or service marks) give their owner dominion over how they identify their product (or service), so their owner need not fear that others will use an identical or confusingly similar name. An example of a trademark is the brand name "Coke®" used to identify a carbonated beverage. Trade secrets give their owner dominion over valuable "secrets" properly guarded by the owner. An example of a trade secret is the recipe for the Coke® brand beverage. Copyrights give their owner dominion over the way an idea is expressed in some tangible medium. An example of a copyrighted work is a book, movie, or song. U.S. patents (utility patents) give the owner temporary dominion over new advances in technology as embodied in a new and useful invention. The invention may be a process, machine, manufactured item, or composition of matter. An example of a (formerly) patented invention is Samuel Morse's telegraph. The term "patent" as used in this book, refers to a utility patent. There are other types of patents, namely design patents and plant patents, which are beyond the scope of this book.

If an invention is both novel and unobvious, the invention may be patentable. Patents are granted for a limited term, which historically expires 17 years from the date the patent is granted. For patent applications filed after June 8, 1995 (with limited exceptions), the patent term will expire 20 years from the date the patent application is filed. Through its life, a patent gives its owner the right to exclude others from making, using, or selling the invention in the United States and its territories. If someone uses a technology covered by a patent without permission from the patent owner, the patent owner will be legally entitled to recover damages no less than a reasonable royalty, and may be able to have the unauthorized use stopped for the remainder of the patent's term.

Obtaining patents is more involved and expensive than other types of intellectual property. In order to obtain patent rights, for example, an applicant must undergo an application process akin to a judicial proceeding. In addition, receipt of a patent may require waiting two or more years and paying thousands of dollars in government fees as well as tens of thousands of dollars in attorney fees. Much more attention and effort must be devoted to deciding when to apply for a patent and the scope of protection needed in order for the patent to be of sufficient value to the business. Therefore, a decision to pursue patent protection will not be automatic. The cost and burden of filing for a patent need to be weighed against its anticipated benefit. Before applying for a patent on an invention, a technology search is frequently obtained.

A copyright registration may be obtained in less than a year for a modest filing fee, without the help of an attorney. Copyright, and also trade secret, procedures allow the applicant to employ a standard process to secure his or her rights, without concern as to whether or how the rights should be secured. For example, if an author desires copyright protection for a work (e.g., a computer program or a painting), the author simply places a copyright notice on the work and optionally also files an application to register the copyright with the U.S. Copyright Office. In fact, these steps are not even necessary, as the mere creation of a work will give the author rights under the copyright laws.

Each type of intellectual property offers its own degree of protection for its owner. In order for there to be copyright infringement, the accused infringer must have had access to the work, and there must be some evidence of copying (e.g., the works are very similar to each other). In order for there to be trade secret infringement, there must have been an improper taking of the secret information. If someone independently creates the same technology or discovers the secret technology by reverse-engineering, they cannot be liable for trade secret infringement. Patents are easier to infringe unintentionally. Liability for patent infringement does not require copying or deriving the technology from a patent. If a company uses patented technology without permission, even if the company independently develops the technology, it is liable for patent infringement. Risks to a patent infringer may include being banned from using the technology altogether and having to pay up to three times the calculated profits lost by the patent owner, plus costs, attorney fees, and interest. At a minimum, a patent infringer would be liable for a reasonable royalty for its use of the patented technology.

1.8 OVERVIEW OF THE BOOK

This book proposes a general approach to patent policy which includes four main objectives.

1. The first objective is to minimize liability for patent infringement to third parties. To achieve this objective, the firm should be aware of patents owned by competitors and obtain patents covering competitors' activities as a deterrent to being sued by those competitors.
2. A second objective is to obtain patents for technological advancements which are already being developed within the business. An investment has already been made to develop these advancements. By obtaining patents, assets which can be bought and sold like personal property, the business can leverage additional value from this investment, thereby increasing the value of the business.
3. A third objective is to obtain patents in order to strengthen the business' position in dealings with third parties. As one example, when entering into a business venture with another company, the business that owns key patents may be able to negotiate a larger ownership interest in the venture. As another example, a standards committee may be considering

adopting a new technological standard. In that situation, the owner of a patent covering the proposed standard is in a better position to utilize the standard technology than another business with no patent.

4. A fourth objective is to use patents as a source of income for the business. The income could be substantial, greatly increasing the business' profit margin, or it could be more modest, merely offsetting the cost of a patent acquisition program.

CHAPTER 2

An Overview of Patents

2.1 INTRODUCTION

A U.S. patent gives its owner the right to exclude others from making, using, or selling the invention throughout the United States and its territories. If someone uses the technology covered by a patent without permission from the patent owner, the patent owner may sue the infringer, and may be legally entitled to lost profits or at least a reasonable royalty, plus pre-judgment interest. The patent owner may even have the infringer prevented from continuing its unauthorized use of the technology. If the infringement was willful, the damages could be increased. By giving these rights to a patent owner, the patent laws were created to give an incentive for innovation.

Before patent rights are given to an applicant, the patent applicant must show that it has contributed something deserving of these valuable rights. For example, the invention must be thoroughly disclosed so that someone who is skilled in the pertinent technology could make and use the invention without an undue amount of effort or experimentation. In addition, the invention protected must be novel (i.e., not in the public domain) and not obvious in view of technology in the public domain. That is, the invention must not be suggested or taught by prior activity (usually limited to non-secret activity) in the pertinent technological area. In short, the applicant is only given the property rights to a defined range of technology in exchange for fully disclosing a new, nonobvious invention. Ideally, the applicant is given an economic advantage, and the public benefits by having early access to the disclosed know-how (see Exhibit 2.1).

2.2 THE INITIAL STAGES OF A PATENT PROGRAM (BEFORE PROSECUTION)

A business' interface with the patent system begins with its technological research and development. Technological developments are monitored, and patent protection is considered for valuable developments. The patent protection process should be started as soon as possible to prevent losing patent

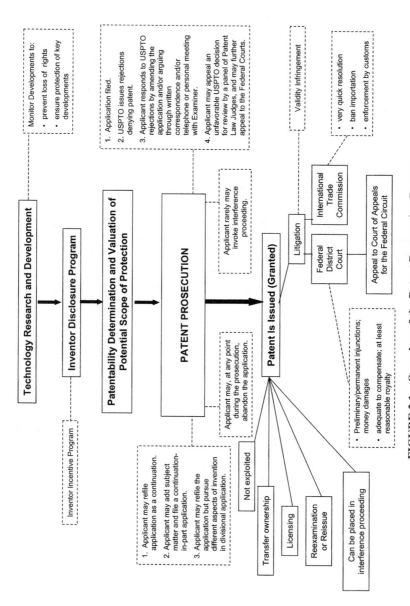

FIGURE 2.1 Overview of the Patent Prosecution Process

Technology Research and Development

Inventor Disclosure Program

Patentability Determination and Valuation of Potential Scope of Protection

PATENT PROSECUTION

Patent Is Issued (Granted)

Litigation

Federal District Court

International Trade Commission

Appeal to Court of Appeals for the Federal Circuit

Monitor Developments to:
• prevent loss of rights
• ensure protection of key developments

1. Application filed.
2. USPTO issues rejections denying patent.
3. Applicant responds to USPTO rejections by amending the application and/or arguing through written correspondence and/or telephone or personal meeting with Examiner.
4. Applicant may appeal an unfavorable USPTO decision for review by a panel of Patent Law Judges, and may further appeal to the Federal Courts.

Validity Infringement

• very quick resolution
• ban importation
• enforcement by customs

Applicant rarely may invoke interference proceeding.

Inventor Incentive Program

Applicant may, at any point during the prosecution, abandon the application.

1. Applicant may refile application as a continuation.
2. Applicant may add subject matter and file a continuation-in-part application.
3. Applicant may refile the application but pursue different aspects of invention in divisional application.

Not exploited

Transfer ownership

Licensing

Reexamination or Reissue

Can be placed in interference proceeding

• Preliminary/permanent injunctions; money damages
• adequate to compensate; at least reasonable royalty

12

rights. For example, failing to file a patent application before a public use or disclosure of the technology could cause forfeiture of foreign patent rights. Special attention should also be devoted to identifying key technological developments and obtaining sufficient patent protection, as key technologies are most likely to be used by the business and its competitors.

An invention disclosure program may be in place whereby inventors, typically including members of the technical staff, will record their ideas and innovations and present them in the form of a shortened disclosure form to a patent coordinator.

An evaluation is then made for each technological innovation of interest to determine whether patent protection should be sought. It is very important to determine not only whether a patent could be obtained, but also whether the probable scope of patent protection is broad enough for the patent to be of value to the business. Patentability does not guarantee patent value. Patents are easier to obtain if the scope of protection being sought is narrow. However, if a patent's scope of protection is too narrowly defined, it may then be easier for competitors and prospective paying licensees to avoid infringement, using equally effective technology not covered by the patent.

If it appears that a patent can be obtained, and the scope of protection will be sufficiently broad, a decision may be made to apply for a patent. The patent application process is called patent prosecution. During patent prosecution, a patent attorney will embark on an ongoing negotiation process with a patent examiner employed by the U.S. Patent and Trademark Office. The patent attorney represents the patent owner, and will attempt to obtain a patent with a maximized scope of protection surrounding a particular technology or a technological development. The patent examiner represents the public interest, and requires each patent application to comply with several statutory requirements before the application issues into a patent.

2.3 PATENT PROSECUTION IS COMMENCED

During patent prosecution, the applicant is presented with a number of different options and strategies from which to choose. The applicant may pursue patent protection for a particular technology in one single patent application, or it may file several related patent applications covering concepts directed to that same technology. An applicant may prosecute an application directed to one concept of a technology, and then later file a continuation application stemming from the first application directed to another aspect of the same technology. If the original patent application contains different inventions, divisional applications stemming from the original parent application may be filed, with each divisional application focusing on a separate invention. If the applicant wishes to add material, or add other inventions to a patent application, the applicant may file a continuation-in-part application stemming from the parent application.

A provisional patent application may be filed before filing a regular patent application. Provisional applications allow businesses to secure an early filing date, but before a patent can be obtained, the provisional must be supplemented with the filing of a regular patent application within 12 months of the provisional filing.

Provisional patents do not receive an examination, and their government filing fees are much less than those of a regular application. Thus, the costs associated with filing and the examination process can be deferred for up to one year.

During patent prosecution, the U.S. Patent and Trademark Office administers the patent laws, and assigns a patent examiner to examine the application for compliance with pertinent statutory requirements such as novelty, non-obviousness, and sufficiency of disclosure of the invention. The patent examiner acts as a quasi-judge in determining, for example, whether the subject matter defined by each claim defines an invention which is novel and non-obvious.

After a patent application is filed, the examiner will perform a first examination. The examiner will search for evidence known as "prior art" (for example, patents and published articles), which indicates the status of the pertinent technology when the application was filed. The examiner will then evaluate the application with respect to the located "prior art" to determine novelty and non-obviousness.

The examiner may, and customarily will, issue an initial and at least one subsequent Office Action, an official document which rejects the application as attempting to claim technology which is unpatentable because it is not novel and/or it is obvious.

In response to each Office Action, the patent attorney will prepare and submit a response which can include remarks addressing the examiner rejections and amendments to the claims and other parts of the application.

If a patent examiner cannot be persuaded to grant a patent with a broad enough scope of protection, the applicant may appeal the patent examiner's decision, and have it reviewed by a panel of patent law judges. The applicant may further appeal an unfavorable decision by the patent law judges to the federal courts.

An interference proceeding may be initiated if the scope of protection being sought during patent prosecution is very close to, or identical to, the scope of protection sought by another in a patent application, or to the scope of protection defined in a recently issued patent. In an interference proceeding, a panel of patent law judges, called the Board of Patent Appeals and Interferences, determines the rightful owner of the technology and, accordingly, who may claim that technology in a patent. The proceeding mainly revolves around determining who was first to conceive the invention and diligently reduce it to practice. Issues of patentability may be raised in an interference proceeding. Therefore, once involved in an interference proceeding, any or all parties to the proceeding could end up forfeiting the ownership rights of the technology if it is shown not to be patentable.

Only a small percentage of patent applications and newly issued patents end up in interference proceedings. When they do, however, the proceeding can be very distracting and costly. An interference can be difficult for any party to endure, and the financial strain can be even more detrimental to small companies.

2.4 AFTER THE PATENT IS GRANTED

Once a patent is issued, the patent owner has several options, assuming the patent is not placed in an interference proceeding, or a reexamination of the patent is not commenced by the U.S. Patent and Trademark Office. Reexamination may be ordered if new evidence has been discovered that brings the patentability of the invention into question.

Once past these obstacles, the owner may exploit the patent in order to obtain income for the business by using one of several methods. The patent owner may transfer ownership of the patent or license the patent. Alternatively, the owner may litigate to obtain damages for past infringement, to obtain royalties for future use, and/or to stop the infringing party from continuing to use the patented technology for the remaining term of the patent.

The patent owner also can sue any party who is making, using, or selling the invention, or any party who is inducing or contributing to such infringement. Therefore, defendants of a patent infringement suit can include manufacturers, wholesalers, retailers, and ultimate consumers.

Patent litigation, however, presents risks for the patent owner. During litigation, the accused infringer can assert that it does not infringe the patent, and it can challenge the validity as well as the enforceability of the patent. If the accused infringer is successful in court, the patent owner could find its patent invalid or unenforceable. Patent litigation also is quite costly, and often involves complicated legal and technical issues. In addition, patent litigation can last for several years. According to a survey conducted in 1999 by the American Intellectual Property Law Association, the median total costs (of those estimated by respondents to the survey) for patent litigation (where the dollar amount at risk is $10–$100 million) through the end of the suit was $2,225,000. The survey determined also that the median cost for a similar litigation through discovery was $1,491,000.

Of course, equally damaging risks are present for the accused infringer. The accused infringer could have to pay substantial money damages, up to three times the damages to the patent owner if its infringement is willful. The accused infringer might also be legally prevented from using the technology for the remaining life of the patent. For these reasons, the majority of all patent controversies are settled without a trial, and a patent licensing arrangement is entered into by the patent owner and the accused infringer.

In many instances, patents are litigated not in the federal courts but before the International Trade Commission (ITC). The ITC disposes of patent issues much faster than the Federal courts, because it imposes shorter time frames within which to handle the various aspects of the case. Thus, the effort that must be expended by a plaintiff or defendant during ITC litigation is quite intense, and large costs can accumulate in a short amount of time.

CHAPTER 3

Strategies for Managing Patent Liability

3.1 PATENT LITIGATION AND ITS COSTS

Patent liability can harm, even cripple, a technology-driven business. Many such businesses use information-age technologies in their products or services, and derive profits from those technologies. Patent liability can either preclude a business from using technologies, or cause it to pay a toll for that use. An internet service provider (ISP) may have to pay patent royalties in order to legally implement a network platform providing access to certain internet services. If the patent owner seeks to enjoin the ISP from using certain technologies, the ISP may be forced to purchase the network platform from another vendor or even utilize an outdated network platform. An equipment manufacturer may be required to pay a high royalty to develop and manufacture computer and communications hardware, making it difficult for the manufacturer to compete with other manufacturers. Similarly, a database software vendor may need to pay royalties to patent owners because of the technologies it is incorporating into its software. Those royalties can put a strain on the software vendor's ability to compete as well.

The cost to defend a patent suit can by itself cripple some businesses. As mentioned above, the median costs for patent litigation through trial can be $2.2M or more. Even if the business survives defending a patent suit, the cost of patent litigation could offset any added profits the business could make by avoiding the cost of patent royalties. If a business is successful in its plea, and the patent is declared invalid, the business' victory will be worthy of limited celebration as its competitors will then be free to use the technology as well.

Litigation itself will subject the business to other costs as well. The drain on management and key company personnel is a major one. Management must be careful not to focus its attention on core business efforts at the expense of giving the needed attention to a patent suit. If the litigation is neglected, the lawsuit could be lost and/or legal resources could be inefficiently utilized.

A patent suit can severely hinder management especially where the company has less than $100 million in revenue. The company may need to hold off on making certain sales, and customers may hesitate before purchasing products or entering into license agreements. Customers may even be co-defendants in the lawsuit. If the company is public, the marketability of the company's shares may be affected, lowering the value of the stock. These effects are over and above the cash an intellectual property lawsuit will consume on a monthly basis, easily $100,000 per month and more. For a smaller company spending between $500,000 and $1 million per month in cash for overhead, $100,000 of added monthly expense can be detrimental.

The President, the CEO, the CFO, and other key technical personnel cannot be insulated from the law suit, and will inevitably be distracted from other efforts. This can divert the company's efforts not only over the short term. It can also adversely affect the quality of products and services, sales, and re-engineering or streamlining efforts. The patent suit may also have long term effects, such as delaying an entry into a new market, which may become critical to the company's continued growth or presence within a particular industry. If the delay is too long, the company could forego entry into the market altogether.

The time and energy intellectual property litigation will drain from key personnel will be significant. The time required may involve several hours per week in discussions with legal counsel and personnel within the company, as well as in investigative efforts and strategy discussions pertaining to the litigation. Undoubtedly numerous company personnel will be called to testify in depositions, responding to questions of opposing counsel. Time must be spent gathering documents in response to discovery requests and in reviewing those documents, and preparing for the depositions.

The patent owner also faces dangers in suing an accused infringer for patent infringement, although those dangers may be outweighed by the expected returns. In addition to the high cost of litigation, the patent owner runs the risk of having its patent declared invalid or unenforceable. Nonetheless, there are many benefits to litigating patents, and there are many plaintiffs who will aggressively assert their patent rights. Exhibits 3.1 and 3.2 show the rising litigation in the computer and communications areas. Businesses using technologies in these and other areas should not be surprised if they face the threat of patent litigation.

The following are examples of instances where patent rights have been litigated by their owners.

- In 1994, Connor Peripherals, Inc. was sued by Iomega Corp. for using Iomega's patented tape-drive technology. The patent lawsuit was settled shortly thereafter.[1]
- In 1994, IBM Corp. was sued by Data General Corp. for patent infringement.[2]

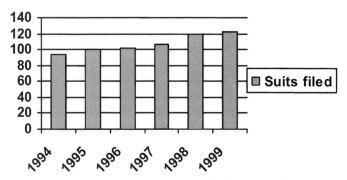

EXHIBIT 3.1   Patent Litigation: Communications and Telecom Technologies*

*The litigated patents were classified in the following technology classes (established by the USPTO): 348, 386, 358, 382, 345, 342, 343, 370, 381, 379, 178, 375, 455, 341, 367, 334, 332, or 329

- On October 9, 1990, 900 Million Productions was sued by First Data Resources Inc., a subsidiary of American Express Information Services Corporation.

    First Data charged patent infringement of certain telephone technologies in 900 Million Productions' "900" service called "The Game," and sought damages as well as an injunction prohibiting the 900 Million Productions company from further use of the technology. The patents were licensed at that time to Call Interactive, a joint venture of the American Express Company and AT&T.

- Early in 1994, Health Payment Review sued GMIS, asserting that a GMIS product called "ClaimCheck" was infringing Health Payment Review's patent rights.[3]

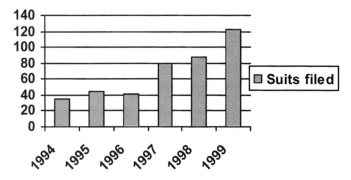

EXHIBIT 3.2   Patent Litigation: Computer Technologies*

*The litigated patents were classified in the following technology classes (established by the USPTO): 364, 395, 737–741, 701, 702, 704, 705, 706, 707, and 711

- In 1993, Intel Corp. asserted its patent rights against several companies, including Microsoft Corp. and a Taiwanese computer maker, for allegedly infringing on its microchip patent rights.

  Intel also requested an International Trade Commission (ITC) patent investigation against Twinhead International, Inc. (a producer of laptop computers).

  Further, Intel charged Cyrix Corp. with infringing its Crawford '338 patent by producing chips in a non-licensed foundry.

- Early in 1993, InterDigital Communications Corp. filed a patent infringement suit against Qualcomm, Inc.[4] Qualcomm later settled its patent litigation with InterDigital.[5]

- RedLine Research Laboratories, Inc. sued Naki Electronics, Inc. for infringing RedLine's patents covering technologies utilized in rechargeable battery packs for the Nintendo Gameboy and the Sega Gamegear.

  The U.S. District Court in Los Angeles ordered Naki to pay $450,000 plus costs, and to stop making, using, or selling the battery packs or any similar product which infringes the patents sued on, for the life of the patent.

- In 1990, the National Telephone Service, Inc. was sued by MessagePhone, Inc. for infringing MessagePhone's patents concerning automatic message delivery service technology. The lawsuit was filed in the U.S. District Court for the northern district of Texas.

- In 1994, Microsoft Corp. and Stac Electronics, Inc. settled a patent infringement suit. Microsoft had been sued by Stac Electronics for allegedly infringing Stac Electronics' patented technology relating to data compression. Stac Electronics received a judgement of $120 million against Microsoft.

- In 1994, a judge upheld an award against Nintendo Co. for violating a patent owned by Alpex Computer Corp.[6]

- In 1993, BankAmerica found itself as a defendant in a patent infringement suit brought by Dr. Roger Billings against Novell, Inc. Dr. Billings had a patent covering client/server technology, and sued Novell and BankAmerica for damages in connection with infringing his patent.

  BankAmerica apparently was chosen as a defendant because of its use of NetWare, a networking software product sold by Novell. BankAmerica settled the suit before trial, and agreed to pay Dr. Billings $125,000.

- On July 17, 1992, Bell Communications Research (Bellcore) sued Vitalink Communications Corp. for its unauthorized use of Bellcore's patented technology for interconnecting broadcast networks. The U.S. District Court in Alexandria was requested to enjoin further infringing activity and to award damages, including "enhanced damages" because Vitalink was allegedly infringing "willfully."

Apparently Bellcore and Vitalink Communications Corp. were having discussions earlier during 1992. In the complaint filed by Bellcore, Bellcore stated that Vitalink promised and represented that it would provide Bellcore with its final position and decision with respect to its infringement and a possible patent license agreement with Bellcore. Presumably, Vitalink failed to take action which was considered acceptable by Bellcore, and continued to manufacture and sell allegedly infringing devices. Bellcore also asserted in its complaint that Vitalink had sold more than 22,000 networking products covered by the patented technology as of July 17, 1992, and that Vitalink's net sales of those products exceeded $200 million.

- In 1992, Theis Research, Inc. began a campaign to enforce its patent rights against equipment manufacturers and Bell operating companies including Ameritech. Theis' patents were directed to automated voice processing technologies.
- In 1993, Conner Peripherals, Inc. was sued by IBM Corp. for using IBM's patented disk-drive technology. The suit charged that Conner infringed nine IBM patents, and sought to enjoin Conner's use of the technology, as well as money damages.

3.2 SOME INITIAL STEPS TOWARD PREVENTING PATENT LIABILITY

In managing a business' patent liability, the ultimate goal is to avoid being sued and paying substantial royalties to other patent holders. An even more important goal is avoiding being enjoined from using a particular technology which could force the business out of a lucrative market. If possible, and if necessary to prevent significant liability, the business should refrain from using technology infringing patents of others altogether. However, in most cases, in order to participate in a particular market, patented technologies (patented by others) will be employed by the business. In those cases, certain steps can be taken to reduce the liability, the likelihood that patent holders will assert their patent rights against the business, and the amount of royalties that will be paid in those cases in which patent liability could not be avoided.

It is especially important for a business to manage its patent liability by monitoring the patent activities of its closest and biggest competitors. Competitors may be particularly sensitive to any infringing activities that the business engages in.

- Advanced Micro Devices (AMD), Intel Corp., and Cyrix Corp. are fierce competitors, and their patent disputes reflect their rivalry. Early in 1994, apparently in response to threats of litigation, AMD planned further litigation with Intel, with Cyrix possibly joining in.[7] Apparently, AMD intended on challenging Intel's Crawford microprocessor patent.

- Another example of fierce competitors entering into patent litigation is the rivalry between AT&T Corp. and MCI Communications Corp. For example, in May of 1993, AT&T and Unitel Communication, Inc. filed a patent infringement suit in the federal court of Canada in Toronto, charging MCI and the Stentor Group with infringing AT&T's intelligent network patents in Canada. In November, 1992, AT&T had notified MCI and the Stentor Group that their expected use of MCI's intelligent network technology in Canada might infringe the AT&T patents.

  Earlier in 1992, MCI filed a pre-emptive suit against AT&T in the U.S. district court for the District of Columbia, asking the court to declare several AT&T long distance service patents invalid and to enjoin AT&T from enforcing other AT&T patents. AT&T filed counter-claims for patent infringement for 10 U.S. AT&T patents directed to intelligent network technologies. The case was assigned to Judge Harold H. Greene to decide issues related to the Modified Final Judgment (MFJ) as well as issues regarding patent infringement and validity.

- Compaq Computer Corp. and Packard Bell Electronics, Inc. are direct competitors in the retail PC market. In 1994, Compaq filed a patent suit against Packard Bell, alleging that Packard Bell infringed three patents covering certain computer technologies.

- There also has been fierce competition in the market of providing in-room television programming for hotels and other members of the lodging industry. In July, 1992, Communications Satellite Corp., an affiliate of On Command Video, filed suit charging Spectradyne Corp. with infringing its patents covering on-demand movie technology. The suit was filed in the Federal District Court in San Francisco, California. This lawsuit followed another patent infringement suit filed in November, 1991 by Spectradyne against On Command and its owner, Comsat Video Enterprises.

The business should implement an aggressive campaign to obtain defensive patents to deter competitors from enforcing patent rights against the business. A search might be performed periodically for all the patents owned by the business' fiercest competitors, and, in some instances, the business might consider modifying its products or services so that it does not include technology patented by those competitors. In some situations, the business may consider staying out of a particular market area.

When patents surface that are close to the business's technologies, a legal opinion should be obtained from a qualified patent attorney to determine whether the technology infringes the patent, and whether the patent is valid. This opinion should be obtained before the company starts or continues any potentially infringing activity.

Just So You Know . . .

Patents give the owner a negative right—to exclude others from making, using, and selling the invention defined by the patent's claims patent. However, a patent does not give the patent owner an affirmative right to make, use, or sell the invention.

Another company may own a patent having claims that prohibit the owner's use of the very technology for which the owner has obtained patent protection. For example, suppose "House Building Company" invents the first door with hinges, applies for a patent, and obtains a patent covering the door. The claims of the patent define a door as a flat, large member having hinges. Anybody who makes, uses, or sells the door having a flat, large member having hinges would be considered an infringer of House Building Company's patent.

Suppose another company, Construction Associates, improves the door. They invent the first doorknob, and apply for a patent directed to a door with a doorknob. If Construction Associates obtains a patent to the door with the doorknob, they would not be able to make, use, or sell doors with doorknobs without permission from House Building Company, which owns the first patent. Similarly, House Building Company could not make, use, or sell any door with a doorknob without infringing the patent owned by Construction Associates. The only way for each of the companies to sell doors with doorknobs, without the threat of being sued by the other for patent infringement, is for them to enter into a cross-licensing agreement.

Once a business becomes aware of a potentially relevant patent, it has a duty to have a patent attorney thoroughly evaluate the patent before it can proceed using its technology without paying royalties to the patent owner. If the business fails to obtain an opinion clearing its technology in the face of the patent, continued use of the technology will likely be considered willful infringement. A well done, competent clearance opinion cannot guarantee that the business will not be sued or that the business would win if sued. However, a proper opinion will reflect that the patent attorney is of the opinion that the business' technology does not infringe any valid claim, and will explain and substantiate that opinion. This can prevent a finding of willfulness in a patent litigation and thereby prevent a loss in court from being compounded by increased damages and attorney fees.

The business should also obtain patents covering technologies used by its competitors, so those competitors will think twice before suing the business, for fear of being sued themselves. This defense mechanism fosters cross-licensing, and serves as a deterrent to being sued for patent infringement.

Using Patents Defensively . . .

Suppose a scuba diving company is located near a strip of beachfront property. The beachfront property is owned by another who prohibits trespassing.

The scuba diving company has the opportunity to buy the only access road leading to the beachfront property. If the scuba diving company does not buy the access road, the road will either be bought by the owner of the beachfront property, making it even more difficult to gain access to the beach, or it will become public property.

The scuba diving company will lose an essential opportunity if it does not buy the access road. If the owner of the beachfront property wishes to use its own beachfront property, he or she will have to use the access road. If the scuba diving company owns the access road, it can require, in return for use of the access road, permission to use the beachfront property.

Similarly, a company, then, can obtain patents covering the technology used by one of its key competitors to deter the competitor from bringing a patent suit. Using the example in the previous sidebar, Construction Associates is limited in that it cannot make, use, or sell doors unless it obtains permission from House Building Company. However, Construction Associates has already been making and selling doors for the last year or so, and did not know about House Building Company's patent because the pending application was kept secret by the U.S. Patent and Trademark Office until it was recently granted. Construction Associates must decide whether it is going to continue to infringe the patent, and incur liability, or simply stop selling doors. Since Construction Associates pursued and obtained patent protection for the doorknob it invented, Construction Associates is in a good bargaining position. House Building Company has an incentive to license their technology (doors) to Construction Associates in return for the right to place doorknobs on House Building Company's doors.

3.3 WHAT TO DO WHEN APPROACHED BY A PATENT OWNER

A technology-driven business likely will encounter patent liability. In most cases, technology-driven businesses have a present market in which they develop and market technology. As they are developing and marketing technology in their present markets, such businesses may be approached by patent owners in a number of ways. Some may offer to license patented technology to the business. Others may threaten the business with a patent lawsuit, demanding that the business pay royalties to avoid the lawsuit, or even requiring that the business stop using certain technologies. Others may simply sue the busi-

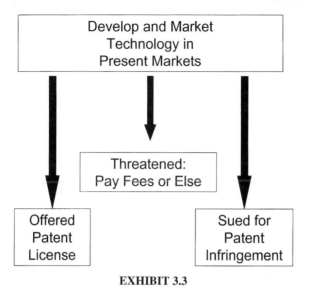

EXHIBIT 3.3

ness for patent infringement, leaving the business without the often-preferred option of negotiating a settlement before a lawsuit is filed. See Exhibit 3.3.

(a) When Offered a Patent License

If a high-technology-driven business is offered a patent license, it may initially check its patent portfolio to determine if it owns any patents covering technology used by the approaching licensor. If it has patents controlling the approaching licensor's use of certain technology, it may wish to assert those patent rights against the approaching licensor or offer those rights in a cross-licensing agreement. The business may also consider its patent portfolio for the purpose of entering into a partnership arrangement with the approaching licensor, or it may simply offer the approaching licensor a license, expressing no interest in the patents of the approaching licensor. See Exhibit 3.4.

The approached business must determine whether or not it is using the technology covered by the patents being offered for license. If it is not involved in any activity which could possibly be considered to infringe the patents being licensed, it can then decide whether or not it is interested in incorporating the technology in its present dealings. If the business is not interested, and is not using the technology, it may be prudent for the business to send the patent or patents back to the approaching licensor. Once the business has knowledge of a patent, its potential liability can be magnified if it ever uses a technology close to that covered by the patent.

If, however, the business is interested in licensing the technology, it should then evaluate the patents. An evaluation of one or more patents will typically

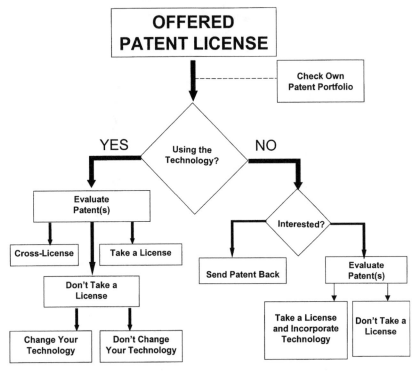

EXHIBIT 3.4

include reviewing the patents to determine their scope of protection, (i.e., what activities will infringe the patents). Another aspect of evaluating patents is to determine the strength of the patent, that is, how easy it would be to invalidate the patent. In determining the strength of the patent, the evaluating party should determine what prior art there is, and what advances the patent has contributed to the prior art. Depending upon the results of the patent evaluation, the business may decide not to take a license, for example, because the patent is very narrow and would not be infringed, or because the patent is not valid. Otherwise, if the business is still interested, and the patent is reasonably broad and appears to be valid, the business may decide to take a license and look into incorporating the technology into its present activities.

If the business is already using the patented technology covered by the patents being offered by the licensor, it should immediately evaluate the patents. While doing so, the business will determine the strength of the patents, the scope of protection provided by the patents, and how clearly they encompass the technology being used by the business. With this knowledge, the business may respond to the license offer in one of several ways. It could cross-license with the licensor, offering a license to its own patents in exchange for permission to use the technology covered by the approaching licensor's patents. It could simply agree to take a license and pay a reasonable royalty. The business could also decide not to take a license.

If a decision is made not to take a license, the business may decide to change the technology it is using so that it is clearly distinguished from the technology covered by the patent. The other choice, of course, is not to change the technology and proceed under the assumption that the business is unlikely to be sued for patent infringement. Bases for this decision might be a strong indication that the patent is invalid, not infringed, or even unenforceable because of improper conduct during prosecution.

(b) When Threatened with Patent Infringement

Technology-driven businesses frequently are charged with patent infringement suits. In this situation, as with a friendly licensor, it makes sense for the business to check its own patent portfolio to see if the business owns patents covering the activities of the threatening patent owner. If the business is not using the technology in question, it should attempt to quickly resolve the matter and make that clear to the threatening party. If the business is using the technology

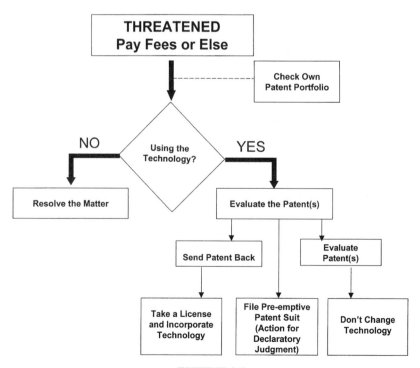

EXHIBIT 3.5

arguably covered by the asserted patents, the business should perform an evaluation of the strength (i.e., validity) and infringement issues as they relate to those activities. The business may persuade the threatening party not to pursue a patent suit, and license its technology for payment of a royalty, or for a right to use certain technology covered by patents owned by the business. In the alternative, the business could cross-license its technology in exchange for use of the threatening party's technology, take a license with reasonable terms as agreed to by the threatening party, or refuse to take a license. See Exhibit 3.5.

If the business is using a technology close to the technology covered by the threatening party's patent, but does not want to be taken to court at an inopportune time, the business may file a pre-emptive patent suit called an action for declaratory judgement. By requesting an action for declaratory judgement, the business may ask the judge to declare the patent invalid and/or not infringed by the business' activities. In addition, the business filing a pre-emptive patent suit can choose the forum, (i.e., the court), in which the suit is filed, and can resolve the dispute more quickly, rather than continuing to use certain technology at the risk of increasing their liability.

(c) When Sued for Patent Infringement

If a technology-driven business is sued for patent infringement, it again should check its own patent portfolio. At this time, it is particularly critical to have strong patents covering the opposing party's activities. If the defending business has one or more patents covering the activity of the party enforcing their patents, they may file a counterclaim or even a separate patent infringement suit based upon those patents. This action can nullify the effects of the patent suit, or at a minimum, provide a strong incentive to the suing party to resolve the issue quickly and settle before litigation costs mount, and their potential liability increases. See Exhibit 3.6.

Depending upon the defending business' situation, it may decide to settle without proceeding with the litigation, or it may decide to defend its position in litigation, arguing that it does not infringe the patent and attacking the validity of the patent. If the business decides to settle, it could work out a licensing arrangement, or it could cease its use of the technology altogether. When proceeding with litigation, however, other strategies might be available to some accused infringers. The following are examples of companies responding to threats of litigation using creative strategies. The first example requests intervention from the Federal Communications Commission, and the second requests intervention from Judge Harold H. Greene, overseer of the antitrust consent decree Modified Final Judgement (the "MFJ") that at the time governed AT&T and the regional Bell operating companies.

1. On May 22, 1988, Allnet Communications Services, Inc. asked the FCC to direct AT&T Corp. to answer a number of questions as to whether it

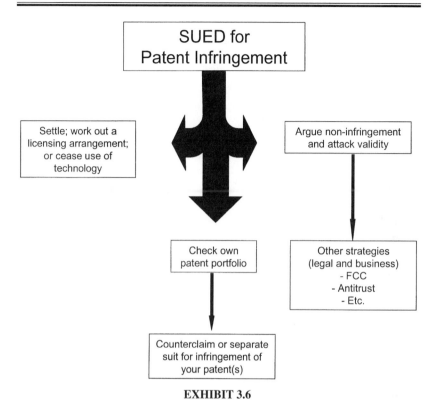

EXHIBIT 3.6

considered a proposed nationwide "800" database system to be an infringement of AT&T's "Weber patent", filed in 1978 for AT&T's "Common-channel Interoffice Signaling System," an inward-WATS (800) service. Allnet filed this request with the FCC because the FCC was involved with a proceeding on 800 database issues, and Allnet believed that AT&T's answer to this question would be necessary to clarify if non-Bell companies would have a right to use the proposed 800 database. Allnet asked several specific questions as to what AT&T's intentions were regarding the Weber patent, under what circumstances it would bring a patent law suit against any local or interexchange carriers that employ the database arrangement, and whether there are any limitations on the types of activities that AT&T might consider to infringe the Weber patent.

2. At the beginning of 1993, MCI Communications Corp. asked U.S. District Judge Harold H. Greene to issue a declaratory ruling, in connection with the MFJ, that AT&T Corp. may not use patents developed prior to the 1984 divestiture of the Bell Operating Companies to impede competition in the interexchange telecommunications market. MCI cited

AT&T's "Weber patent" covering technologies used in "800" database systems, and other patents that could conceivably impede free competition in the interexchange telecommunications market. Together with this request, MCI filed a civil complaint in the federal court for the District of Columbia seeking a declaration that certain AT&T patents are invalid and an injunction barring enforcement of other AT&T patents.

3.4 WHEN CONSIDERING INTRODUCING A NEW TECHNOLOGY AND/OR ENTERING A NEW MARKET

There are times when a business should consider conducting a patent infringement search and patent evaluation in order to familiarize itself with all pertinent patents that may control its activities, and to assess at an early stage the extent to which the business' activities are affected. If the business is not going to introduce any new products, and its behavior will remain the same, it may not be necessary or advisable to look for patents that cover the business' activities. Such a study may just create complications that are not necessary at the present time.

However, there will be certain points in time at which the business is going to change its behavior. For example, the business may make and sell more products, increase its international sales, or introduce a new technology. In these situations, the decision to proceed and the way in which the business proceeds could change depending upon the existence of any infringed patents. For example, a business may decide not to increase its international sales of a product if it will increase its patent liability, and if key competitors likely will enforce their patent rights against the business. If the business is considering introducing a new product, it may modify the way the product is designed in order to avoid infringement of one or more patents of which it is aware. In 1993, Eastman Kodak terminated one of its subsidiaries dealing with imagery after Wang Laboratories, Inc. brought a patent infringement suit against the subsidiary.[8]

In order to avoid incurring patent liability, a business entering a new market should first evaluate the market and its competitors. It should evaluate whether its competitors will be protective of their patented technology, and whether they will be sensitive to the business's new activities. It also would be prudent to evaluate how vigorously those competitors have enforced their patent portfolios in the past. See Exhibit 3.7.

Depending upon how fierce the competition is in that particular market, and how vigorously the competitors in that market have enforced their patent portfolios, it may be prudent to perform a complete clearance search to locate all patents that may cover the technology the company is considering using. This may include an exhaustive search at the U.S. Patent and Trademark Office for

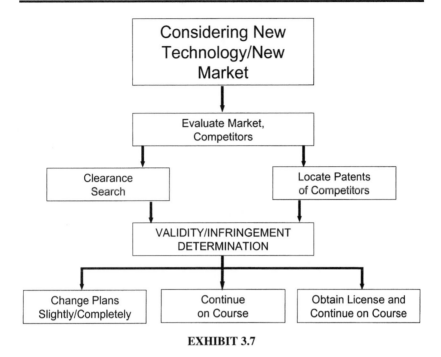

EXHIBIT 3.7

all patents that could be considered relevant and that might cover the technologies to be adopted by the business. In any event, the business should identify and have its patent counsel consider all of the patents owned by its key competitors in the market of interest. For each relevant patent that is identified, the business should evaluate whether it is valid and infringed by the technology it is considering using. If no patents are found that appear to be infringed, or if any apparently relevant patents are not believed to be valid, the business may decide to continue on its course of introducing a new technology or entering a new market.

If the evaluation reveals potentially infringed patents, the business may only need to change its plans slightly to avoid infringement, or it may have to alter its plans completely. A business may decide to change its plans completely if it determines that a key competitor has significant patent protection covering that area, and has vigorously enforced those patent rights in the past. That information may indicate that the risk is not outweighed by the expected benefits of entering into a new market. Thus, a thorough patent evaluation may help the business decide whether market entry is worth the cost before investments are made and momentum is achieved in the new market. Alternatively, the business may decide to pay licensing fees for patented technologies, and to continue with their new plans.

3.5 IT IS SAFER TO ASSUME THAT KNOWN STEPS OR ELEMENTS ARE PATENTED

In managing patent liability, the business should not subscribe to a common misconception, that the business' use of technology combining only old or commercially available components, for example, computer and software packages purchased by other vendors, cannot create patent liability. Many businesses have incorrectly, albeit understandably, presumed (to their detriment), that the various steps in a process (or the various pieces of a system) are each publicly available technology (e.g., they can be purchased or they are freely disclosed in technical journals), and therefore a patent could not be obtained covering the combined technologies. They accordingly assume others could not get (or already have) a patent to the combination. Patents can be, and have been, granted to new combinations of old elements. If several old systems are used in a new manner, or combined together to form a system which did not exist before, that overall system could be patented or patentable. The company bringing those pieces together might apply for and obtain patent protection, and it also might infringe other patents covering the overall system.

When a business forms a system or device by combining components it purchases from others, it cannot rely on the indemnifications provided by the respective vendors. They will only indemnify against patent liability for use of the component itself, not for a new use of the component, combined with other components to create a new system or device.

3.6 EXPERT ADVICE WHEN EVALUATING A PATENT IS ESSENTIAL

A company should be extremely hesitant before ignoring a patent, and should never assume that a patent is either invalid or not infringed without obtaining an informed opinion from patent counsel. Further, if a business allows a lay person to make the determination of patent relevancy, and that person proves to be wrong, the patent owner can sue the business and receive possibly up to three times their lost profits plus attorney's fees and costs. In such an instance, the business would be considered a willful infringer for failing to have obtained an opinion by a qualified patent attorney that their activities do not infringe a valid claim of the patent.

The lay person is likely to be wrong in making an infringement determination because of the standards (at times counter-intuitive—and ever changing) used to interpret the scope of a patent and the technology that it protects. The claims of a patent play a major role in defining the scope of protection provided by the patent. Depending upon several factors and legal principles, too involved for a complete discussion here, features of the invention described in the specification of the patent may or may not have a limiting effect on the scope defined by the claims. Each claim of the patent is considered separately, that is, as a separate definition of a particular aspect of the invention, and thus of the scope of protection provided by the patent.[9]

In addition, legal doctrines have been designed to prevent efforts to design around a patent. One such legal doctrine, called the "doctrine of equivalents," might be asserted by a patent owner in such a way that an implementation infringes even though it does not fall within the literal definition of a claim.

In determining the validity of a patent, each claim is considered separately and evaluated to determine whether it meets the various statutory requirements specified under the patent law. Some of those requirements include sufficiently disclosing details of the invention as well as claiming an invention that is neither in the prior art nor obvious in view of the prior art. In this regard, a claim cannot be rendered invalid for lack of novelty or for obviousness in view of technology that is not prior art. Some trade secret use may not be considered prior art, even though it is an indication that the technology has been used before by others.

Since each claim is treated separately for a validity determination, the existence of one invalid claim does not prevent other claims from being upheld in court as valid and infringed by the business' technological activities.

It is difficult to invalidate a claim; and a patent attorney must be cautious when providing an opinion that clears his or her client's activity based solely on invalidity grounds. The courts will presume all claims of the patent are valid, and validity must be proven by clear and convincing evidence. The presumption of validity is strong, and holds true even in the face of art not considered by the patent examiner during prosecution of the patent's application. The presumption of validity is especially strong if the same prior art or similar prior art was considered by the examiner during the patent prosecution, and the examiner still granted a patent.

In any event, proving the validity of a claim is an uphill battle, and a business should not rely solely upon the opinion of a lay person (even one who is technically conversant) in deciding to continue use of a technology that appears to be covered by the patent. As a legal matter, if a patent attorney does not make that determination in a thorough, well-documented written opinion, and a court determines that the patent was indeed valid and infringed by the business' activities, the business could be liable for increased damages (up to three times the damages incurred by the patent owner) and possibly also attorney's fees and costs incurred by the patent owner. However, the attorney's opinion cannot prevent a law suit from being filed, and cannot guarantee a victory in litigation. At a minimum, however, liability for willful infringement might be avoided by obtaining an objective legal opinion ahead of time.

(a) Why do you need to obtain the advice of counsel?

The business has an affirmative duty to obtain the advice of counsel once it is aware of a patent covering its activity, or possibly covering its technology.

More generally stated, a potential infringer has an affirmative duty to exercise due care to determine whether or not he or she is infringing. This duty includes the duty to seek and obtain competent legal advice before the initiation of any possible infringing activity. This affirmative duty was established by the appeals court having exclusive jurisdiction over all patent appeals in the United States, the Federal Circuit. That decision arose out of a lawsuit between Underwater Devices, Inc. and Morrison-Knudsen Co. decided in 1983.

The potential infringer that fails to obtain the advice of counsel, and is hailed into court for patent infringement, can face liability as a willful infringer. When this happens, the damages awarded can be increased up to three times, and attorneys' fees and costs can also be charged to the infringer.

For example, in another case, the defendant accused infringer, Krauss-Maffei Corp., was found to have committed willful infringement, and the patentee plaintiff, Afros, s.p.a., was awarded three times the actual damages determined by the court as well as its attorneys' fees. The court stated "defendant appears to have blithely gone ahead with manufacturing and marketing . . . without stopping to consider whether it infringed a patent . . . legal advice was sought only upon plaintiff filing suit, a full two years after the patent issued."

The accused infringer avoided a finding of willfulness in Rastv Edt. Johnson, Inc. v. Brandt, Inc., 805 F.Supp. 557, 569 (N.D.Ill. 1992). In that case, Brandt, Inc., the accused infringer, was found to have continuously solicited and faithfully heeded to oral and written opinions of competent counsel beginning years prior to the filing of the lawsuit. This was a significant factor in the courts' finding that Brandt, Inc. did not willfully infringe the patent at issue.

(b) At what point does knowledge of a given patent give rise to the duty to obtain advice of counsel?

The need may occur when the business discovers or is made aware of a patent applicable to its technology. It may discover the patent (i) when it monitors new patents as they are announced in the Patent Office's biweekly publication called the Official Gazette, (ii) when it performs searches of issues patents, or (iii) when it investigates the patentability of a given invention for which it is filing a patent application. A relevant patent may also come to the attention of the business through an offer for a license, or when it is threatened with patent litigation based upon the patent.

The advice of counsel regarding the strength of a patent will also help the business determine how and when to come to an agreement with the patent owner. If a royalty rate is to be negotiated for a license under the patent, information obtained from the legal opinion can be very helpful in negotiating the royalty rate. The opinion will address issues having a direct bearing on the strength, and therefore the value, of the patent, such as the scope of protection, validity, and enforceability.

However, the law does not clearly explain the moment when the business should be charged with being aware of a patent, (i.e., when it needs to obtain an opinion from counsel). In Stryker Corp. v. Intermedics Orthopedics, Inc., 891 F.Supp. 751, 815 (E.D.N.Y. 1995), *Aff'd*, 96 F.3d 1403 (Fed. Cir. 1996), counsel for the defendant Intermedics Orthopedics, Inc. conceded that it saw a reference to the patent, including a drawing well prior to being notified by counsel for plaintiff of the patent. The Court held that such awareness of the patent created the affirmative duty to have an opinion rendered regarding the patent. In Grambro Lundia AB v. Baxter Healthcare, Corp., 896 F.Supp. 1522, 1548 (D. Colo. 1995), the district court of Colorado found that there was no willfulness on the part of the accused infringer who obtained an opinion from counsel within a reasonable time after it was charged with infringement, and relied in good faith on that opinion.

Do you need the opinion before you start possible infringing activity?

There are times when a patent attorney's opinion is not obtained before a decision is made to continue potentially infringing activity. For example, in King Instrument Corp. v. Otari Corp., 767 F.2d 853, 867, 226 USPQ 402, 412 (Fed. Cir. 1985), the accused infringer obtained no opinion from counsel. However, the defendant studied the patented machine, developed its own different construction, and filed a patent application based upon the new construction. The Federal Circuit considered these design around efforts and the "totality of the circumstances," and affirmed the lower court's refusal to find that the defendant willfully infringed the patent at issue.

The courts do not make it crystal clear when a delay in obtaining a written opinion will be forgiven by the court when it considers whether the infringement was willful. The business should establish clear procedures on patent opinions and exercise diligence to ensure that an opinion is obtained as soon as practical, given the circumstances. If the business has been using the technology at issue for quite some time, before becoming aware of the patent, a small delay in the obtaining of an opinion might be forgivable. However, if the technology has yet to be incorporated into a product, and the business is aware of the relevant patent, it would be prudent to obtain a clearance opinion before the technology is incorporated into a commercial product.

The Federal Circuit has held, in Ralston Purina Co. v. Far-Mar-Co., 772 F.2d 1570, 227 USPQ 177 (Fed. Cir. 1995), that rejecting a license offer without consulting patent counsel, where the patented technology was already in a commercial product, can result in a charge of willful infringement. In the Ralston Purina decision, the Federal Circuit states a strong preference that a written opinion contain within its four corners a patent validity analysis, properly and explicitly predicated on a review of the file histories of the patent at issue, and an infringement analysis. The opinion should compare and contrast the potentially infringing product with the patented invention, and it should contain sufficient internal indicia of creditability to remove any doubt that a competent opinion was obtained. The opinion cannot contain only bald, conclusory, and unsupported remarks regarding validity and infringement.

(c) Benefits of the advice of counsel and certain caveats

There are many benefits to seeking and following the advice of counsel. If the business finds itself accused of patent infringement in a patent lawsuit, and it cannot present a written opinion by qualified patent counsel that it is not liable for patent infringement, the court may determine that there is infringement and that the infringement was willful. The business may be able to avoid litigation by simply avoiding infringing activity in accordance with its attorneys' advice. The advice of counsel can also give the business information which will allow it to make a calculated choice as to whether or not to use a given technology, and the business can use that information to avoid or reduce the payments of royalties. Before deciding to use a given technology, the business can consult with the patent owner to determine if a license is available at a reasonable royalty, and if the royalty demanded by the patent owner is unreasonably high, the business can simply avoid its use of the technology altogether.

Perhaps the strongest argument for obtaining the advice of counsel, before incorporating a new technology or continuing to use an old technology in the face of a patent, is that the liability incurred by such use of the technology may be senseless and unnecessary. In many cases an easy solution may exist to designing around the patent, which can be done with the help and advice of the attorney.

Obtaining and following the advice of counsel is not enough. The potential infringing business must take part of the responsibility to ensure that the opinion is well-based, and must provide counsel with all relevant information at its disposal, so the business can justifiably form a reasonable basis for believing, in good faith, that no valid claim is infringed.

An opinion giving the green light must be thorough enough, or otherwise sufficient considering other factors, for the accused infringer to believe that a court will reasonably hold the pertinent claims are invalid, not infringed, or unenforceable. In looking at this issue, the courts will consider the intent and reasonable beliefs of the accused infringer.

It is also critical that the client inform patent counsel of *all relevant facts* within his or her knowledge that might reasonably impact on the opinion. Many cases have resulted in a finding of willfulness, and increased damages, even though an opinion was obtained by the accused infringer, because the accused infringer failed to provide relevant information to its patent attorney when seeking the opinion. For this reason, it is very important for the client to take an active role in evaluating a given patent, and to be forthcoming and provide all information relevant to the opinion. This includes information regarding the composition of the product being considered. It also requires that the client look closely at the technical assumptions made by the patent attorney in rendering the opinion to assure that there are no errors or misunderstandings of any important facts.

A change in the design of the product after the rendering of the opinion can render the opinion no longer useful. It is recommended that all pertinent facts be provided to counsel as a basis for obtaining a reliable opinion. However, one exception to this rule is that the failure to give a first opinion of one lawyer to a subsequent lawyer considering the same patent is considered by the courts a plus, not a minus. The second lawyer can thus make his own independent evaluation without being influenced by the first opinion.

In supplying the attorney with all pertinent information, it is important that the individuals most knowledgeable about the pertinent facts within the business be involved in the review process. The attorney should be given access to these individuals and they should review the written opinion, once rendered, to confirm that all of the assumptions are accurate, complete, and based upon complete information.

In another case, Kori v. Wilco Marsh Buggies & Draglines, 761 F.2d 649, 656-57, 225 USPQ 985, 989-90 (Fed. Cir. 1985), counsel's opinion stated "I have every reason to believe that the validity of the aforesaid patent cannot be maintained and that it will be declared to be null and void by the court handling the litigation." The court stated that this was merely an expression of the counsel's aspirations for winning an infringement suit without any supporting reasons. The opinion did not constitute an authoritative opinion upon which a good faith reliance may be founded on invalidity.

Endnotes

1. *The Wall Street Journal*, October 18, 1994.
2. *The Wall Street Journal*, November 8, 1994.
3. *Best's Review-Life-Health Insurance Edition*, May 1994, p. 99.
4. *San Diego Business Journal*, April 5, 1993.
5. *The Wall Street Journal*, November 3, 1994.
6. *The Wall Street Journal*, December 5, 1994.
7. *Electronic News*, June 14, 1993.
8. *PC Week*, August 30, 1993.
9. The scope of protection provided by a patent may not be limited by a specific feature recited in one claim, if another claim does not require the same feature.

CHAPTER 4

Strategies for Leveraging Value from R&D: Implementing a Patent Program

4.1 HABITS AND MECHANIZATION

Of course, such things as revenue goals, cash requirements, development deadlines, and sales and marketing activity will take precedence over patent acquisition and management efforts. Therefore, it is important that when the company is started initially and is not at a critical juncture, certain mechanisms are put in place and certain habits are formed which will carry the company through critical times without throwing away important patent rights. For example, when a company needs to obtain financing, in order to have sufficient cash to meet payroll and other critical expenses, the efforts of management will be prioritized and focused on obtaining the financing. Management will not spend time dealing with patent issues, (e.g., deciding what patents to apply for, or making sure technology is properly documented to protect patent rights).

Patent portfolio development and management is to a business like weightlifting is to the NFL lineman. The day before the game, the lineman should not be in the weight room. Similarly, in the midst of a critical juncture for the company, senior management will not have time to concern themselves with forward-looking patent activities, except that patents can be attended to with minimal effort if they are part of the business' normal patterns and if a mechanized process is already put into place.

The underlying purpose of a patent is to provide its owner with the right to exclude others from making, using, or selling the invention the patent covers. The underlying value of a patent is that it can deter others from using the invention, and, if they are using it, the patent owner can file a lawsuit seeking a remedy for such use. The patent owner is the one who enforces its patent rights.

Section 281 of the patent law states that "[a] patentee shall have remedy by civil action for infringement of his patent."

The ability to file a civil action and exert control over infringers will dictate the value of the patent in other areas, such as in transferring ownership of the patent, in licensing, and in deterring others from taking aggressive action (such as by filing a patent lawsuit) against the patentee.

For example, in 1993 Microsoft only held 24 patents and was struggling with IBM over software licensing. When the two companies could not come to terms, IBM wielded a portfolio of over 1,000 patents as a strong-arm tactic to get Microsoft to the table. Analysts said Microsoft eventually had to ante up an estimated $20–30 million in patent and licensing fees. In the wake of this, Bill Gates told financial analysts "Our goal is to have enough patents to be able to take and exchange intellectual property with other companies." As of October 2000, Microsoft held 1,391 patents.

Open disclosure of the technology is a prerequisite to obtaining patent rights. It is this open disclosure of information to the public which furthers the advance of technology, and the patent exclusionary rights are given to the patent owner in return for this open disclosure. Thus, while the law may say that you have the right to exclude others from making and using a particular invention, there is no way to physically prevent another party from taking the invention and incorporating it into an infringing device or product. If someone does make, use, or sell an infringing product, the patent owner cannot simply call the authorities and ask them to apprehend the infringer and destroy the infringing products.

Thus, patents require a lot of effort to enforce, and it is important that patent rights be respected.

In the past, much of the business community, particularly software developers, assumed that copyright and trade secret protection were sufficient to protect an information age company's rights. Copyrights and trade secret rights do not prevent others from independently creating the same technology, or similar improved versions of that technology. In addition, copyrights and trade secrets do not provide property rights that can be repeatedly used defensively to counter (or deter) litigation initiated by others against the business. While a company might be able to obtain a patent covering the "next step" of their key competitors, it could not get copyright protection or trade secret protection giving exclusive control over such a feature.

Patents are a form of personal property. Although they are intangible, they can be bought and sold as personal property, and therefore can be treated as assets of the business. In addition, they may be licensed to obtain supplemental licensing income; and they may be used to deter litigation and offset royalties being paid to competitors. Many companies have employed patent acquisition programs to realize these benefits.

Many say that for certain technologies, such as computer technologies, the life span of the technology is very short and that new technology will frequently be incorporated just a couple of years later, thus rendering a patent obsolete. However, this is a grave misconception regarding applicability of patents. A look at a sampling of U.S. patent lawsuits filed in 1998 shows that several lawsuits filed were based upon patents issued three, five, or even more than 10 years ago.[1,2]

4.2 A SUGGESTED APPROACH FOR A PATENT PROGRAM

One of the initial considerations in employing a patent acquisition strategy is to evaluate the costs of obtaining patents versus the return in value to the business, and whether the business will be able to utilize the patents in a beneficial way. Costs are discussed more fully in Chapter 7. As to the value of a patent, an initial determination must be made as to the types of technology that can be patented. Many businesses will frequently overlook key technologies, not realizing the technologies are capable of being patented. For example, software developers in the recent past have assumed that software could not be patented. If an overall system or process is new, even if it involves old technologies or old elements, it could be patentable.

Depending upon the scope of protection pursued, it will be more or less difficult to obtain. If narrower protection is sought in patent prosecution, the patent will be easier to obtain but the value of the resulting patent may be of minimal use to the business if the protection is too narrow. For example, if a patent is obtained directed to a doorknob on a door, and all the claims of the patent required that the doorknob be made of styrofoam, that idea would probably be new and unobvious (and therefore patentable). However, if the use of styrofoam adds nothing to the marketability of the doorknobs, then the claims would be too narrow. It is unlikely that any competitor would use styrofoam in its doorknobs, and even if a competitor contemplated using styrofoam, it could easily design around the patent by changing its doorknobs to overcome the claims of the patents. The doorknobs would still function properly if they were not made of styrofoam.

There are certain technologies for which it makes sense to obtain patent protection. If it is likely that the business, or its competitors, will be incorporating certain features in their products or services, then a resulting patent to those features could be valuable, assuming that the claims of the patent are cleverly drafted to hinder designing around the patent. Therefore, before a patent application is applied for, the business may consider the likelihood that the technology will be used in a meaningful way in the marketplace, and the state of the prior art, and the limitations that the prior art will place upon any patent protection that might be obtained.

An ideal goal is to obtain patents for technologies that are "essential" to competing effectively in a particular market. Essential technologies must be used in one way or another by those competing in the market. They may even form the basis of a standard, such as the GIF (Graphical Interchange Format) format for accessing graphics through online services, the V.42bis data compression standard, and the TDMA (Time Division Multiple Access) wireless telephone standard.

- Unisys Corp. holds a patent covering a data compression/decompression algorithm in at least two widely-used communications standards. One of the standards is GIF, a method used by CompuServe Information Service and many software developers to enable viewing of graphics information. The other standard is British Telecom's BTLZ algorithm, which is used in an international V.42bis standard for high-speed data compression.

  Unisys has licensed its LZW patent to users of GIF and the BTLZ algorithm. For its use of GIF, several years ago, CompuServe has agreed to pay an initial royalty of $125,000 and $5,000 per month thereafter. Software publishers could use the GIF standard in connection with CompuServe's online services by paying CompuServe 15 cents per copy of software, 11 cents of which was passed on to Unisys.

  Many modem makers used the V.42bis data compression standard in their modems, and paid a one-time licensing fee of $20,000.

- InterDigital Communications Corp., a small company based in suburban Philadelphia, owns several patents covering the use of TDMA (Time Division Multiple Access), a standard technology in new digital cellular telephone equipment.

  InterDigital originally had trouble convincing licensees to pay for their use of TDMA. However, AT&T and InterDigital entered into a cross-licensing deal, by which InterDigital received a $2.5 million advance. Other licensees included OKI, Qualcomm Inc., Siemens, and Matsushita. Siemens and Matsushita each paid lump sums of $20 million to InterDigital. Motorola refused to pay InterDigital royalties, and a jury trial was conducted in Wilmington, Delaware in February, 1995.

More than likely, the first step of a patent program is already underway: technological research and development. Throughout the R&D process, appropriate personnel may monitor developments in order to ensure that the rights to certain technologies are not lost, and that the patent process is immediately started for all developments of value, especially for those critical developments that may become essential to competing in the marketplace.

The second step is the creation of an invention disclosure program. Businesses may have an invention disclosure program by which technical personnel are asked to disclose their ideas in an invention disclosure form and submit them to patent personnel within or outside the company. In some businesses, the invention disclosure program includes an inventor incentive program which encourages inventors to submit their ideas. After a disclosure is obtained, a determination is made as to whether a patentable innovation has been developed, and the scope of protection that might be obtained if a patent is applied for. At this stage, a decision is made as to the likely value of a patent and whether the business should pursue patent protection. Then, a patent application may be prepared and filed, commencing the patent prosecution process.

There are a number of critical events that should be avoided, if at all possible, in a patent program. For example, businesses will want to avoid barring patentability in the United States or abroad. As a general rule, every effort should be made to have patent applications prepared and filed with the U.S. Patent and Trademark Office as early as possible. Due diligence will help in any priority contests with other companies filing for similar patent protection.

In addition, it is recommended that the patent application preparation and prosecution be started before implementing a system or method, in order to avoid having to disclose too much detail about the implemented system. The patent laws require an inventor to disclose the best mode he or she contemplates for carrying out an invention at the time a patent application is filed. When an invention is in the final stages of implementation, there are many details that may be part of the best mode that the business may be forced to disclose. This necessary disclosure can significantly increase the cost of the patent application preparation, and may also result in forfeiture of valuable trade secrets the business would not have had to divulge if it had filed its application earlier, when the inventor had not yet conceived of the final best mode.

Before allowing any technology to be publicly used, disclosed, published, or involved in any commercial activity, it is recommended that a patent application be filed with the U.S. Patent and Trademark Office. This filing is to preserve both U.S. and foreign patent rights. In most (but not all) circumstances, the U.S. patent laws provide for a one-year grace period after such public activity, within which a patent application may be filed without jeopardizing the U.S. patent rights. However, although a company can, in most cases, delay filing an application for up to a year after such activity occurs, most foreign patent laws do not provide a grace period of any sort. Once an invention is publicly used, published, disclosed, or commercialized, in most foreign countries there is an absolute bar to patentability. If the application is filed in the United States (as a provisional or a non-provisional application) before any such activity, that U.S. filing date may be considered an effective filing date for most foreign countries, and would thus preserve the patent rights not only in the United States but also in those foreign countries.

Endnotes
1. *Popular Mechanics*, August, 1994.
2. *PC Week*, April 18, 1994.

CHAPTER 5

Licensing, Selling, and Buying Patents

5.1 VALUING THE PATENT

If a competitor contemplating infringement believes the patent is weak or that the penalty for infringement will be small, the competitor will be less likely to respect the patent owner's rights. If the patent owner is willing to license the technology under an apparently weak patent, the competitor will not be inclined to pay high royalties. If the patent owner wishes to preclude the competitor from using the technology of a weak patent, the competitor is most certainly going to ignore the patent.

Therefore, the patent owner wishes to ensure that its patents are valid and enforceable, and that all steps have been taken to maximize the impact the patent laws will have on competitors should it become necessary to enforce the patent with civil litigation.

Both the patent owner considering how and whether to wield its patent rights and the competitor contemplating respecting such patent rights will want to understand what the patent can do, and just how strong it is. The patent owner will want to take steps to maximize the strength of the patent, and the competitor will want to capitalize on any apparent weaknesses.

The above general factors will, of course, set outside limits on the value placed on a patent in any license or sale transaction. In addition to the above factors, there is a virtually unlimited number of techniques for valuing a patent, some simple and some complex. The author recommends posing the following questions when analyzing the monetary value of a patent. Of course, this list is not exhaustive; there are sure to be situations where yet other factors affect the "ultimate question"—the price the buyer is willing to pay and the price the seller is willing to accept.

- Will the purchaser or licensee benefit strategically by the deal? For example, access to the technology might open a starting business about to go public to an attractive market and its accompanying revenues, thus justifying a higher valuation. The increase in value could be tens of millions or hundreds of millions of dollars.

- Is there a noninfringing substitute; can the purchaser/licensee simply focus on other equally lucrative markets?
- What is the size of the market controlled by the patent's claims? How much of that market (in annual revenue) can be captured by the purchaser/licensee? Of that, what portion of the revenues will be profit? Some argue it is reasonable for the patent owner to seek 25 to 33 percent of the before-tax profit.

5.2 EXPLOITING YOUR PATENTS

A patent portfolio can be exploited in order to generate income for the business. Depending upon how patents are exploited and what goals are set, patents can be used to increase the business' profit margin, or simply to offset the costs of the business' patent program. Income can be derived for the business by licensing the patents without litigation; by licensing the patents with litigation where necessary; and by litigating, settling for significant damages before trial where appropriate. See Exhibit 5.1.

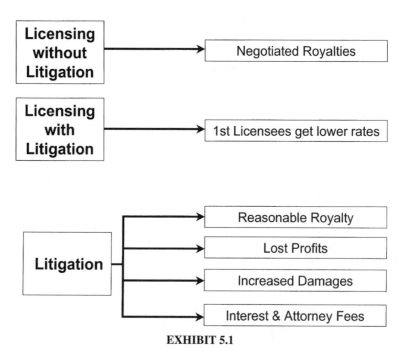

EXHIBIT 5.1

When a patent owner licenses its technology, the licensee is granted freedom from being sued for patent infringement from the patent owner. However, the patent owner cannot grant permission to use the technology, a right the patent owner may not have, as another business could conceivably have an overlapping patent covering the same technology. Therefore, when a patent license is essentially granted, the licensor is agreeing not to sue the licensee. See Exhibit 5.2.

Depending upon what profit margins exist for a particular product or service, and the value of the technology covered by the patent, the royalty rates could range anywhere from a fraction of a percent for high quantity production goods or services, to royalties as high as 50 percent for extremely valuable technology used in products or services having high profit margins.

If a licensor recognizes the importance of enforcing a patent, and takes whatever steps are necessary to enforce its patent rights, it may embark upon litigation. Once the patent owner has litigated a patent, and its validity has been upheld in court, the license rates may be increased due to a corresponding increase in confidence that the patent will not be invalidated. The licensor whose license agreement precedes the patent litigation is typically rewarded with a lower royalty rate by virtue of not waiting for the patent litigation to be resolved before agreeing to pay licensing fees.

According to an article published in *The Journal of the Patent and Trademark Office Society*, titled "Overview and Statistical Study of the Law on

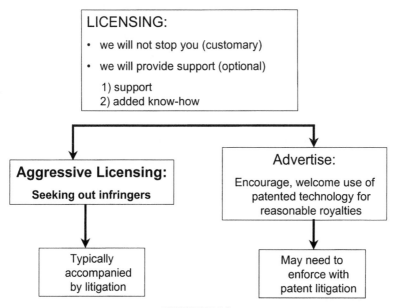

EXHIBIT 5.2

Patent Damages,[1] "out of 54 reported reasonable royalty patent decisions, 17 (or 31 percent) had reasonable royalty rates of under 5 percent, 21 (or 39 percent) had rates of between 6 and 10 percent, 11 (or 20 percent) had rates of between 11 and 20 percent, and 5 (or 9 percent) of the cases had rates of over 20 percent."

Royalties may be calculated in many different ways including a percentage of the selling price of the product or the service; a percentage of the cost to manufacture a product using the patented technology; and/or a fixed sum per discrete product or service sold by the licensee. These licensing charges may also be accompanied by an initial sum paid to the licensor, or an agreement to pay a set sum of money in fixed installments. Other arrangements include in kind exchanges, for example, providing the licensor with an interest in the licensee company.

Licenses may be exclusive, meaning that the licensee is the only licensee, or non-exclusive, meaning that other licensees may, upon payment of appropriate royalties, use the technology and be free of suit by the licensor. Licensees may also pay for the right to sublicense.

The following are examples of patent licensing arrangements:

- Spectrum Information Technologies, Inc. managed to derive a substantial amount of income from licensing its patent portfolio. For example, AT&T Corp. entered into a license agreement to manufacture, use, and sell Spectrum's patented and patent-pending technologies relating to computer systems and wireless transmission equipment. The agreement called for AT&T to pay an up-front licensing fee and continued royalties. In addition, AT&T agreed to issue a $10,000,000 note to Spectrum that it would pay in five years.

  Spectrum also signed a license agreement with Megahertz Corp. of Salt Lake City, Utah, giving Megahertz permission to use certain cellular technology with modems that can be used with cellular phones. The agreement called for Megahertz to give Spectrum $1,500,000 up front and continued royalty fees.

- Celeritas Technologies, Ltd. was successful in licensing its patented technology to companies such as Toshiba, Apex Data, and Pacific Communications Sciences. Celeritas obtained patent protection for a technology called TX-CEL, which enables portable computers (notebooks) to transmit at 14.4 baud (14,000 bits per second) through a cellular phone. Celeritas was reported to receive up to $2 per modem incorporating the patented technology.

- Unisys Corp. has a patent covering the LZW data-compression technology, which is used in the GIF (Graphical Interchange Format) graphic standard used in connection with online and Internet services. LZW is also used in the data-compression standard V.42bis incorporated in high-speed modems. Unisys charged CompuServe an up-front payment of

$125,000, and $5,000 a month thereafter, and additionally charged CompuServe 11 cents per copy of software sold utilizing the technology (with a right to sublicense granted to CompuServe). In addition, Unisys received royalties from many modem makers using the high-speed data-compression standard, charging each modem-maker a one-time license fee of $20,000.

• Competing games makers, including Sega, Nintendo Co., and 3DO charge royalty rates to software developers to make software compatible with their games. Some of the higher rates, charged by Sega and Nintendo, have been between $9 and $12 per unit.

As an alternative to licensing, a patent owner can assign (sell) all or a portion of its rights in the patent.

Litigation is another means by which a patent owner can obtain substantial income from its patents which are being infringed by others. A patent owner who litigates a patent is entitled to at least a reasonable royalty, but may receive additional amounts in money damages, including lost profits of the patent owner, and in some cases, increased damages up to three times the amount of profits lost by the patent owner. In addition, a patent litigation may result in the patent owner being awarded interest, sometimes even attorney fees and costs over and above a reasonable royalty or lost profits.

The following are examples of reported cases in which damages were awarded:

• On January 25, 1990, in Datascope Corporation v. SMEC, Inc., the patent owner was awarded $3.28 million in damages, which included royalty damages of $14,747, increased damages of $763,307, attorney costs of $988,043, and lost profits of $1,511,867.

• On March 29, 1990, in Motorola, Inc. v. Hitachi, Inc., two patent damage awards were given in a single reported decision. In the first instance, the patent owner was awarded $500,000 in total damages, all of which were reasonable royalty damages. In the other instance, the patent owner was awarded $1.9 million, $1.5 million of which was reasonable royalty damages and $0.4 million of which was characterized as lost profits damages.

• On October 23, 1990, damages were awarded to the patent owner in Manville Sales Corp. v. Paramount. The total patent damages awarded was approximately $1.15 million, all of which was lost profits damages.

• On February 27, 1991, $26.23 million total patent damages was awarded to the patent owner in Micro Motion, Inc. vs. Exac Corporation, $1,294,617 of which was royalty damages, $4,877,819 being lost profit damages, $14,649,089 being damages for price erosion, and $5,409,481 being awarded for pre-judgment interest (i.e., interest on the damages for the time during which the company was waiting for the judgment to be rendered).

- On April 23, 1991, in the Hayes Microcomputer Products patent litigation, the patent owner was awarded $7,019,622 in total patent damages. That total damage award included $3,509,811 in royalty damages, and $3,509,811 in increased damages.
- On June 25, 1992, in another case, American Medical Systems vs. Medical Engineering, the patent owner was awarded a total of $1,429,605, of which $46,264 was royalty damages, $476,535 was increased damages, and $906,806 was for profits lost by the patent owner.

Endnotes
1. Article by Ronald B. Cooley, in the *Journal of the Patent and Trademark Office Society*, Volume 75, pp. 515–537 (July, 1993).

CHAPTER 6

Partnering, Strategic Alliances, and Deals

As can be seen in Exhibit 6.1, patents can serve as an added bargaining chip in dealing with others, whether it be in adopting a proposed standard, entering into an alliance with another company, or selling shares.

6.1 WHEN A NEW STANDARD IS ADOPTED

When a new technological standard is proposed, there are two positions in which a business may find itself. It either will or will not have patents covering one or more technologies to be used in the proposed standard. If the business has patents covering technologies used in the proposed standard, it has more options and is in a better position than others who do not have patent protection. As one option, the business may charge a reasonable royalty to all users of the new industry standard. The business may also use its patent rights to offset patent royalties demanded by others for use of the new standard. The patent rights in the business also may be used as a bargaining chip in determining what the standard will be before it is adopted. The business may have an interest in having a particular standard adopted, and in being able to use the standard without having to pay royalties.

Some groups are trying to reduce the applicability of intellectual property rights on standards technologies. In testimony before Congress in the spring of 1998, John Major, Executive VP at Qualcomm stated, "Qualcomm holds more than 130 patents relative to CDMA, has approximately 400 patent applications pending around the world, and has licensed 55 companies to manufacture equipment based on this standard. . . . We believe that the third-generation standards process should recognize and respect the intellectual property rights of patent holders. We believe that markets and not governments, should guide the timing and deployment of third-generation services." A Working Group for the European Union has proposed alternatives to the standard royalties

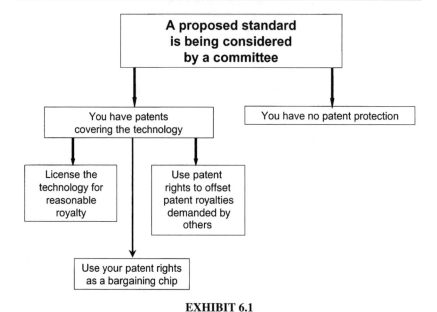

EXHIBIT 6.1

agreement in connection with third-generation mobile communications standards which, if adopted, could go so far as to extinguish certain businesses' royalty rights if the patent is not "essential" for implementation of the standard.

Beware that standards organizations may require full disclosure of patents or patents pending that might relate to a proposed standard. For example, a proponent of the standardization of a given technology may be under a legal obligation to disclose its patents or pending applications covering such technology, if they have any.

6.2 WHEN ENTERING INTO ALLIANCES AND OTHER RELATIONSHIPS INVOLVING TECHNOLOGY

The business may wish to enter into an alliance or venture with another company. If the business has no patent protection, then it must bargain under normal circumstances (e.g., offering certain resources, including technical know-how, and capital contributions). However, if a company has patents covering one or more technologies that will be needed by the venture, that company may be in a better bargaining position. The business may offer to license the patented technology to the venture, and thereby obtain income in addition to its share of the venture's profits. In addition, or alternatively, the business could obtain a larger ownership interest in the venture. See Exhibit 6.2.

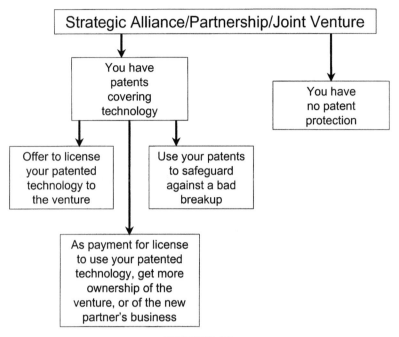

EXHIBIT 6.2

- Early in 1993, *AT&T Corp.* formed an alliance with *Unitel Communications, Inc.*, apparently to better compete with MCI Communications Corp. and the Stentor Group of telephone companies in Canada. Its patent portfolio presumably helped AT&T's standing when it entered into a relationship with Unitel. Unitel, a Canadian long distance carrier, agreed to give AT&T a 20 percent ownership interest in its business, reportedly in exchange for an AT&T license to use patented intelligent network technology.
- Another relationship that has been formed and strengthened, in part, by patents is the cross-licensing arrangement between *Coherent, Inc.* of Santa Clara and *Lumonics Industries* of Ontario, Canada. In a January, 1995 announcement, Coherent's president Hank Gauthier, stated: "In reaching this agreement, the intellectual property rights of Coherent and Lumonics relating to excimer laser systems have been fully recognized and reconciled. We have previously stated Coherent's intent to license our competitors under these patents and we are pleased that the cross-licensing agreement with Lumonics has further expanded the portfolio of excimer-related patents that we will be offering for licensing or otherwise protecting from infringement."

Each of these companies is heavily involved in laser technology. Coherent makes lasers for scientific, medical, commercial, and micromachining markets. Lumonics participates on an international level in the development, manufacture, and support of laser-based systems in industrial settings.

- Another partnership of sorts announced in January, 1995 was between *Corel Corp.* and *Strategic Mapping, Inc.* of Santa Clara, California. Corel agreed to license its ability to use certain mapping technology developed and patented by Strategic Mapping on a non-exclusive basis. The purpose was to give Corel a continuous license to use the technology in the development of its Windows '95 products. The companies also entered into an agreement to work jointly on the development of products.

- Another example of a partnership assisted by the strength of patents was a cross-licensing agreement in 1992 between *Motorola, Inc.* and *Philips Electronics NV*, in the area of digital cellular radio technologies. The cross-licensing agreement concerned several technologies covering many radio technology standards, including the European GM, the personal communication network (PCN), and the U.S. TDMA standard known as IS-54. Both Motorola and Philips stated that the intention of the cross-licensing would be to make it easier for suppliers of radio communications systems to implement cellular systems complying with international standards.

  In 1990, Motorola and *Alcatel* of France also entered into a cross-licensing agreement for "essential patents" covering the GSM pan-European digital standard. Motorola had been awarded contracts for GSM-related validation systems in many European countries. Alcatel was also a member of the ECR 900 Consortium with *AEG* of Germany and *Nokia* of Finland, and signed an agreement with *Italtel* for directly introducing GSM in Italy.

Patents may also help buttress a business' position when an alliance or partnership is dissolved or goes sour.

- In 1995, *Checkfree Corp.*, a leading provider of electronic bill paying services, sued *National Payment Clearinghouse*, a subsidiary of a former Checkfree ally, personal finance software maker, Intuit, Inc. Checkfree was seeking to ban National Payment from further use of the bill-paying technology, and unspecified damages. Formerly, Checkfree had an alliance with Intuit, the software company that makes the Quicken personal finance program. However, Intuit subsequently bought National Payment Clearinghouse, a user of competing electronic bill-paying technology. Finally, Microsoft agreed to buy Intuit and National Payment Clearinghouse for $1.5 billion. This change of relationships apparently prompted Checkfree Corporation to take action. The former close relationship with Intuit did not last, and Checkfree's patent position apparently gave them some recourse to losing that relationship.

In addition to asserting its patent rights, Checkfree forged an alliance with Mastercard International, to offer its services through banks.

In contrast with the above examples, a company's improper use of patented technology can be a deal breaker.

- In 1998, AgrEvo GmbH, a German biotechnology firm withdrew its $650 million offer to buy Cargill Inc. AgrEvo GmbH rescinded its offer after Cargill was forced to admit, during a patent lawsuit, that it improperly used genetic material from seeds purchased from competitor Pioneer Hi-Bred International Inc.

(a) Clarity Regarding Ownership

Do not forget to make sure intellectual property ownership is clearly delineated before entering into any relationship. This applies to individuals who are employees of the company, individuals working part-time or as contractors, individuals hired on an hourly basis through an agency or a third party contractor, as well as any third party contractors.

A business can run into problems when an employee freely accepts technology from another company, or when an employee jointly works with another company to work through certain issues or to create certain enhancements to the business' product. This collaboration can result in intellectual property, the ownership of which is uncertain. The resulting intellectual property, at least part of it, may be owned jointly by the two different parties. Joint ownership impacts on what can be done with the intellectual property—who has permission to use it and who reaps the benefits of it. When two entities commonly own rights to patent rights, the enjoyment of that ownership right is shared equally by both parties. Thus, neither party can be excluded by the other from using the technology, and either party can grant a full license to anyone else without having to seek permission of the other party.

Common ownership frequently occurs, and, if a dispute arises, can create severe problems especially for the smaller company who has less leverage. Suppose a fictitious company called ACME Products develops and manufactures consumer products, and those products incorporate certain control and sensing circuits. ACME Products contracts with to design and produce the circuits. The original equipment manufacturer (OEM) is supposed to develop, from the ground up, the circuitry details, while ACME Products is supposed to develop the functionality of the product. The companies agree that ACME Products will own patent rights in the operational aspects of the product, while the OEM will own rights in the circuitry.

Assuming the appropriate contract language was drafted to make this delineation, a problem arises because operation of the device and its circuitry depend, to a certain extent, upon each other. In fact, in developing and refining the operation of the product, and in developing the corresponding circuitry, the two companies collaborate. Various features of the product are refined in discussions back and forth between the two companies.

Thus, the OEM company invents features related to the operation of the product, while ACME Products invents features related to the circuitry.

The agreement does not contain an assignment clause, by which ACME Products assigns any ownership interest it acquires, by its inventing efforts, in the circuitry, and by which the OEM company assigns to ACME Products its rights in the operation of the product. Therefore, when the product is developed, many patentable aspects of the product are subject to joint ownership.

ACME Products now is at risk. It cannot keep others from making a competing product, if the OEM company decides to license the technology to third parties.

If the agreement assigned all the patent rights in the circuitry from the OEM to ACME Products, and the OEM was given a license to use the circuitry technology, ACME Products would be in a better situation, since the OEM as a licensee, would not be permitted to sublicense the technology to other companies. If ACME Products had a patent application pending, directed to the operation of the device, before any collaborative efforts with the OEM, the ownership of such technology per any resulting patent would lie solely with ACME Products.

(b) A Few Notes about Contractual Provisions

A given company may purchase technology from a third source, who may indemnify the company for infringement of certain types of intellectual property. An indemnification will typically not cover unintended combinations of the technology with other things, nor will it cover any modifications or any unintended/unauthorized uses. Once the purchaser adds value to the technology, it risks liability for patent infringement without indemnification.

An indemnification clause cannot protect the purchaser from an injunction. Even when the vendor pays the tab for a patent defense, the vendor cannot shield the purchaser from a patent owner's right to exclude others from the technology. All the vendor can do is try to negotiate a compromise or provide the closest non-infringing substitute. Be careful, as the indemnification clause may not even require this.

The importance of considering patent strategy issues in all contractual activities cannot be overemphasized. Every time the company interacts with third parties it can either support or undermine the company's efforts to claim ownership to its developments. The inclusion of too much information in a response to an RFP can result in forfeiture of substantial trade secret rights. The disclosure of important technological developments in a user conference before a patent application is filed can result in the forfeiture of foreign patent rights, and if a U.S. patent application is not filed within one year, it can result in the forfeiture of U.S. patent rights as well.

Business dealings with other companies can create express or implied (written or oral) licenses by which large companies, perhaps customers, are given permission to use the intellectual property of the company, perhaps even patents, without any compensation. Some companies provide clauses in their general contracts which require that the vendor grant a blanket license to all of its patented technology. Even before a contract is granted, and the company chooses a vendor, the vendor must sign this agreement which includes a clause granting a blanket license to all its intellectual property rights. The contract presumably is maintained on file by the company, and can be resorted to should the vendor ever decide to seek compensation for the larger company's use of its technology.

Customers are frequently larger companies. The contractual practices of those companies are frequently designed to undermine or nullify any legal rights the vendor may have for obtaining compensation or otherwise restricting the use of technology.

Intellectual property is seldomly asserted offensively by the smaller vendor against its customers. However, the vendor may wish to obtain and preserve its rights to assert those rights in the future, as a defensive measure. The larger company could very well be in a position of great strength, and have an active patent licensing program. Should the larger company approach the smaller vendor and demand license fees for its use of certain technology covered by the larger company's patents, the smaller company might have no bargaining position to convince the larger company to reduce its royalty demands. Alternatively, if the vendor has patents which cover technology used by the larger company, the vendor can simply cite those patents as a means to offset the royalties demanded by the larger company.

(c) Initial Public Offering (IPO) Due Diligence Efforts

In today's age, patents are playing a more crucial role in the success of businesses of all types. Therefore, when a company goes public, an underwriter will want to take more care to ensure that patent rights and other intellectual property rights are handled appropriately, and, as part of its due diligence efforts, the underwriter should assess all risks pertaining to intellectual property rights which may materially affect the company. As part of this process, counsel for the underwriter will investigate the status of the technological developments of the company, the steps the company has taken to protect its intellectual property, and the state of its intellectual property efforts at the time of the investigation. In addition, the underwriter's patent counsel may inquire as to whether there are allegations that the company is infringing third party patents and whether the company is aware of any patents that could be relevant to its business activities.

When a company goes public it will negotiate an underwriting agreement with the underwriter that will typically include warranties and representations regarding intellectual property. The underwriter may want the issuer to represent, in writing in the agreement, that the company possesses adequate rights in all patents, licenses, inventions, copyrights, and technology. In addition, the underwriter will want to know that the company possesses adequate rights in all its know-how. These intangibles are typically defined as those rights currently employed by the company in the operation of its business and which is material to the business.

In addition, the underwriter may want to know whether any third parties have any rights to any patents or patentable inventions of the company. If the company is aware of any infringing activity in which it is engaged, this should also be brought to the underwriter's attention. Otherwise, the company may be required to represent that it is not aware of any infringing activity in which it is engaged. In addition, it is important that the company not be aware of infringement, misappropriation, or violation by others of its own intellectual property. If there is a conflict with the intellectual property rights of the company, or if the company is aware that it is violating the intellectual property of another, the company should bring that to the attention of the underwriter.

In addition, the underwriter may wish to obtain an opinion from the issuer's intellectual property counsel making certain representations regarding intellectual property issues. This serves to supplement the due diligence efforts of the underwriter's counsel.

CHAPTER 7

Budgetary Issues

7.1 THE COSTS OF PATENT ACQUISITION EFFORTS IN THE UNITED STATES

There are many facets to the patent system. There will be costs before, during, and after patent prosecution, all related to acquiring patents. In addition, there will be costs for exploiting the business' patent portfolio and for enforcing the business's patent rights. The costs of exploiting a patent portfolio can vary widely, and will partly be a function of the number and value of patents owned by the business.

Therefore, it is difficult to provide an accurate picture of the expected costs in exploiting a patent portfolio in any given business. The costs that might be incurred in enforcing a patent portfolio are even less predictable. The one aspect of enforcement costs that is easy to predict, however, is the fact that it will be substantial.

The costs incurred in patent acquisition are somewhat more predictable. Before patent prosecution, the company will monitor developments and determine whether patent applications directed to certain technologies should be filed. Then, novelty searches may be performed and the expected patent protection evaluated, before a decision is made to prepare a patent application and file it with the U.S. Patent and Trademark Office. Once an application is filed, patent prosecution will last an average of two years. Some technologies, including computer software, can take three or more years before a patent is obtained. After the patent is obtained, the main patent acquisition expenses are the first, second, and third maintenance fees which must be paid at 3.5, 7.5, and 11.5 years, respectively, from the date the patent is granted.

Exhibit 7.1 illustrates some of the costs that can be expected in acquiring a patent, including filing a single patent application, prosecuting the application until a patent is issued, and maintaining the issued patent for its term.

Exhibit 7.1 also includes some information based upon a survey performed in 1999 by the American Intellectual Property Law Association's Committee on Economics of Legal Practice. Other data is estimated by the author. The survey values are medians taken from a sampling of estimated averages. These

EXHIBIT 7.1

	Attorney Fees (excluding disbursements)	US Patent and Trademark Office Fees (Others may be incurred)
Helping Client Develop Disclosure and Description of invention	$1,500–$3,000	N/A
Patent Novelty Search and Report	$1,000–$2,000	N/A
Preparing and Filing Patent Application— Relatively Complex Electrical/Computer	$8,000–$15,000	$710 (plus charges for extra claims)
Preparing and Filing Two Information Disclosure Statements	$440 ($220 each)	$480 (possible charge if prior art discovered late)
Patent Application Prosecution Fees	$2,000–$6,000	Fees required if, e.g., ■ late filings ■ extra claims
Reviewing Allowed Patent Application and Paying Issue Fee	$400	$1,240
SUBTOTAL	**$13,340–$26,840**	**$2,430**
Paying First Maintenance Fee (3.5 years after patent issues)	$350	$850
Second Maintenance Fee (7.5 years after patent issues)	$350	$1,950
Third Maintenance Fee (11.5 years after patent issues)	$350	$2,990
TOTAL	**$14,390–$27,890**	**$8,220**

figures are somewhat out-of-date, especially in view of the recent rises in attorney salaries. Without taking into account any increases that might have occurred or be occurring in law firms throughout the country, these costs represent typical attorney charges, excluding disbursements (e.g., mailing costs, telephone costs, copy costs, and government fees). The government fees estimated are fees charged to a large entity applicant by the U.S. Patent and Trademark Office (USPTO) effective as of October 1, 2000. If the applicant qualifies for small entity status, the government fees are generally half of those indicated. Other costs, including special legal advice and travel costs for attending interviews at the U.S. Patent and Trademark Office are not included.

The government fees can significantly increase depending upon the situation, because the government imposes various fines for filing documents late and for filing continuation applications in order to get an application reconsidered by a patent examiner. In addition, if a patent application presents more than a certain number of claims, additional government fees will be charged.

These charges are provided to give the reader a general idea of the costs that may be incurred in a streamlined patent acquisition process. It is important to note that patenting an invention can be (and often are) more involved and therefore more costly.

The difficulties encountered in obtaining patent protection can vary widely depending upon such factors as the complexity and quantity of technical information that must be conveyed to describe the invention and the hard to predict reactions and opinions of the patent examiner. Some patent applications contain two or more times the amount of subject matter and claim numerous technological features, thus being the equivalent (in terms of cost, effort, and value) of two or more typical patent applications. Additional continuation or divisional patent applications may need to be filed to adequately protect all the features of a single application, driving costs up further.

Exhibit 7.1 also illustrates that bringing a simple patent application from its first evaluation through payment of the issue fee will likely cost well over $15,770 ($13,340 in estimated attorney fees, and $2,430 in estimated government (USPTO) fees). To maintain a patent for its complete term after it is granted, first, second, and third maintenance fees will have to be paid at predetermined intervals. Bringing a technology from its conception through the end of the term of the patent can cost at least $14,390 in attorney fees and $8,220 in USPTO fees, not counting other expenses and miscellaneous costs.

(a) Doing It Right vs. Budget Constraints

It is imperative that management set appropriate budget limits on the business' patent efforts, while freeing the parties involved, including the inventors and the patent attorney team, to produce intellectual property that will withstand challenge by an accused infringer in court and by a potential licensee during license negotiations. The business world and the patent laws are changing every day in ways that are increasing the amount of effort that should be made in preparing and filing a patent application. Once a patent owner enforces a patent or otherwise exploits it, thereby exposing the patent to close scrutiny, the patent owner may then wish more effort was spent on the process of obtaining the patent.

CHAPTER 8

Patent Litigation

8.1 PRACTICAL ASPECTS OF LITIGATION*

The outcome of trial in intellectual property litigation is not always determined by the true merits of the case. Aside from whether infringement really exists or whether a patent is valid and enforceable, a case is sometimes decided by obscure, non-merit factors, such as perseverance and stamina of the parties, character and demeanor of crucial witnesses, predispositions of a judge towards patents and monopolies, or dislike of counsel or witnesses by the judge or jury. Consequently, a decision to litigate strictly based upon objective factors may not always lead to the expected result.

From this perspective, the discussion herein focuses on some of the undeterminable and unforeseeable factors which should be considered prior to engaging in intellectual property litigation. Such factors are identified for considering whether to settle, litigate, or, in the case of an accused infringer, to simply cease and desist from the alleged infringing activity.

Fortunately, the merits of a case at the appeal level are substantially more likely to determine the ultimate outcome—that is, assuming all parties have the stamina, resources, and will to litigate to the end. This is because the Federal Circuit is much better equipped to handle patent and trademark matters as a result of, among other things, substantial prior experience in reviewing Patent and Trademark Office decisions, employment of neutral technical advisors who address technical issues for the court, and an in-depth knowledge of intricate patent and trademark laws. This presentation is limited to considerations at the trial level.

(a) Options: Settle, Litigate, or Cease and Desist

A preliminary decision to license, litigate, or cease and desist will be made, in part, in light of a fair assessment of available evidence and legal argument. On questions of validity and enforceability, the evidence available to the accused

---

*By George M. Sirilla. Reprinted (some portions edited or updated) from the Pillsbury Madison & Sutro LLP 1997 Intellectual Property Spring Seminar Materials.

infringer will generally consist of publicly accessible documents regarding the patent, its prosecution history, and prior art. Regarding infringement questions, a comparison should be made between the accused activity and claim language as interpreted by patent counsel and the accused infringer's engineering staff or technical experts. The potential litigant may also consider possible counter-suits for antitrust violation, patent misuse, or unfair competition. Based upon these preliminary assessments, the economics involved, and business judgment, the potential litigant will decide his course of action. No certainty in outcome, however, can be projected at this stage of the deliberation.

Unknown factors which add uncertainty to the decision include: whether the case is tried before a jury; the discovery after litigation ensues of previously unknown evidence; the random assignment upon filing of a lawsuit to a possibly biased judge; the availability of crucial witnesses during pendency of the litigation; new precedent established by the Federal Circuit during the pendency of the suit; and (particularly in computer and electronics litigation) the evolution and obsolescence of the litigated technology during pendency of the litigation. Some of the unknown factors have nothing to do with the true merits of the case. Yet they may affect the ultimate outcome. Thus, if the litigation route is chosen, the litigant may be faced with unpredictable odds.

Rather than litigate a threatened controversy, settlement is one way to remove the uncertainties. Sometimes a patent owner will not press for or need injunctive relief, but if the patent owner simply refuses to license on reasonable terms, and the accused activity is critical to the alleged infringer's business, litigation may be the only practical option. Alternatively, the matter in dispute may not be worth the trouble to pursue, either by settlement or litigation, even if there was a favorable assessment of the risks and ultimate outcome. In that case, a potential litigant may simply back off and cease the accused activity, if he can walk away without any significant liability.

With this background, we begin the discussion by explaining the consequences of settlement and the risks of litigation. We also discuss how litigation is conducted, a typical litigation time-table and schedule of events, the effects of litigating in certain forums and before certain judges, the costs and other burdens imposed upon litigants, the assessment of risk and consequences, and the selection of trial counsel. Counsel's potential conflicts of interest are also discussed. By acquiring an understanding of litigation risks, the trial process, and the consequences of settlement, the potential litigant may meaningfully choose an appropriate option.

(b) Settlement

As earlier stated, settlement is an alternative to litigation and generally is the preferred option, both for the patent owner and the accused infringer. Whether settlement can be reached lies for the most part within the patent owner's discretion, because he has no duty to offer a license, or any duty to offer the license on less than exorbitant terms. Compulsory licensing does not exist in the United States. From an accused infringer's perspective, the question inevitably reduces to how he will posture himself to negotiate favorable licensing terms. The patent owner thinks of what pressure it can bring to bear upon the accused infringer in order to secure favorable licensing terms, higher royalties, or improvement in its competitive position.

Of course, an accused infringer will be highly motivated to settle whenever it faces a preliminary injunction and the prospect of being forced out of the market while the litigation is pending. But issuance of a preliminary injunction will be highly dependent upon such factors as prior successful litigation of the patent, industry recognition and acceptance of the patented technology, and a strong showing of infringement. An accused infringer may also be motivated to settle if it faces an investigation at the United States International Trade Commission ("ITC") or is subject to personal jurisdiction in a court having a rapid calendar.[1]

(i) Settlement Minimizes Losses. Where the accused infringer desires to continue the alleged infringing activity without the threat of an injunction, entering into a settlement agreement *before* rather than *after* commencement of litigation has definite advantages. Settlement, for example, avoids possible treble damages under 35 U.S.C. § 284[2] for "willful infringement." The Federal Circuit has found "willful infringement" where the infringing acts were committed "without concern for the rights of the patentee" or without a "good faith belief" that the patent is invalid.[3] In essence, the law imposes an affirmative duty upon manufacturers and importers to obtain independent and competent advice of counsel *before* beginning any commercial activity which might infringe another's patent rights. Because increased damages for willful infringement can emerge from what may seem like innocent circumstances, the potential litigant should give serious thought to settlement before commencement of suit, particularly in view of the increasing trend in patent litigation to seek and secure enhanced damages.

The advice of counsel may include interpretation of the patent's claims and instructions on how to design around the claims. This advice must be competent, and not just based on a perfunctory review of the patent and the accused products. It must include a thorough analysis and investigation of the patent's prosecution history. Without competent advice, willful infringement may be found.[4]

In addition to exposure to enhanced damages for willful infringement, the accused infringer may have to face other potential monetary liabilities based, for example, on the patent owner's lost profits, price erosion, pre-judgment interest on damage awards, and an award of opposing counsel's attorneys' fees. Attorneys' fees ranging from a few hundred thousand dollars to well over a million dollars have been awarded in patent cases in the last ten years. When damages, legal fees, and other costs involved in defending a patent suit are added to the possibility of an injunction, the litigant's potential financial exposure can become staggering. Thus, settlement prior to litigation has very real and definite advantages.

(ii) Settlement Postpones Potential Litigation. Considering that a patent owner may have spent months or years investigating a potential infringer before giving notice of infringement, any delay in suit during pre-litigation settlement negotiations will provide time for the alleged infringer to evaluate and develop his or her position so as to be on more equal footing with the patent owner before commencement of the civil action. During this pre-suit negotiation period, for example, the accused infringer may conduct validity searches, obtain advice of counsel, prepare its defenses, redesign its product, and, generally, prepare for minimizing damages in potential future litigation.

(iii) Settlement and Licensing Strategy. Even if there are strong defenses against the patent's validity, it may be wise to consider accepting a license if the terms are reasonable, rather than risk the far more serious consequences of a jury verdict for the patent owner and the issuance of an injunction that would keep the alleged infringer out of the market for at least a year (the time for an appeal to the Federal Circuit). If the patent would expire before an injunction could be secured, the strategy, of course, would be different. Then you could risk taking a more aggressive stance in settlement negotiations.

In cases where a license has been entered into and the licensee later learns of an invalidating defense or develops a new non-infringing device, the licensee can stop paying royalties while challenging the patent in court. Any provision in the license agreement requiring the licensee to continue paying royalties while challenging the licensed patent in the courts would be ineffective and unenforceable under the law.[5]

The licensee should be forewarned, however, that cessation of royalty payments during the litigation may terminate the license, thereby placing the licensee in the undesirable position of having an injunction entered against it should the invalidity or non-infringement court challenge fail. The licensee cannot circumvent this result or prevent termination of the license simply by paying royalties into an escrow account.[6]

A licensee is thus placed in a quandary of choosing between, on the one hand, acquiescing to the continued enforcement of the license agreement or, on the other hand, terminating the license agreement and challenging the patent in court while facing the risk of being permanently enjoined if the court challenge fails.

A third option, however, is available to the licensee. The licensee may challenge the validity or infringement of a patent in court while continuing payment of royalties due under the license and, thereby, avoid termination.[7] Although the Federal Circuit has not squarely addressed the issue, in *dicta* the Court has seemed to indicate that a licensee may be entitled to the return of all royalties paid after the filing of the complaint (*i.e., pendente lite*) should the licensee prevail.[8]

The terms of a pre-suit settlement agreement, even after recission or breach, procedurally may control the rights of a party in any subsequent litigation that may occur. Those terms can affect the strength of a charge of willful infringement, the scope and applicability of claims relative to the accused devices and products, and more importantly, jurisdiction of subsequent litigation.

To broaden protection against charges of willful infringement, for example, a well-advised licensee might insist on a provision in the license agreement which settles, once and for all, all past claims of infringement (including willful infringement issues) by a lump sum payment for any past sales of the patented invention.

Structuring the terms of the license agreement may also resolve a licensee's jurisdictional concerns. A breach of a license agreement can give rise to either a state court action or a federal action in the district courts. The ensuing controversy may be released to state courts if the licensor sues for failure to pay royalties, thereby possibly foreclosing the licensee's opportunity to immediately attack the validity of the patent. This contract action may also be tried in federal courts if there is diversity of citizenship between licensee and licensor or if issues of infringement and validity could be raised. Alternatively, the licensee could file a declaratory judgment action of patent invalidity in the federal courts before the licensor sues for breach of contract in state court. In order to preserve the licensee's strategic pre-emptive strike capability to file the federal action, the license agreement might provide a 30–90 day pre-termination notice period prior to effective cancellation of the license. During this notice period, the licensee may then make his pre-emptive strike by filing a declaratory judgment action in any of the permissible federal courts of its choice.

Although the validity question may still remain open for challenge, the license agreement and acts that follow may foreclose the ex-licensee from pursuing non-infringement defenses. For example, if the licensee places a Section 287 marking on its products, advertises its products in any manner indicating coverage by the licensor's patent, or acknowledges coverage of licensed products by the patent, it may be later estopped from denying infringement. To afford the greatest protection to the licensee, the definition of licensed products or services should be narrowly defined so as to better enable the licensee to design around or substitute the licensed products or services with non-infringing substitutes. Further, the licensee should perform no extraneous acts that overtly acknowledge coverage of licensed products by the patent.

(c) Redesigning Products

Before putting a product into commercial production, good business practice compels a party to conduct a pre-production infringement study as one measure of litigation avoidance. This infringement study should aid in any required redesigning effort before making substantial expenditures for commercial production. In addition, a competent infringement opinion at an early stage of product development giving appropriate clearance for a product design will surely mitigate against a finding of willful infringement in any subsequent litigation over that product.

If a party has failed to clearly avoid infringement during early product design, however, redesigning may still be an available option where suit is threatened after commercial production. A party's attempt to redesign after suit is threatened may be relied on to show good faith, thereby diminishing the likelihood of a willful infringement finding. To have the greatest benefit, however, the redesign effort should involve a competent opinion of independent counsel and, if feasible, outside technical experts.

(d) Litigation

There are circumstances where an accused infringer has no choice but to litigate, such as where the patent owner relentlessly pursues him or her for past infringement even though the alleged infringing activity has ceased. Whenever there is no concern of an injunction or exclusion order, the asserted patent may still be challenged in order to gain the option of being able to use or manufacture the patented invention. This situation may arise where loss exposure is minimal and/or where the potential gain far outweighs the potential loss.

Where the alleged infringer has elected to continue the accused activity, and the patent owner refuses to license, or is demanding outrageous terms so that litigation follows, the accused infringer will have to defend, for example, on grounds of non-infringement, invalidity, and/or unenforceability, despite the financial burden and the possibility of an injunction or an ITC exclusion order.

If the expiration date of the patent is sufficiently close, the alleged infringer may litigate liability with little risk of business disruption due to an injunction.

(i) Assessment of Risks

A. Statistical Assessment The value of statistical data concerning litigated intellectual property cases is questionable because the data does not reflect any peculiarities of the cases decided. Some of these peculiarities are described below.

Since 1982, an average of 1000 or more intellectual property law suits have been filed each year in the U.S. district courts, but less than 100 of these cases actually go to trial.[9] The remainder are dismissed or settled for various reasons. If a case is tried before a jury, a verdict instead of a written opinion will be rendered. Verdicts carry little information for statistical analysis and may not be reported at all in the legal report. In contrast, a full written opinion with findings of fact and conclusions of law are issued in non-jury cases. Written opinions provide a good basis from which to draw statistical inferences; but again, not all of the written opinions are actually published, so we still do not have a full picture of events at the district court level.

A significant number of jury and non-jury intellectual property decisions are appealed to the Federal Circuit. The Federal Circuit issues written opinions for those appeals which are not dismissed or settled by the parties. Annually, that court decides between 100 and 120 appeals from the district courts. Of those decisions, only about 60 percent are published.[10] From this limited body of published decisions, only narrow statistical inferences can be drawn. Based upon trends indicated by Federal Circuit decisions, it is fair to say that nowadays, somewhere between 50 percent and 70 percent of the patents adjudicated were ultimately held valid, and infringement is found in nearly 50 percent of the cases adjudicated.

B. Evidentiary Assessment A complete assessment of the risk factors associated with the body of evidence available for trial may not be possible until well after the filing of a lawsuit, because a good part of the evidence may not be known until completion of discovery. Even so, a litigant can still assess the force and effect of witnesses and available evidence before engaging in the lawsuit. That assessment will be made in light of the complexity of the litigated issues and in light of whether the case will likely be tried before a judge or a jury. Complexity usually favors the patent owner, as do trials before a jury.

To overcome the barrier of complexity, witnesses testifying on behalf of an accused infringer need extremely good communication skills in order to impart meaning to complex principles in such a manner that the trier of fact may logically discern what is right or wrong. Expert witnesses having this quality can be found, but the litigant's officers, employees, fact witnesses, and engineers may not always possess the necessary communication skills.

The burden of proof on various issues in patent trials follows either the "preponderance of evidence" rule or the "clear and convincing" rule. The preponderance rule is akin to "more likely than not," whereas the more difficult "clear and convincing" rule is somewhat like "thorough conviction" or "clear belief." The burden of proof on infringement follows the preponderance rule. The patent owner must prove that it is more likely (*e.g.*, 51 percent) that the accused activity infringes than that it does not. Conversely, the accused infringer has a much higher burden of proof on invalidity or unenforceability questions. There, the burden is clear and convincing evidence, that is, the accused infringer must show that the asserted patent is invalid or unenforceable by thorough conviction or firm belief—a much greater than 51 percent probability.

With such a high burden to prove invalidity or unenforceability, it is almost a virtual necessity that for an accused infringer to challenge the patent, it should have some very strong evidence. Otherwise, the risk of loss may simply be unacceptable.[11]

Assessment of other evidence developed during the course of discovery will undoubtedly affect risk determination. Such evidence may include business records of the adverse party, deposition transcripts of third-party witnesses and employees, responses to discovery requests, and deposition testimony of expert witnesses.

C. Assessment of the Forum   Notwithstanding that decisions of the Federal Circuit since 1982 have promoted some uniformity and predictability in the substantive U.S. patent laws, the philosophies and pre-dispositions of district court judges, if not known to counsel, can still have an unpredictable effect on the outcome of litigation at the trial level. One author[12] characterized the influence of judicial philosophy and oral advocacy by surveying 45 of his judicial colleagues before and after oral arguments in general civil litigation. Each colleague described himself as being liberal, moderate, or conservative. Based on the individual descriptions, the survey established a significant correlation between their individual philosophies and the projected outcome.

Although no similar surveys are known for intellectual property cases, information on prior rulings by different judges is available through computerized searches. Knowledge of these prior rulings may aid litigants in predicting outcomes and may help counsel tailor arguments and approaches to fit the sensitivities and personal philosophies of the presiding judge.

Some district courts severely limit the amount of time for discovery unless good cause is shown for extensions of time. The nature of the defenses being developed, however, may require extensive and prolonged discovery and the court, due to a lack of familiarity with complex patent issues, may not be impressed with argument for extensive discovery. Discovery may be further complicated for the accused infringer if it is seeking information about a patented invention or prior art that occurred 10, 20, or more years before the suit was filed. It is possible that due to corporate mergers or acquisitions, relocation and death of witnesses, and/or document destruction polices, etc., the relevant events may be impossible to reconstruct without extensive discovery. Without sufficient time to pursue these defenses during discovery, a potential litigant could be severely prejudiced. Hence, the rules of the forum as to length of time for discovery could play a significant role in the outcome of the case.

It is also true that in a jury trial, a court will instruct the jury on how to apply the substantive patent laws to the facts of the case. The judge, however, controls what factual evidence will be submitted to the jury. So, despite submission of a factual question to the jury, the judge may still substantially influence the ultimate result by controlling what evidence the jury will receive. That influence may manifest itself in subtle favoritism of the judge toward one counsel over another, or in the judge's inherent biases for or against patents or particular parties. As a result, borderline hearsay evidence, uncorroborated or unreliable business records, and/or the testimony of incompetent witnesses, for example, may be admitted into or excluded from evidence over objection. What's more, because an appellant must show "clear error" or "abuse of discretion" on appeal of evidentiary rulings, reversible error as to such rulings is difficult to demonstrate on appeal. Accordingly, an assessment of the outcome in a jury trial may depend in large measure upon which judge has been appointed to hear the case.

In sum, despite the fact that appeal will only lie to the Federal Circuit, a prospective or actual litigant still needs to consider the forum and/or the individual judge before whom the case will be tried.

(ii) Identifying, Selecting, and Evaluating Trial Counsel Inasmuch as advocacy and capabilities of counsel will also influence the outcome of litigation, identification and selection of counsel play an important role in the process of committing to litigation. A typical district court action requires a two- to three-year engagement of trial counsel from filing of the complaint through trial and/or settlement. An appeal in the Federal Circuit averages another 10-12 months. Considering crowded dockets in some jurisdictions, a typical civil action could last four to six years at the district court level.

At the other end of the spectrum, a rapidly moving ITC investigation will ordinarily be tried within five to seven months after the investigation is instituted. Because ITC proceedings progress so rapidly, they generally require more intensive effort in a shorter time period than district court actions. Thus, for complete representation through an appeal, trial counsel's engagement (and the costs of such engagement) should be expected to span for at least four to five years for a district court action and at least two to three years for an ITC investigation.

Changing trial counsel during litigation can be very costly, both in terms of counsel fees and the additional risk of losing the litigation. Trial courts generally will not delay trial solely for the benefit of a party who has decided to use new counsel because of dissatisfaction with existing counsel. For this reason, reasonable care should be exercised in selecting trial counsel. If trial counsel is not engaged early enough in the litigation, it may be very difficult to get up to speed before the trial begins. While changing counsel during rapidly moving district court or ITC litigation is possible, and it has been done with success, it may require herculean efforts on the part of the new trial counsel and his or her team.

Changing counsel, of course, may not be within a party's control. An involuntary change resulting from disqualification of counsel, for example, will bring about similar risks and hardships. Usually, an opponent will bring a motion to disqualify early in the litigation, but there are circumstances where an opponent may only learn of a basis to disqualify near the close of discovery. In any event, if the motion is brought too late, the court might deny it because it would cause an undue hardship to the non-moving party, particularly if the movant waited too long to file it. In any event, conflict questions should be thoroughly investigated before engaging trial counsel.

Ideally, counsel's technical expertise should match the technology involved in the litigation. Litigation concerning complex electronics or data processing devices or equipment, for example, suggests that counsel should have an electrical discipline, while litigation involving chemical compositions or biotechnology suggests that counsel should have expertise in those arts. Matching counsel's technical expertise with the technology at issue, however, is only a general rule, since any particular technical discipline, or lack of it, has no necessary bearing on counsel's ability to make an effective presentation at trial. If required, the subject technology can ordinarily be explained to competent trial counsel by the technical experts, including co-counsel within the firm. Competent and experienced trial counsel can then present the technological issues in an understandable manner to a court or jury. Technological expertise, therefore, is not necessarily a decisive factor in selecting lead trial counsel.

Furthermore, jury trials require superior advocacy skills, because juries commonly cannot be expected to fully comprehend complex technological issues. Frequently, a jury's findings on such issues is determined more by counsel's ability to communicate and his credibility, and by the ability of technical experts and other witnesses to present clear and simplified explanations. Juries are also known to possess greater sentiment for small individual inventors in suits against large corporations. At times, social moods and contrasting ethnic orientations of juries, counsel, and parties may even influence fact finding to an unpredictable degree. Thus, social awareness and sensitivity of counsel to these issues may be important factors in the ultimate outcome.

How does a prospective litigant identify and select capable intellectual property counsel? Probably the best indication of capability and competence is peer recognition. Many corporate attorneys and general practice firms are very likely to know about exceptional intellectual property counsel, either through years of prior association or by general knowledge of counsel's reputation. Victories in reported decisions, for example, in the U.S.P.Q. could be another important qualification. Authorship of scholarly and insightful articles in patent journals may also provide an indicium of knowledge, but that is not necessarily an indication of performance and capability as trial counsel. Knowledge of the substantive law is only *one* of many factors affecting ultimate success in litigation. Other factors include experience, confidence developed through successes in prior litigation, good judgment, superior cross-examination skills, and effective writing and speaking skills, all of which make up the art of trial advocacy.

(iii) Identifying and Selecting Expert Witnesses Expert witnesses play an important role in intellectual property litigation. Categories of expertise required in intellectual property litigation are technical, legal, and economic. In a patent suit, a technical expert is a virtual necessity at trial to testify on such issues as whether an accused device or process falls within the scope of a patent claim, or whether an invention is obvious to skilled artisans in view of the prior art.[13] Engineering professionals, such as those employed by the party involved in the litigation, are in a good position to identify potential technical experts, and as such, they normally assist trial counsel in the selection process. Typi-

cally, technical experts are field practicing engineers specialized in the patented technology. In some cases, the inventor himself, or an engineer employed by the party, may effectively serve as a technical expert.

Because of the complexity of the patent laws and difficulties in their application, a legal expert may be permitted by the court to testify on such matters as claim interpretation and patent practice. Since this is purely a legal function, some judges may not permit use of such a legal expert. In any event, trial counsel are generally well aware of possible legal experts who can provide such testimony.

Economic experts may be employed for one of two reasons. On validity questions, an economic expert may testify about "commercial success" of the invention, that is, sales and sales trends, sales of competing products, industry growth trends and projections in the product area, and the like. This evidence will be submitted to demonstrate that features of the patented invention are or are not responsible for the commercial success.[14] Assuming liability is found and the patent is held valid and infringed, an economic expert as well as marketing, manufacturing, licensing, accounting, and/or financial experts may testify in the damage phase. Testimony on damages may embrace lost profits, reasonable royalties, price erosion, pre-judgment and post-judgment interest, and the like.

What are the criteria for selecting an expert witness? Obvious criteria include experience, publications, peer recognition, and renowned foundational knowledge in the area to be covered. Since practically every trial will bring together conflicting expert witness testimony, it is most important that an expert project an honest, trustworthy character and the required level of knowledge. Questions of technical or economic merit frequently are resolved by the trier of fact based on which expert is more believable. A second criteria is the expert's ability to communicate effectively with the court or jury. Regardless of pre-eminence, the expert's testimony will be of no avail unless he or she can convey thoughts clearly. Also, the expert must accept and believe in the positions taken in the litigation and his or her opinions on a particular point should be consistent with opinions taken in prior publications or in prior litigation. There is also the question of an expert witness' conflict of interest. It is not uncommon that experts working in a particular field have previously performed consulting services for the adversary, in which case a court may disqualify the expert. In addition to substantive knowledge, the expert should have sufficient skills and training to withstand vigorous cross-examination.

These are the principal requirements for an expert witness, but because every case has its own peculiarities, there may be some other special requirements for an expert witness in a particular case which will have to be determined on a case-by-case basis by competent counsel.

(iv) *The Costs and Burdens of Litigation* Litigants are sometimes faced with extremely high attorneys fees to defend or prosecute a patent infringement

action. According to a bi-annual economic survey conducted by the AIPLA in 1991,[15] median U.S. patent litigation averaged about $2.2M through trial in 1999. Attorneys' fees in major intellectual property suits through trial can exceed $2 to $4 million. Attorneys' fees are virtually unpredictable in advance because the amount of time required to be spent by counsel varies directly in proportion to the effort put forth by the adversary, an effort that cannot be accurately estimated in advance. Other expenses of trial include expert witness fees and, often, substantial travel and lodging expenses for counsel, parties, and witnesses. In-house counsel may help to reduce expenses, but their participation is frequently limited by prohibitions against disclosure of an adversary's confidential business information.

In addition to legal fees and expenses, litigation imposes an extraordinary burden on the officers and employees of a party-litigant. The greatest burden stems from the amount of time required for consultation with counsel on strategic matters and to respond to discovery demands from the adverse party. It has become common practice for parties in important litigation to submit extensive discovery requests that can be very burdensome and expensive. An adversary may target for deposition officers and directors who can ill afford to take time away from their regular duties and responsibilities for depositions. A deposition of a corporate officer, for example, may last from one to several days, and preparing for the deposition may also require one or more additional days. A party's engineers and technicians may similarly be deposed for numerous days. The burdens on the company become clearer and heavier if the litigation is vigorously pursued and contested, as it frequently is when the stakes are high.

Counsel's consultation with his or her client's officers and employees will be required not only for preparing for depositions but also for preparing responses to discovery requests (e.g., interrogatories, requests for admission). Consulting sessions are also needed in order to learn about the opponent, the subject matter of the controversy, and what direction the lawsuit or settlement posture shall take. It may be necessary for a company to dedicate one or more professionals to serve as liaison between the company and outside counsel to assure effective and timely communication and preparation.

Production of documents generally requires the litigant's employees to search for, compile, identify, and assemble the requested documents. Searching for and copying voluminous documents may take weeks, and it may even disrupt files and work in progress. Counsel or the party's staff must also screen company documents to mark and/or classify confidential business and technical information, to redact or expurgate wholly irrelevant information, and to categorize attorney-client and work-product privileged information. It is not uncommon that tens or even hundreds of thousands of documents may have to be processed for production to opposing counsel in an important patent infringement action, especially between head-to-head competitors.

A litigant's counsel and expert witness may also be permitted to enter the adversary's production plant to inspect and photograph equipment or products related to the patent claim. Such an entry, of course, is an unwanted intrusion, for it exposes trade secrets and production facilities to persons adverse to the disclosing party and, although a protective order might be in place to protect against any unauthorized disclosure, there might still remain an unacceptable risk of disclosure of valuable trade secrets or know how.

An accused infringer's relationship with its vendors and/or customers may also be affected by discovery intrusions from opposing counsel. For example, third-party vendors or customers may be involuntarily brought into the action by subpoenas for depositions and document production that inevitably cause some business disruption, if not great inconvenience.

Thus, the burden of litigation will encompass, among other things, interference with regular business activities, commitment of substantial time of key personnel for consultation with counsel and preparing for discovery, disruption of files and work-in-progress, potential damage to customer and vendor relations, and significant attorneys' fees and costs.

(e) Conclusion

A decision to litigate or settle can have grave consequences. Prediction of outcome cannot be made with any real certainty. A conservative approach would be to settle to remove as many uncertainties as possible, if settlement is a practical and real option. Litigation avoidance by prudent planning with competent legal counsel is undoubtedly the best policy.

8.2 A WALK THROUGH PATENT INFRINGEMENT LITIGATION*

(a) Introduction

Patent litigation has naturally increased rapidly as companies have recognized the importance of their ideas and sought to protect and maximize the competitive advantage that patents provide in the marketplace. According to the New York Times (December 27, 1998), the "combination of more patents and more companies built around patented technology has driven up the number of lawsuits. . . . The richer the prize, the bloodier the warfare and the greater the likelihood that the case will be tried rather than settled. The median cost to each party in a patent trial is $1.2 million . . . complex trials run to $6 million or more."

Unfortunately, the management in many companies lacks an understanding of what is involved in this specialized form of litigation. In turn, such high level decisionmakers often find themselves without sufficient information to

---

*This section was written by Blair Jacobs

effectively evaluate and weigh the risks and benefits of making the difficult decision to protect one's property through litigation. This chapter seeks to provide an overview of patent infringement litigation in an attempt to provide decisionmakers with a realistic but generalized view of the complexities and burdens associated with patent infringement litigation.

One thing that must be kept in mind at all times, however, is that patent litigation in the United States is very complex and therefore consumes large amounts of time for many individuals within a company. Patent litigation is also typically extremely expensive. Costs, of course, vary with the complexity of the case, but The American Intellectual Property Law Association (AIPLA), an organization that surveys its members around the United States to estimate the costs of patent litigation, estimates that the average patent infringement litigation through trial could cost each party millions of dollars.

Patent litigation is highly specialized, involving expert witnesses and voluminous and time-consuming production of documents. Furthermore, because competitors in patent infringement litigation almost always seek to learn the most sensitive trade secrets of opposing parties, this results in much consternation for companies that place a significant value on protecting trade secrets. While most courts will enter protective orders to minimize the dispersal of such confidential information, it is still difficult for most companies to reveal sensitive documents to competitors who obviously have incentive to steal or copy proprietary secrets. All of these factors stress the importance of not entering into patent infringement litigation lightly.

However, the monetary stakes in patent infringement litigation are often staggering, so much as to dwarf the attorneys' fees and inconvenience associated with being involved in such litigation. So in some circumstances, depending upon a company's patent portfolio strategy and the diversity of its business, litigation is the best course for maximizing and protecting one's competitive advantage in the marketplace. What follows is a general discussion of the types of issues and stages of litigation that a company will typically see in a patent case.

(b) Pre-filing Evaluation and Obligations

In evaluating the merits of initiating an infringement lawsuit, a patent holder not only has to consider the potential upside if it wins, it must evaluate the risks it runs by placing all matters concerning the patent at issue. In terms of the upsides, the patent holder will obviously want to obtain competent legal advice regarding the issue of infringement and evaluate the range of damages which might be awarded against the infringer if the patent holder prevails. Equally important is an assessment of whether a judgment, if any, can be enforced. The patent holder must then balance the possibility of success with the expense and time necessary to pursue the litigation, while also factoring in the likelihood that its business operation may be impacted by the loss of resources necessary to handle the litigation.

The largest potential downside to patent litigation is that the counterclaims that are inevitably brought against a patent holder who files an infringement lawsuit often include an allegation that the patent is invalid. The possibility of losing on the issue of invalidity presents a significant downside for the plaintiff because, if that occurs, it no longer will have any rights under the patent. This risk is one of the most significant that a patent holder must evaluate when deciding whether to bring a claim for infringement. Thus, the prudent patent holder contemplating filing a lawsuit for infringement will not only first obtain a legal opinion as to whether the competitor is infringing, but also some level of advice regarding the validity of its own patent. Rushing into litigation with a patent of suspect validity can create far more potential downside than may be justified, so obtaining legal guidance on this issue is essential.

If any questions at all exist regarding the validity of a patent, consideration should be given to alternatives to litigation such as entering into a licensing agreement, thereby minimizing the exposure of your own patent to an unfavorable ruling and strengthening the patent in the eyes of others.

Before a plaintiff can file a lawsuit in a federal district court, the plaintiff's attorney must investigate the facts and law to determine that there is a nonfrivolous basis for the lawsuit. Rule 11 of the Federal Rules of Civil Procedure requires that if an attorney signs a court document, the attorney must certify there is sufficient factual basis for it and that it is supported by the law or a nonfrivolous extension of the law. In a patent case, it is typical to obtain an infringing device and analyze it before filing a suit. Indeed, recent Federal Circuit cases have stressed the importance of taking this step. When the accused device is compared with the patent, one or more claims of the patent must read on, and thus infringe, the accused device. After it is established that at least one of the claims of the patent is infringed, the suit can be filed.

The filing of a complaint initiates a patent lawsuit in federal court.

(c) The Complaint

A patent infringement action begins with the plaintiff filing and serving a complaint, a document which sets out the grievances of the party seeking damages. Usually, it identifies the plaintiff and the defendant and states under what theory the defendant is liable to the plaintiff. A complaint will conclude with a prayer for relief, which is a statement of what the plaintiff seeks from the defendant. The location or venue of a case is generally determined by the location of the parties and/or where the infringement took place. Counsel for each side will strive to keep the case in a location which is favorable to their client. For example, while some federal courts typically take three years from the filing of suit until trial, others, like the Eastern District of Virginia, average approximately nine months from filing of suit until trial. Plaintiffs tend to favor courts that have a faster track to trial because this makes the job of presenting a defense more difficult.

Following service of the complaint, the defendant has 20 days in which to answer. In answering, a defendant either admits or denies the allegations in the complaint and, in most patent cases, files counterclaims against the plaintiff. The Federal Rules also provide, in certain circumstances, for the filing of a motion in lieu of filing an answer. These motions are typically concerned with whether a defendant is subject to the jurisdiction of the court, whether the court has jurisdiction to hear the particular issues raised by the complaint, whether the location of the lawsuit is the most convenient for the parties, whether the defendant was properly hailed into court and whether the appropriate parties are present in the lawsuit. Each of these issues should be examined carefully by an attorney prior to filing an answer because some defenses can be waived if they are not raised.

Either party can request that a jury hear the case. If no such request is made, the judge will decide the case when it gets to trial. The decision of whether to demand a jury is important in patent cases. In general, jurors are thought to be more reluctant than federal judges to find patents invalid. Thus, plaintiffs often desire a jury trial. This may not be true, of course, if the judge has a record of upholding patents or has a specialized technical background advantageous to his or her hearing the case alone.

(d) Preliminary Injunction

More and more frequently, courts are willing to grant preliminary injunctions in the early stages of a case which preclude the alleged infringer from using the invention during the pendency of the litigation. Many courts hold an "evidentiary hearing" following a request for an injunction. An evidentiary hearing can be expensive to conduct since it is, in effect, a "mini-trial." Such a hearing is often necessary because it is rather difficult to obtain a preliminary injunction in patent cases.

A preliminary injunction, however, will be entered only in extraordinary circumstances. A patent owner must show that he or she has a strong likelihood of success against the infringer, that the balance of hardship between the patent owner and the infringer favors the patent owner, and that the preliminary injunction would not be contrary to the public interest. These requirements are normally difficult to meet unless the patent previously has been litigated and found valid. If a patent holder is successful in gaining a preliminary injunction, a case usually will settle because a court has decided that the patent owner has a strong likelihood of success even before the case has gone to trial. In addition, the defendant's inability to continue its sale or use of the product will often be detrimental.

After the case is framed by the complaint, and after an answer and counterclaims and plaintiff's motion for preliminary injunction, if any, are resolved, the case proceeds to the discovery phase.

(e) Discovery

In most instances, the most time-consuming and expensive portion of any lawsuit is the discovery period. During this period, each party has the right to inspect documents of the other party or third parties related to the issues in the suit. They also have the right to ask written questions of each other regarding contentions and facts related to the suit. They have the right to take verbal testimony of each other and of third parties in the form of depositions. In a sense, discovery is designed to elicit every possible fact about a case so that there are no surprises at trial.

These procedures, which vary in time from three or four months to two years depending on the assigned judge and federal district, are expensive and time-consuming. The procedures also intrude on the regular business activities of both parties.

The following sections briefly describe some relevant discovery procedures.

(i) Initial Discovery Disclosures At the outset of a lawsuit, many, but not all, districts, require a party to locate and produce to the opposing party information that typically would be requested during the course of the lawsuit. This information will include the names and addresses of individuals that are likely to have relevant information regarding the dispute, a copy or a description of all documents and tangible items that are relevant to the dispute, and a computation of damages along with supporting evidence. In practice, these disclosures are typically less than complete because parties require additional discovery to ascertain complete relevant facts in a suit.

(ii) Document Requests Each party can request relevant documents from another party and can also seek the production of documents from third parties who are not in the suit but who possess relevant documents nonetheless. The party receiving the document requests must agree to produce the requested documents or must object to the production of those documents within 30 days. A party agreeing to produce documents has the option of producing those documents for inspection as those documents are kept in the ordinary course of business or, producing the documents labeled and categorized to correspond to each of the categories in the document request. Most businesses prefer the former to the latter.

Patent holders engaged in litigation need to realize that the details of their business will basically be an open book during discovery. A large commitment of time, resources, and cooperation throughout the company will likely be required during this phase of the litigation. While certain procedural devices can help minimize concerns in this regard (i.e., "protective orders" which can limit what information needs to be divulged and/or what uses an opponent can make of a company's information), litigants must be prepared for the possibility that their detailed financial information, customer information, trade secrets, and otherwise similarly confidential or proprietary information may be required to be turned over to the opponent/competitor. Clear communication with counsel can minimize the burdens associated with discovery.

(iii) Interrogatories   The parties may serve written questions on each other after a lawsuit is started. Interrogatories may not be sent to parties outside the suit. Depending upon the jurisdiction in which a suit is brought, each party is limited typically to 25 to 30 interrogatories, unless the parties agree to an increased number.

Interrogatories must be answered or objected to within a limited period of time, generally 30 days. In answering interrogatories, a party may either answer the interrogatory directly or, in certain circumstances, produce business records in lieu of answering the interrogatory. A party may only produce business records if the answer to the interrogatory may be derived from business records and the burden of abstracting or summarizing the information in the business records is substantially the same for either party. In practice, parties typically provide a response to each interrogatory, but carefully phrase each answer to minimize disclosure.

Experiences in discovery can vary from a fairly cooperative exchange of necessary information to a war, where each party goes in front of the judge on a regular basis accusing each other of intentionally withholding information in disregard to the rules. Some judges keep tight reins on the discovery activities of the parties, while others allow much more latitude. The extent of discovery allowed by the court and the cooperation or, conversely, the refusal to cooperate exhibited by the parties during this phase has a substantial impact on the overall cost of the litigation. If, for example, your opponent is intent on conducting broad-based, aggressive, and pervasive discovery, and the judge is unwilling to do much to limit such tactics, there is little else you or your attorney can do to minimize the expenses incurred by you in response. Conversely, if the opponent is fighting your every effort to conduct legitimate discovery, then the costs associated with such delays, and with repeatedly asking for the court to intervene and compel cooperation, amount to a contingency which must be taken into account. The cost of discovery is often unpredictable and, to a large extent, beyond the control of a party or its attorney. In most instances, patent infringement litigation involves contentious discovery because the stakes are so high.

Despite the heightened cost of discovery, the effectiveness of these efforts plays a crucial role in the eventual outcome of a case or, equally as important in many instances, a party's position when negotiating an out-of-court settlement. Effective and efficient discovery can maximize a company's settlement position.

(iv) Limitations on Discovery   Discovery is not a fishing expedition. Only relevant information that is not already possessed by the other side must be turned over during discovery. Typically, an attorney will raise a number of ob-

jections and will attempt to limit the intrusion caused by discovery as much as possible. Moreover, there are few instances in which information or documents need not be revealed. Nevertheless, most businesses find that discovery has the detrimental impact of sapping resources and personnel.

Generally speaking, communications between an attorney and a client are privileged and not discoverable by the opposing party. In order to qualify for the privilege, a communication must be between only an attorney and a client under circumstances of confidentiality. If a communication is conducted in a situation where other people reasonably may hear it or discern its content, the privilege may be waived. As a result of the negative affect of potential waivers of the privilege, it is best to limit the people who receive correspondence from an attorney. Wide dispersal of such information may result in the information being received by entities or people not entitled to the privilege, thereby waiving privilege for the entire communication.

A party can also usually withhold production of documents and information covered by the attorney work product doctrine. This doctrine protects all documents and information prepared in anticipation of trial. The rule stems from the fact that it would be unfair for one attorney to reap the benefit of the work of another attorney or to allow one attorney to intrude upon another's preparation of a case. In certain limited circumstances, however, a court may order an attorney or party to turn over attorney work product. The attorney work product doctrine thus is not as broad a protective as the attorney-client privilege

(v) Discovery Motions   As mentioned above, a party receiving discovery requests such as interrogatories or document requests usually objects. If the party asking for the discovery feels that the objections are unwarranted or unjustified and that a party has not properly complied with a request, the party may bring a motion to compel discovery.

If a court grants a motion to compel discovery, it will enter an order to that effect and the party must then produce the withheld information. Although such motions are commonplace in patent cases, obtaining discovery from a reluctant party is usually an expensive and time-consuming process.

(f) Pretrial Preparation and Motions

After completing fact discovery, the parties will begin to prepare for trial. They will engage experts to testify on their behalf, make arrangements to have fact witnesses testify on their behalf, and examine the other party's arguments. They also will probably take the depositions of their opponent's expert witnesses. These depositions are important in patent cases because they tend to highlight an opponent's positions.

One or both of the parties usually bring a motion for summary judgment after the close of discovery. Summary judgment is a procedure that allows a court to decide the case without going to trial. A person is entitled to summary judgment if there are no significant facts in dispute and judgment is warranted as a matter of law. In reality, the chance of obtaining summary judgment is remote. Nonetheless, summary judgment motions are very important because they can end a case short of a timely and expensive trial.

A central issue in most cases, and thus a common subject of motions, involves the interpretation, meaning, and scope of the claims(s) at issue. The U.S. Supreme Court confirmed in the Markman case that it is the judge's job to interpret and "construe" the patent claims, and the jury's job to decide whether the accused device is covered by the patent as construed by the judge. Frequently, however, once the scope of the claim is determined and interpreted by the judge, it is readily apparent whether the accused device infringes or not. As a result, a judge's construction may render a case ripe for resolution without further proceedings.

The Markman case has given rise to what is known as a "Markman hearing," which is an opportunity for both sides to present arguments, and possibly expert testimony, in order to advance what they believe to be the proper construction of the claims of the patent. Markman hearings are being used with ever-increasing frequency in an effort to bring cases to a prompt resolution and avoid the time and expenses associated with proceeding through a full jury trial on the patent infringement issues.

While there can certainly be significant time, effort, and expense associated with preparing for and conducting a Markman hearing, these efforts will likely be minimal compared with what would be required otherwise.

In certain cases, however, there still may be factual issues that remain even after the court construes the claims of the patent. This can occur, for example, when it is alleged that even if the device does not copy the patented invention literally, the accused device does essentially the same thing, in essentially the same way, to achieve essentially the same result. This is referred to as infringement under the "doctrine of equivalents," and is often a jury question. Thus, while a favorable construction of the patent by the judge at a Markman hearing will be very helpful in prevailing under the doctrine of equivalents, in such cases a trial will probably still be necessary.

If summary judgment is not granted, the parties must begin arduous preparation for trial. District courts generally order pretrial submissions, voir dire, proposed exhibits, jury instructions, and a variety of other procedural devices before trial commences. Through this course, the court attempts to streamline the trial process as much as possible and to minimize the risk of surprise.

(g) Possibilities for Settlement before Trial

Settlement is generally encouraged in all civil cases. Judges tend to actively encourage settlement because it saves the litigants time and money and lightens the court's caseload. Furthermore, many patent suits are settled by the parties entering into a licensing/royalty agreement. By entering into such arrangements, a patent holder maintains rights under the patent, does not have to worry about challenges to the validity of the patent, and receives compensation. For the alleged infringer, a settlement similarly provides a means to avoid costly patent litigation and provides a fixed business cost instead of a potentially enormous damages award. Most importantly, such an agreement allows the alleged infringer to continue practicing the technology at issue; this benefit, in some instances, may make the difference between staying in business and being shut down.

Most courts today have mandatory settlement conferences during the pendency of litigation. Others require parties to engage in mediation or arbitration, alternative dispute proceedings where parties essentially present their cases to an independent third party. Of course, in some instances settlement is not possible and a case must proceed to trial.

(h) Trial

A court will set the case for trial after discovery is completed, the pretrial motions decided, and the pretrial papers submitted. After the selection of jurors (if applicable), trials commence with the presentation of opening statements. The plaintiff's statement typically covers the Patent Office's grant of a U.S. patent after thorough examination by an expert patent examiner; the inventor's struggle to make the invention work, overcoming problems that others had been unable to solve; commercial success won by the inventor's efforts; and the infringement of the invention. The defendant's statement will highlight the defenses. The defendant may, for example, suggest that the patent should never have been granted because the invention was already known or obvious, the owner deceived the examiner to get the patent, or that by independent effort the defendant created a product different from what the patent covers.

The inventor, the engineers responsible for the defendant's product, and the expert witnesses have leading roles in a patent suit. The inventor's account of difficulties he or she overcame to achieve success with the invention tends to play a significant role in the patentee's case. The testimony of the defendant's engineers' can be equally critical since the questions of whether the defendant's product was the result of copying or independent design can make or break a jury case. In the end, however, technical experts often determine the outcome of a patent case. On validity issues, technical experts provide a comparison of the differences and similarities between the patented invention and prior art and may give their opinions on the ultimate issues of anticipation or obviousness of the claimed invention. On infringement, the technical experts' conflicting comparisons of the application of the language of patent claims to the accused product and on technical issues of equivalency may strongly influence a jury's decision. Believable and understandable expert testimony is critical since those issues are highly technical.

Another common expert witness in patent lawsuits is a patent law expert, often a prominent patent lawyer with past experience in the U.S. Patent Office. Such an expert's role is to explain the mechanics of obtaining a patent, U.S. Patent Office procedures, the prosecution history of the patents at issue, and the relationship between the claim terminology and the accused product. The patent law expert's role can be much expanded, particularly in a bench trial, where opinions on ultimate questions of patent law are often permitted. Interestingly, some judges regard such testimony with disdain, while others openly welcome the particular expert's assistance.

After all the evidence in the case has been presented, the attorneys present closing arguments. Unlike opening statements, closing arguments are not limited to a factual presentation of the evidence. Rather, attorneys typically argue that the facts in evidence demonstrate that the case should be decided in their client's favor. A decision will be rendered after the closing arguments. In a bench trial, the judge will usually issue a written decision at a later date. If the case is a jury trial, the court will read the jury instructions to the jury after the closing arguments. After the jury instructions have been read, the court will dismiss the jury to a closed room where they will deliberate on the facts of the case and reach a decision. When this happens, the jury will return to the courtroom and announce their decision.

If a defendant is found to have infringed one or more claims of the plaintiff's patent(s), possible remedies include damages and an injunction.

(i) Damages

An infringer must pay damages to the patent owner for any infringement. The United States Code provides for recovery in patent actions of damages not less than a reasonable royalty, together with interest and costs, and for damages that may be increased by the court (upon a showing of exceptional circumstances) of up to three times the amount found. This is interpreted to provide for the alternative of lost sales or a reasonable royalty, or a combination of both. If an accused infringer is found to have willfully infringed a patent, he or she may have to pay treble damages and, possibly, attorney fees. However, such increased damages are viewed as draconian by most courts and are only awarded in extraordinary circumstances, typically where an infringer did not seek and rely on the advice of counsel after receiving or being placed on notice of the patent at issue.

As far as lost profits are concerned, a patent owner is entitled to recover the amount of money that would have been made but for the infringement. Courts have interpreted this to mean incremental profit, rather than actual profit lost. Incremental profit is calculated by subtracting variable expenses from the gross selling price of the patented product. As a result, the incremental profit on a product is usually higher than the actual profit realized on the patented product. Such issues as demand for the patented product, the absence of acceptable non-infringing alternatives, and the patent owner's capacity to meet demand all weigh into the calculation of lost profits. Patent infringement damages, there-fore, may actually exceed the amount of profit actually made by the defendant through the infringing activity.

At a minimum, a patent owner is entitled to recover a reasonable royalty for the use of his or her invention by the infringer. Courts generally look at the fol-lowing factors to determine what a reasonable royalty should be:

1. the rates paid by the patent owner and the infringer for the use of similar patents;
2. the royalties received by the patentee for any pre-existing licenses for the patent in suit;
3. the patent owner's established policy of licensing or not licensing others to use his or her invention;
4. any commercial relationship between the patent owner and the infringer, such as, whether they are competitors in the same territory in the same line of business, or whether they are inventor and promoter;
5. whether the sale of the patented product promotes the sale of other prod-ucts that are not patented;
6. the amount of time left until the patent expires;
7. the established profitability of any products made under the patent, the patent's commercial success, and its current popularity;
8. the advantages of the patent over old modes and devices used for similar purposes;
9. the nature and scope of the patent, the breadth of the claim language at issue, and whether such claims are easy to design around;
10. the extent to which the infringer has used the patented invention;
11. the portion of the profit or the selling price that is customarily paid for the use of the invention in the business or in comparable businesses;
12. the portion of the profit that should be credited to the invention as distin-guished from non-patented elements, the manufacturing process, busi-ness risks, or significant features added by the infringer;
13. the opinion testimony of qualified experts;
14. the amount that a licensor and a licensee would have agreed upon in a hy-pothetical negotiation if both had been reasonably and voluntarily trying to reach an agreement; that is, the amount that a licensee who desired as a business proposition to obtain a license to manufacture and sell the patented invention would be willing to pay as a royalty and yet still be able to make a reasonable profit.

Reasonable royalty awards in patent cases tend to be lower than lost profit awards. In addition to collecting damages for infringement of a patent, a patent owner also may obtain a permanent injunction enjoining the defendant from producing future products that infringe. As a matter of course, a court will usually enter a permanent injunction at the end of the trial after a defendant has been found to infringe the plaintiff's patent(s).

(j) Post-Trial Activities

After the trial has concluded, the losing party may file various motions seeking post-trial relief from the court. Litigants typically move for a new trial based on mistakes made during trial and a renewed judgment as a matter of law, claiming that no reasonable jury could have decided the case the way the present case was decided. These motions are rarely granted.

Next, the losing party may appeal the case to the Court of Appeals for the Federal Circuit, the court with exclusive jurisdiction for appeals in patent law. In such an instance, both parties file extensive written pleadings with the court arguing about the existence or non-existence of factual or legal errors, there is sometimes an oral argument in front of a panel of judges, and the panel issues an opinion concerning the case below. This entire process can be time-consuming and expensive as well, though not nearly as time-consuming and expensive as the trial process.

(k) Conclusion

Patent litigation is some of the most difficult, specialized litigation in our jurisprudence system today. Potential litigants must be willing to examine all relevant factors with a careful and unbiased eye before embarking on litigation. All of the benefits, costs, and risks associated with undertaking a lengthy, hard-fought, and often contentious battle must be weighed. The benefits of protecting and maximizing the utility of a patent portfolio can obviously be huge, but they must always be examined with careful counsel of the potential downsides existing based on the set of facts that are present. This increased scrutiny will allow a business to wisely maximize its patent portfolio and competitive positioning with the marketplace.

8.3 AVOIDING AND RESOLVING DISPUTES

Here, the company should separate its needs from its desires. This can be critical. The best course of action to avoid or resolve a dispute is to sit down and talk with the other side. Ideally, at least one individual in each company is able to look at the situation objectively, to provide internal advice to the decision makers, and to discuss the issues with the other side in an objective fashion without being hindered by emotion. In addition, ideally, there are no political considerations or other forces at work that would prevent one company from being reasonable in resolving the dispute. For example, one company may not wish to appear weak, or the attorney for that party may not wish to appear weak and thus may not compromise its adversarial posture in dealing with the dispute. In addition, there may be secret information pertaining to the issue which one company does not wish to reveal to the other company, but which has a lot to do with why that company has taken a particular position.

In situations where face-to-face discussions are unsuccessful in resolving a dispute, companies may resort to litigation. However, more and more companies are learning that an alternative method—mediation—can be used.

Mediation, unlike arbitration or civil litigation, is not binding. Thus, it presents less risk to the parties. If a party does not like the proposed solution to a problem, it is not obliged to adopt that solution. Each party may walk away from a mediation at any time without penalty.

A technology-related mediation, dealing with an intellectual property dispute, can be resolved in as little as one or two days. The mediation will typically involve a business representative who is a decisionmaker from each party as well as a lawyer for each party having expertise in the legal, technical, and business issues at hand.

Mediation tends to focus more on the business objectives of each party and less on the legal merits. However, the legal strengths or weaknesses of each party will be considered by the mediator, who may give feedback to each party as to its relative bargaining position on those issues. On the other hand, the focus is to come to a solution which allows both parties to go on with their business. Frequently, the parties in a dispute have a customer-supplier relationship which, under the best of circumstances, should be maintained.

Mediation also allows for creativity in coming up with a solution. As part of the process, a resolution agreement is drafted, which includes all of the terms of the settlement.

It is important for the executive of a small to mid-size company to keep in mind this solution as an alternative to the more costly arbitration and civil litigation avenues which may be pursued. The interaction with the opposing party is less hostile in a mediation, and a present or possible future relationship with the opposing party is less likely to be foregone or sacrificed.

Mediating Intellectual Property Disputes: Insights from the Cornell/PERC Survey

By Sandra A. Sellers

The Cornell/PERC Institute on Conflict Resolution recently released the results of their 1997–1998 survey of the general counsel or chief litigators for the Fortune 1,000 corporations about their use of alternative dispute resolution (ADR) mechanisms. The response rate was extremely high—60 percent, or 606 respondents. The responses were catalogued in *The Appropriate Resolution of Corporate Disputes: A Report on the Growing Use of ADR by U.S. Corporations,* by David B. Lipsky and

Ronald L. Seeber ("The Cornell Report") (see *ADR Report*, 11/25/98, p. 2). Eighty-seven percent of the respondents used mediation at least once in the last three years; 63 percent preferred mediation to other ADR forms. Mediation was used most frequently in employment and contractual disputes, *but more than a quarter—28.6 percent–of all surveyed indicated that they have used mediation in intellectual property disputes.* The percentage of those who used medication in intellectual property disputes was greatest in the manufacturing (durable, 64 percent, nondurable, 55 percent and service (44 percent) industries.

The Report concludes that the future of ADR appears to lie in mediation. Forty-six percent of the respondents said they were "very likely" to use mediation in the future and an additional 38% said they were "likely" to use it. In particular, the companies indicated they are more likely to use mediation in selected types of disputes, including those involving intellectual property. What accounts for mediation's popularity in the realm of intellectual property? Intellectual property matters are particularly well suited to mediation, as the leading companies surveyed by Cornell recognized.

Mediation saves money. Cornell's survey found that 89.2 percent of all companies surveyed (97 percent of those that use mediation "very frequently") mediate disputes in order to save money. Most intellectual property matters are expensive to litigate. It is not unusual for a patent infringement dispute to cost each side well over $1 million through trial, and such cases often are appealed, adding to the cost. Since cases of this type often are settled via license agreements, sometimes during trial or on appeal, much of the cost of discovery, trial preparation, voluminous exhibits, expert testimony, and diverted executive time could have been spared by using mediation at an earlier stage to craft an appropriate settlement.

Fast results. Mediation provides prompt resolution, while the product is still commercially viable. The Cornell survey found that 80.1 percent of all respondents (97 percent of those that use mediation "very frequently") mediate disputes to save time. It is not clear from the report exactly what is meant by "saving time," but it may mean both saving executive time and reaching a resolution as promptly as possible. Both definitions are significant in an intellectual property context. Many "hot" products are covered by patents, trademarks, or copyrights, and by virtue of their appeal become subject to infringement. But how good is a favorable judicial decision if the patented technology already has been superseded by another patent, or if last season's most popular toy now sits on the self, or if some other copyrighted software game now heads the best seller list? Mediation can resolve the dispute long before a judicial decision may be reached.

Parties stay in charge. With mediation, the parties retain control of the process and the ultimate decision. The Cornell survey found that 82.9 percent of all respondents (100 percent of those who use mediation "very frequently") mediate because it "allows the parties to resolve the dispute themselves." If the judge, jury, or arbitrator might be confounded by intellectual property law concepts such as "prior art" or "doctrine of equivalents," or factual issues concerning the underlying technology, it may be best to avoid the "poor" decision that could proceed from such confusion. The parties can keep control of the outcome by mediating, rather than relinquishing the decision to a third party.

Confidentiality is preserved. Confidentiality was another major reason the Cornell respondents used mediation (44.9 percent of all; 74 percent of those that use mediation "very frequently"). Many intellectual property disputes, particularly alleged trade secret misappropriation, involve confidential business and technical information. Mediation avoids disclosure of such sensitive information, even under a protective order. This minimizes the risk of losing trade secret designation, and of accidental or ill-time disclosure of other confidential information. A company may not want certain knowledge prematurely, out of concern for its affect on investors, or an impending merger or IPO. Finally, a party can disclose certain information, such as sensitive business plans, in confidence to the mediator, who can then use this background information to craft a settlement that meets each party's business needs, without transmitting the information to the opponent.

Mediation fosters creative, business-driven solutions. Since most intellectual property matter ultimately are resolved via license agreement, it is more efficient to utilize the mediation process, which is designed to reach a business-driven settlement. The mediator can help the parties draft a variety of business arrangements, such as licensing (or cross-licensing) agreements, joint ventures, distributor agreements, usage phase-out agreements, etc. The mediated agreement also may extend well beyond the scope of the legal claims in the pending lawsuit and accommodate larger business interests, which may result in more satisfaction with the dispute resolution process and with the settlement itself. Indeed, the Cornell survey found that 67.1 percent of all surveyed (93 percent of those that use mediation "very frequently") mediate because of "more satisfactory settlements"; moreover, 81.1 percent of all surveyed (97 percent of those that use mediation "very frequently") mediate due to greater satisfaction with the process.

Mediation preserves continuity in existing business relationships. The Cornell survey found that 58.7 percent of all surveyed (83 percent of those that mediate "very frequently") mediate because it "preserves good relationships." Many intellectual property disputes arise between parties that have an ongoing business relationship, such as between the intellectual property owner and its customer or distributor. It is good business judgment to mediate these disputes and preserve and strengthen that relationship, rather than create a permanent enemy through the adversarial litigation process. Many industries that are dependent on intellectual property rights, such as software and biotech, have limited channels of supply and distribution, and cannot afford to lose key partners due to a lack of alternatives.

Leveling the playing field. Mediation offers an option for a defendant who may feel disadvantaged in the forum chosen by the plaintiff. In complex intellectual property matters, a defendant may need lots of time (and money) to prepare its defense and cross-claims alleging invalidity of the patent, trademark, or copyright. If time is short, as in investigations before the U.S. International Trade Commission, or in a federal court with a "rocket docket" like the U.S. District Court for the Eastern District of Virginia, it may be better to settle a dispute than to defend under such constraints. Similarly, a defendant may prefer not to defend in a jury trial in the plaintiff's "home" court, or in a jurisdiction with precedent favorable to the plaintiff. Mediation offers a sensible way out of these predicaments.

Why don't more companies use mediation to resolve intellectual property disputes? The largest barrier to using mediation is opposition from their adversaries. Seventy-five percent of all Cornell respondents (93 percent of those who use mediation "very frequently") stated that their opponents are unwilling to come to the mediation table.

There also can be internal opposition to mediation due to lack of management support. The Cornell survey found that 28.6 percent of all respondents (only 18 percent of those who use mediation "very frequently") had no direction from senior management to use mediation. The survey also noted, however, that middle management often failed to support mediation due to a perception that mediation undermined their traditional decision-making authority. This is consistent with the International Trademark Association's informal telephonic survey, in which corporate counsel expressed the view that if the dispute could not be settled in - house, it should be litigated, because later settlement by a mediator would impugn the in-house lawyer's settlement skills, thereby undermining counsel's credibility within the company.

Some respondents perceived certain "benefits" of mediation as negative attributes. Approximately 40 percent of all respondents indicated they do not use mediation because it is nonbinding and results in compromised outcomes.

Many of these barriers to mediation should dissipate as more companies learn to embrace the primary benefits of mediation, such as cost and time savings, and control over the process ad ultimate resolution.

Finding qualified intellectual property neutrals. The Cornell Report also noted some concern about finding qualified neutrals when specialized expertise was required. Twenty percent of all respondents identified the lack of qualified neutrals as a barrier to using mediation. There are, however, a growing number of resources of finding neutrals qualified to mediate intellectual property and other technical matters. The major national ADR providers, such as CPR institute for Dispute Resolution (<www.cpradr.org>), American Arbitration Association (<www.adr.org>), and JAMS/Endispute (<www.jams-endispute.com>) now have specialized neutrals. Technology Mediation Services, LLC (<www.technologymediation.com>), World Mediation Network's IP Mediation Services (<www.worldmediation.com>), and ADROIT, Inc. (<adroit@way.com>) are dedicated to offering neutrals for intellectual property and other technical disputes. The American Intellectual Property Law Association (AIPLA) (<www.aipla.org/ADR_Toc.html>) has a listing of members who provide ADR services. The World Intellectual Property Organization (WIPO) has an Arbitration and Mediation Center (<www.arbiter.wipo.int/about_center/index.html>) with an extensive, worldwide list of neutrals. The International Trademark Association (INTA) (<www.inta.org/adrtoc.htm>), in conjunction with CPR, has a panel of neutrals in the U.S. and Canada who handle trademark, trade dress, false advertising, and unfair competition disputes. The Software Publishers Association (SPA) created the Software Industry Mediation Service (SIMS) (<www.spa.org/mediation>) to fill in the previous gap of neutrals knowledgeable about software issues.

There are other individual mediators throughout the U.S. that may be found through web searches and word of mouth. This list is not exhaustive, but may be a starting point for finding qualified neutrals.

Mediating intellectual property disputes is the future. As noted previously, the Cornell survey found that a large majority of the respondents intend to use mediation in the future, particularly in intellectual property disputes. One hundred percent of those corporations who use mediation "very frequently" indicated that mediation minimizes risk by keeping control of the outcome, which is extremely important when an entire product line (or the company) may be dependent on certain intellectual property rights. Few companies can afford to ignore the time-saving and money-saving benefits of mediation. Mediation has a high success rate— 80 percent—which is consistent with the satisfaction rate of all corporations that responded to the Cornell survey. All these benefits—high rates

of success and satisfaction, realized without foreclosing other options—
suggest that it should be standard corporate policy to try mediation in any
dispute that does not require establishment of legal precedent.

Sandra A. Sellers is president of Technology Mediation Services,
LLC, of McLean, VA and director of the Software Publishers Association's Software Industry Mediation Service. She is a certified mediator,
an attorney, and a former litigator, who now mediates high tech and
other intellectual property disputes. She can be reached at <ssellers@
technologymediation.com>

Reproduced with permission from *ADR Report*, Volume 2, Number 25,
pages 2–4. Copyright 1998 by Pike ad Fischer, Inc. For more information
on *ADR Report*, call 1-800-255-8131, ext. 248

8.4 TAKE STEPS NOW TO PROTECT YOUR ENTITLEMENT TO DAMAGES SHOULD YOU EVER NEED TO LITIGATE

The damages a patentee can recover may be limited in certain circumstances.
If infringement goes on for several years, and the patentee has still not taken action, damages may be lost or the right to recover certain damages may be limited. This is because §286 of the patent statute states that no recovery can be
obtained for any infringement committed more than six years prior to the filing
of a claim for patent infringement. In addition, if a patent owner or its licensee
sell products without properly marking those products with a designation of
"patent" together with the number of the patent, damages may be severely limited or even wiped out in an action for infringement. Unless the patentee can
prove that the infringer was notified of the infringement and continued to infringe after such notification (in which case damages can be recovered for such
infringement occurring after such notice) the patentee's rights to damages will
be foregone.

A patented product must be marked by putting the designation "patent" or
"pat." along with the U.S. patent number. This marking must be substantially
consistent and in a continuous manner for all patented products that enter the
U.S. market. The product itself must be marked unless, from the character of
the article, this cannot be done, in which case, a label may be fixed to the product or to a package containing the product. Package marking is appropriate in
various instances, such as when the article is too small to be marked, the article would be defaced by directly marking the article, the custom in the business
is to mark only the product marketing materials, and the expense of marking directly is prohibitive. Where practicable, the marking should be easily viewable
by consumers.

(a) What to Do with Licensees

Section 287(a) requires patentees and persons making or selling any patented article to mark the patented article. According to the courts, a patent licensor must make reasonable efforts to require marking by its licensees or risk foregoing a right to past damages. Not only should the patent owner provide in its contracts and license agreements that the licensee must mark all products falling within the scope of the patent under license, but it is recommended that the patent owner take additional steps to ensure marking, such as sending letters to the licensee reminding them of their obligation to mark the products, and requesting confirmation that the products are marked.

Endnotes

1. Although the statutory one-year time limit for ITC cases has been repealed, the ITC is still expected to complete cases expeditiously. The U.S. District Court for the Eastern District of Virginia, as an example, averages only about eight to ten months from the filing of the complaint to trial in civil cases.

2. 35 U.S.C. § 284 states:

   Upon finding for the claimant the court shall award the claimant damages adequate to compensate for the infringement *but in no event less than a reasonable royalty* for the use made of the invention by the infringer, together with interest and costs as fixed by the court. When damages are not found by the jury, the court shall assess them. In either event, the court may increase the damages up to three times the amount fixed or assessed . . . (emphasis added).

3. *Power Lift, Inc. v. Lang Tools, Inc.*, 774 F.2d 478, 482 (Fed. Cir. 1985); *Glaros v. H.H. Robertson Co.*, 779 F.2d 1564, 1572 (Fed. Cir. 1986).

   Examples of acts where "willful infringement" was found include situations where the accused infringer has ignored cease and desist letters, rejected offers for a license without opinion of counsel, defied a cease and desist letter based upon self-serving opinions of non-infringement from in-house engineering staff, deliberately copied the patented invention, continued to infringe after notice from the patent owner, or placed goods in commerce without obtaining independent legal advice from competent counsel.

4. See generally *The Advice of Counsel Defense to Increased Patent Damages*, Sirilla, Edgell and Hess, 74 J.PAT. and TRADEMARK OFFICE SOC'Y 705 (1992).

5. *Lear, Inc. v. Adkins*, 395 U.S. 653 at 673, 89 S.Ct. 1902, 1912, 23 L.Ed.2d 610, 624 (1969); *Cordis Corp. v. Medtronic, Inc.*, 780 F.2d 991, 994 (Fed. Cir. 1985), *cert. denied*, 476 U.S. 1115 (1986).

6. *Cordis Corp. v. Medtronic, Inc.*, 780 F.2d 991, 996-96 (Fed. Cir. 1985), *cert. denied*, 476 U.S. 1115 (1986).

7. *Nebraska Eng'g Corp. v. Shivvers*, 557 F.2d 1257, 1260 (8th Cir. 1977); *Warner-Jenkinson Co. v. Allied Chem. Corp.*, 567 F.2d 184, 188 (2d Cir. 1977); *Crane Co. v. Aeroquip Corp.*, 356 F. Supp. 733, 738-39 (N.D. Ill. 1973) (noting that the threat of termination of the license would have "a chilling effect on meritorious challenges of patents"). *See also C.R. Bard, Inc. v. Schwartz*, 716 F.2d 874, 880 (Fed. Cir. 1983).

8. *Cordis Corp. v. Medtronic, Inc.*, 780 F.2d 991, 995 (Fed. Cir. 1985), *cert. denied*, 476 U.S. 1115 (1986) (citing *Warner-Jenkinson Co. v. Allied Chem. Corp.*, 567 F.2d 184, 188 (2d Cir. 1977)) ("Ultimately, all royalties paid after the filing of the complaint *may* have to be returned to the [licensees]").

9. Source: Administrative Office of the United States Courts, Annual Reports of the Director.

10. "The First Two Thousand Days," Report of the U.S. Court of Appeals for the Federal Circuit, 1982–1988, Honorable H.T. Markey, Chief Judge.

11. It is difficult to prevail on obviousness type Section 103 invalidity defenses in view of the statutory presumption of validity, especially in jury trials.

    35 U.S.C. § 282 states:

    > A patent shall be presumed valid. Each claim of a patent (whether in independent, dependent, or multiple dependent form) shall be presumed valid independently of the validity of other claims. . . . The burden of establishing invalidity of a patent or any claim thereof shall rest upon the party asserting such invalidity. . . .

12. "Do Philosophy and Oral Argument Influence Decisions," ABA Journal, March 1991, by Honorable Myron H. Bright, Judge, U.S. Court of Appeals Court for the Eighth Circuit.

13. In accordance with *Graham v. John Deere Co.*, 383 U.S. 1 (1966), the expert will usually develop testimony on the scope and content of the prior art, the level of skill in the relevant art at the time the invention was made, the differences between the prior art and the invention, and his opinion whether those differences would have been obvious to those skilled in the art.

14. Other indicia of unobviousness, besides commercial success, include whether the invention filled a long-felt need, whether there were prior unsuccessful attempts to solve the problem, whether others have copied the invention, and industry recognition and acceptance. These issues may also be addressed by technical experts.

15. American Intellectual Property Law Association, "Report of Economic Survey 1999," conducted in the Spring of 1999.

CHAPTER 9

A Look Inside Patent Prosecution (Obtaining a Patent)

9.1 A LOOK INSIDE PATENT PROSECUTION

This section describes the process of prosecuting a patent application before the U.S. Patent and Trademark Office (USPTO), and several factors which can influence the outcome of the prosecution process.

(a) Sample Independent and Dependent Claims

Note these claims are rudimentary, and do not reflect good claim drafting. They are intentionally simplified to illustrate a few points about claims.

1. A chair comprising a platform and a plurality of legs secured to said platform.

This claim broadly covers a chair, which has a platform and more than one leg secured to the platform. For example, a chair with only two legs would infringe claim.

The following claim depends from claim 1, and thus is called a dependent claim.

2. The chair according to claim 1, wherein said platform has two flat sides, and said plurality of legs comprise ten legs secured to one of said two flat sides of said platform.

This claim should be viewed as a separate definition of the invention, that is, a separate definition of the scope of protection being sought by the patent applicant. Each of these claims is viewed on its own. Even though claim 1 might be rejected as unpatentable over certain prior art, claim 2 might survive the rejection because it has more specific features and is narrower in scope.

A patent examiner probably would reject claim 1 as being unpatentable in view of prior art. The prior art might take the form of a patent that discloses an existing chair having a platform, four legs, and a backrest.

However, claim 2, which recites that the chair has ten legs, might be more difficult for the examiner to reject. It would be more difficult for the examiner to locate prior art showing a chair with ten legs. The examiner might argue that it would have been obvious to provide ten legs on a platform; however, the applicant could argue to the examiner that there is no reason for providing ten legs on a platform to make a chair, and that the examiner is making his or her determination of obviousness improperly using the applicant's own teachings in hind sight.

9.2 THE PATENT PROSECUTION PROCESS

In prosecuting a patent application, a patent attorney will embark on a negotiation process with a patent examiner. The attorney, in representing the client, will attempt to obtain a patent protecting the broadest possible scope of technology. The patent examiner represents the public interest and in so doing, will attempt to minimize the scope of protection that can be obtained before granting a patent. The examiner does this by ensuring that each patent application complies with several legal requirements before a patent is granted.

An application that is filed with the USPTO will typically include, among other items, a technical description of how to make and use the invention (called the specification), a set of drawings, and one or more claims which define the scope of technology for which the applicant is seeking ownership. Illustrative examples of patent claims are provided in the side bar.

The examiner considers many legal requirements for patentability, some of which include novelty, non-obviousness, and sufficiency of the disclosure of the invention. The patent examiner acts as a quasi-judge, and determines, for example, whether the scope of technology defined by a claim is both novel and unobvious in view of the prior art.

More specifically, during the prosecution of a typical application, an applicant, by way of his or her attorney, files a patent application. Some time after receiving the filed application, usually between three months to a year later, the examiner will perform a first examination of the application and search for patents and published articles, known as "prior art," which indicate the state of technology at the time of filing the application. The examiner will then study and evaluate the "prior art," and determine whether the submitted patent claims define a scope of technology that is both novel and unobvious.

The examiner will issue an official document called an Office Action after each examination, in which the claims may be rejected as being unpatentable because they are allegedly anticipated by (lacking in novelty), or obvious in view of, the prior art which the examiner found in his or her search.

In response to each Office Action, the attorney will prepare and submit a responding document (called an Amendment or a Response) which may include remarks addressing the examiner's rejections and also an amendment portion making changes to the claims.

Examiners will typically err on the side of rejecting claims, because they are weary of issuing patents with claims that define a broad range of technology. The examiner's confidence that a claim should be patented is increased if the scope of technology defined by that claim is narrow. It is the job of the patent attorney to convince the examiner that broader claims, defining a broader scope of technology, are patentable, and that the examiner's uncertainty as to the patentability of such broad claims is misplaced.

The reactions that applicants may encounter from examiners can vary widely. There are thousands of patent examiners at the U.S. Patent and Trademark Office, and each examiner has at least some discretion in how he or she treats a patent application.

9.3 THE CONCERNS AND INCENTIVES OF THE EXAMINER

Patent examiners are presented with a number of pressures and individual concerns which can immensely affect their ability to work with and help the patent attorney. Some examiners have their work reviewed by a reviewing patent examiner, and all examiners are subjected to random review by a quality review division. In some rare instances, as was the case with a patent recently issued to Compton's NewMedia and directed to CD-ROM technology, an examiner issues a broad patent, and when the patent is exploited, the industry complains to the U.S. Patent and Trademark Office. In response to these complaints, the Commissioner of Patents may order a reexamination of the patent, causing embarrassment to the examiner who granted it.

With this in mind, the examiner is concerned that an apparently patentable application may not be patentable in the eyes of others. By presenting difficulties to the applicant and by forcing the applicant to narrow the scope of technology defined by an application's claims, the examiner can reduce the chance that a reviewer, or the public, will conclude that the claims were too broad and that the patent should not have been issued. Therefore, the more concessions that an examiner can force upon an applicant, by way of narrowing the claims, the more comfortable the examiner will feel allowing an application to issue into a patent.

Another concern of the examiner is that he or she may be dealing with yet another over-zealous patent attorney whose remarks and suggestions are not to be trusted. The examiner may approach such patent attorneys by demanding more concessions than are really necessary for patentability. For example, a first Office Action may include many rejections which are not well-supported by the evidence or by the law, in the hope that the patent attorney will respond to the rejections by narrowing the scope of the claims.

Some examiners have what might be called "personal patentability requirements." For example, there are examiners who believe a patent application must enhance the wealth of technological knowledge in a particular art before it should be granted patent protection, even though the law does not possess any such requirement.

The examiner may also lack confidence that his or her search for prior art was complete. The examiner may be concerned that pertinent prior art was missed, and therefore may not feel comfortable allowing claims which define a broad range of technology. Difficulties in obtaining all relevant prior art are frequently encountered in computer technologies which contain an abundance of non-patent prior art, including articles, textbooks, and software that is in the public domain.

Other factors and considerations may encourage the examiner to compromise and approve a broad claim. For example, the examiner may need to devote a significant amount of time explaining a particular position in order to convince the applicant's attorney to change the application. The examiner may need to update his or her search for prior art in order to support a particular rejection of the claims. These efforts can be difficult for the examiner placed under tight time constraints, and expected to act on a minimum number of applications per week.

The examiner is also prone to compromise, because the applicant may appeal the examiner's decision to a panel of administrative patent law judges who are members of the Board of Patent Appeals and Interferences. If the examiner's rejections are not well-supported with evidence and arguments, there is a significant chance that the panel will reverse the examiner's decision.

9.4 THE CONCERNS AND INCENTIVES OF THE APPLICANT

As a general rule, the applicant's goal is to obtain the broadest possible claims, claims that define the broadest range of technology without encroaching upon technology that is part of the prior art. In other words, the applicant wishes to obtain a broad, valuable patent that is both valid and enforceable. Since people will have different opinions as to what breadth of claims the law will allow, the patent attorney will typically attempt to obtain very broad claims for which a colorable argument can be made for patentability. This goal will at times be at odds with the position taken by the examiner, who is charged with allowing only those claims for which a well-supported case of patentability can be made.

In addition to acquiring broad claims, the applicant and the applicant's attorney will want to obtain a patent which is enforceable and which will be respected by competitors and licensees as valid. Accordingly, the patent attorney will want to ensure that narrower claims are also in the application which the patent owner can fall back on if a broader claim is found to be invalid. In addition, the patent attorney will ensure that any relevant prior art which the applicant is aware of is brought to the examiner's attention for consideration during the examination process. It is to the applicant's advantage to address all questions regarding patentability during prosecution, rather than later, after a patent is granted, in litigation or in negotiations with a potential licensee. The best prior art should be part of the prosecution process and should be considered by the examiner before a patent is issued. The patent attorney will make sure all relevant information is brought to the examiner's attention for an even more important reason. There is a duty of candor imposed upon both the applicant and the attorney to disclose to the examiner all relevant information that may have an impact on the patentability of the application. If this duty is not fulfilled, the patent, even if it is obtained, could be unenforceable.

During the prosecution of the patent application, the applicant's attorney should take particular care not to limit the claims in a way that eliminates or significantly reduces the value of any resulting patent. Ideally, the claims will define a broad range of technology which must be included in any competing product, thereby making the patent very valuable. The applicant and the attorney must keep this goal in mind and be careful not to make too many concessions to the examiner in order to obtain a patent. The patent attorney must also be careful not to argue too strongly. The claims may be narrowed not only by changing the language of the claims, but also by arguing that the invention comprises specific features not explicitly recited in the claims. If arguments are made that the invention has certain details, the patent owner will later be estopped from asserting a broader meaning of the invention against third parties, such as, in licensing or litigating the patent.

Another concern of the applicant and the attorney as well is to reduce costs and the time it takes to resolve all issues and obtain a patent. This goal may require attending personal interviews with the examiner at the U.S. Patent and Trademark Office or speaking with the examiner on the telephone, and it may also require making concessions and narrowing the claims even when not absolutely required to do so by the law.

CHAPTER 10

More Prosecution Strategies

10.1 THE IDEAL APPROACH

A technology business that produces its own technology and sells it in the form of products or services will want to (where budget permits):

- Require everyone with access to its technology to first sign a non-disclosure agreement,
- Perform searches to keep up with the state-of-the-art as well as to be aware of the patent activity of competitors, present and future partners, and any possible threatening entities who might pose a threat to the company for competitive, strategic, or legal reasons;
- Draft its patent applications so as to have many fallback positions, i.e., alternate features and embodiments, and file continuations to present claims of different scope, thereby capitalizing on those fallback positions. This preserves the flexibility of having an application still pending dating back to the earlier filing date, but which can be amended to cover a given product or service of another party (A patent cannot be easily amended, while a pending continuation application can).
- File patent applications directed to technologies inside and outside the company's core business, yet targeted to cover the activities of competitors, present or future partners, and other possible threatening entities.

By taking these actions, the business will know what is new, know the patent activity of others, including its competitors (limited to published patent applications and issued patents), preserve trade secret rights and the right to file for patent protection, maximize the benefit received by filing for patent protection, and be more likely to have patents that give a better bargaining position vis-à-vis other companies, even where those other companies are not direct competitors in the same market.

(a) Using the Design Around Process During Patent Prosecution

When a patent application is prepared, the patent attorney and company personnel work together to produce a document that tells a story and that clearly presents various technological features. The more features disclosed, the more features that can be claimed. In other words, by disclosing more features in the application, the patent attorney and the applicant will have more flexibility in the prosecution process and more options to choose from when drafting claims.

Some companies boast about the number of patent applications they file each year as well as the number of issued patents they receive each year. This information *can* be misleading. It is helpful to the company reporting those numbers, because the business world, as a general rule, likes to measure success in terms of measurable units. However, the inaccuracy of those numbers results from the fact that a given patent application or patent may have several times the number of claims and/or the amount of subject matter as another application or patent. Another point of value that should be considered when looking at a pending patent application, or an issued patent, is the careful attention that was paid to disclosing an invention so as to preserve the right to claim various aspects of the invention in the best way, avoid problems in litigation, and more clearly cover competing products. Such an application may be the same size or shorter than another application, but its value can be orders of magnitude higher.

What amount of money should a company set aside for the preparation and filing of a given application? The patent application process is a subjective one, and patent attorneys will charge for their efforts on an hourly basis. Therefore, it is difficult to place a dollar amount on a given patent application, or a patent resulting from such an application. Moreover, without the benefit of hindsight, it is even more difficult to decide ahead of time what the budget should be for a given patent application or a group of applications to be prepared and filed to protect certain technology.

Typically, patent attorneys will work with the inventors to disclose the features of an invention in a clear manner and to draft a set of claims covering those features so as to place the company in the best possible position to hinder others from practicing the same essential invention. In this effort, the company and the patent attorney should consider how competitors might try to design around those claims. When a competitor designs around a patent, it works closely with its own patent counsel and its engineers to identify alternative ways (not covered by the claims) of achieving the same results or functionality. The courts have been publishing decisions that make it easier to avoid a patent's claims. In other words, if the patent doesn't, word for word, clearly and precisely cover a given product, there is a risk (increasing week by week as new decisions are published by the Federal Circuit) that competitors will be able to circumvent (get around) that patent.

The efforts to avoid a patent will be substantial, and the competitor will consider all options at its disposal.

How can the company applying for a patent anticipate and hinder its competitor's design around process once a patent application issues into a patent?

One option is to simply submit varying claims of varying scope, while being careful not to argue features before the Patent Office that are not necessary to achieving a given key function or result of the claimed product. As part of this process, it is important that the patent attorney work closely with company marketing and technical personnel so they can together best understand the more important and less important features of the technology.

Another strategy is to keep applications pending and to file additional applications to embellish the same technology, (e.g., by claiming alternative ways of achieving the same functions and results.)

In any event, a patent applicant will reach a point at which a given claim or set of claims is indicated as allowable by the patent examiner. If the applicant pays the issue fee, that application will issue into a patent. If a continuing application (child application) is not filed before its parent issues into a patent, then the patent owner will be limited to claims in that issued patent only. That patent will be the only basket in which all of its eggs are placed. However, if a continuing application is timely filed before the parent application issues into a patent, that continuing application will allow the patent applicant to submit alternate claims with more clear and direct language covering features of the technology which a competitor might use to circumvent or design around the parent application (which is now a patent.) This can be a powerful tool, as this continuing application will remain secret (with some exceptions—due to a new optional 18-month publication of pending applications). Thus, competitors will not know the types of claims being submitted in that continuing application, nor will they know the type of reaction the continuing application receives from the patent examiner.

(b) Joint Development Activity and Ownership: When Claiming Separate Ownership to a Given Technology Can Hurt You

Section 102(g) of the Patent Law provides that a claim cannot be patentable if it was first invented by another. Section 103 states that section 102(g) shall not preclude patentability (of a claim) where the earlier subject matter and the claim were, at the time of inventing, owned by the same entity or subject to an obligation of assignment to the same entity.

Jim, Scott, and Mary meet to discuss a new idea of how to provide a new service over the internet. Jim and Scott (owners of company A) come up with the idea first, but ask Mary to help them smooth out the details. Mary plays an important role in making the technology viable, and contributes with Jim and Scott to several enhancements which increase the technology's marketability.

Mary then decides to start a separate company (Company B) using some of the technology as the foundation for a new business model. Mary then proceeds to develop further enhancements to the technology.

To support Mary in her effort with her new company, Jim and Scott purchase a collective 66 percent interest in Company B.

When Jim, Scott, and Mary were working on the basic technology, they discussed giving the technology to the new Company B. However, no clear document was produced requiring that the developed technology be assigned to Company B.

Now, Jim and Scott are considering filing a patent application, to be assigned to Company A, to the basic technology. However, they want Company B to do well, especially since Company B's market is much larger than Company A's market, and Jim and Scott's collective 66 percent interest in Company B is likely to be worth 5 to 10 times as much as their interest in Company A. Nonetheless, they file a patent application and assign it to Company A. To help Company B, they grant it a license under their patent application.

Company B then files a patent application to the improvements to the technology, which Company B wishes to incorporate in its business.

Because the improvements filed in the patent application assigned to Company B were developed with an obligation to assign those improvements to a different company than the basic technology in Company A's application, the earlier application of Company A will be used as prior art against the subsequent application of Company B. Thus, by retaining separate ownership of the technology, Company A, as well as its sole shareholders Jim and Scott, have hindered the success of Company B by creating "prior art" under 35 U.S.C. §102(g) against possibly the biggest asset they ever had in their life—Company B.

(c) Valuing a Given Patent Application as Early as Possible

The claims of a patent application can be related to a specified dollar value, which can serve to guide the patent application drafting process as well as the budget that should be set for the patent application. Is the technology sought by the claims directed to an existing or likely future market, and if so, what is the dollar value of that market? Is the company the first to enter into this technology area, or is the technology area congested? If the company is first, then patent efforts may present an enormous opportunity to gain exclusivity in the market. Even where the technology area is congested, the patent application may still be valuable to the company. For example, if the company has already committed to a presence in the market, and the dollar value of the market is very high, the value of the patent application could be quite high, especially because potential adversaries will likely have competing and overlapping patent rights (See Using Patents Defensively. . ., in Chapter 3).

An attempt can be made to estimate both the size of the market, in terms of annual revenue, as well as the size of the portion of the market the company can control—either by selling its own products or by charging a license fee to others selling products in the same market. That annual revenue may be attributable to the patent rights, provided that the claims cover those features which command the allotted market segment. In other words, if competitors can use features that fall outside the claims and still compete in the same market segment, there is no need for a competitor to either stay out of the market or pay a license fee for the right to continue its use of those features in its products.

Accordingly, the company can look at the market, define the product features that command a portion of that market, and estimate the size of the market that is likely to be commanded. This information can be used to determine the claims that the company must achieve in a patent and decide on the budget for pursuing such claims.

The difficulty of obtaining access to the budgets of companies of various types and sizes makes it difficult to compare the amount of money spent by a variety of companies in comparison to their success. Success can be measured as achieving exclusivity in a given market, enforcing one's patents, and/or generating revenue (e.g., royalties) from a patent.

File patent applications early to avoid losing rights, and create a patent pending status which can be represented to competitors as well as investors and underwriters. When an application is pending, you need not disclose when the application was filed. Accordingly, competitors will not know whether a patent might issue tomorrow, or two years from now.

Have everyone sign non-disclosure agreements. This includes officers, directors, founders, employees, customers, business partners, independent contractors, and anyone to whom you might have given access to your technology. Having such agreements signed before access is given help preserve trade secret rights as well as patent rights in the United States and abroad.

Before entering into a new market, (i.e., developing a new product or an enhancement to an existing product), perform a collection search to determine if there are any patents relevant to the technology incorporated into that product. The collection search may be limited to the United States, if that is the primary market of concern, or it may also include other regions (and thus patents from other regions). It is always easier to consider potential patent problems before a substantial amount of money and effort is spent to enter into a given market or market segment than it would be if the product was already developed at the cost of several million dollars or more. At worst, the company may be forced to forego marketing that product altogether, as was the case when Kodak started a subsidiary called Kodak Imaging, and after being sued for patent infringement by Wang Laboratories, decided to close down the subsidiary. Even if changes can be made to the product to avoid infringement, or a license fee can be paid, either of these situations can result in delay to the delivery of the product (and a sacrifice of some of the market advantage associated with being first into the market) as well as additional costs.

In devising a patent strategy, consider the possible threats to the company in general, to the company's markets by competing activity, and to the company's product due to others asserting their intellectual property rights. A given technology area may require the filing of more patent applications to discourage others from entering into the same market/space, and/or to deter others from asserting their intellectual property against the company and thereby preserving the company's present ability to participate in that same market/space.

Do not ignore technology developments outside of your business. By filing for patent protection to other technologies, you may put the company in a position of strength against larger companies using that other technology. Suppose a multi-billion dollar company (Company X) is marketing several different products in many different areas, one of which directly competes with your product. They could pose a threat to your market share simply by undercutting your prices or otherwise competing in the marketplace, or even by filing an intellectual property lawsuit (patent, trademark, copyright, or trade secret) against your company. Since Company X has other large markets that are important to it, an opportunity is presented to the company who files for patent protection to technologies outside its own markets yet covering those of Company X.

(d) Process

It is important to create a process for dealing with intellectual property and patents. Process is important because if a good process is not in place, valuable patent rights can slip through the cracks. If a clear process is not provided and responsibilities for these tasks are not clearly assigned, there can be no assurance that a given intellectual property right will be preserved or that action will be taken to avoid liability for infringing the intellectual property of another.

When it comes to preserving rights, obtaining patents is not enough. Those patents will preferably be pursued in a way that preserves and obtains patent rights that are of strategic importance to the company, thus putting the company in a better position to get the most mileage out of its technology.

There are few patents which, with additional effort, could not have been provided with additional broader or otherwise valuable claims at a certain stage in the patent process. At some stage during the patent program, someone should make sure that there is some type of iterative communication between the patent counsel preparing the patent applications, the person responsible for managing the company's intellectual property efforts, personnel creating the technology and the company's products, and marketing personnel. The patent attorney will craft the patent application and will make sure that claims of a certain scope and type are presented and pursued. The patent manager will give the patent attorney instructions on how to pursue patent protection and what to pursue, and will facilitate the exchange of information between the patent attorney and the development and marketing personnel within the company. The development personnel will, by being more involved with the patent process, make sure that key technologies are clearly communicated to the patent attorney, and make sure that those key technologies do not slip through the cracks. The marketing personnel will make sure the company's most critical markets are pursued in claims.

(e) Assignment Documents

It is critical that the company own all patent rights that are applied for. The best way to ensure such ownership, and the first step, is to make sure that every individual or entity contributing to the company's technology has signed an agreement expressly assigning all patent rights to the company. Accordingly, all independent contractor agreements and all employment agreements should include a paragraph assigning all intellectual property rights to the company. In addition, the company should be careful when it acts on its customers' suggestions. Such back and forth interaction between the company and its customers can amount to collaborative efforts in developing a given technology that is claimed in a patent application. This is frequently overlooked, and, if identified through discovery, and in litigation can severely hinder any efforts to enforce that patent.

Therefore, the company should be careful not to involve the customers too much in its inventive process, and when it does, the company should take steps to ensure that it is not obtaining patent rights that are co-owned by the customers.

When a company is preparing an application which has not yet been filed with the Patent Office, it should make a careful determination as to any and all possible inventors contributing to the subject matter in the claims. If there is subject matter described in the specification, which is not claimed, but the company may end up claiming that subject matter in the future, it is better to include the claim at an earlier stage and add the person contributing to that subject matter as an inventor. For example, if an inventor works for a different company, or is not otherwise affiliated with the company, it is better to get that inventor to execute an assignment agreement as early as possible. The law is more forgiving if you err on the side of including too many inventors, where there is a legitimate and reasonable basis to do so, than if inventors are left off the application.

If an inventor assigns an invention to the company, but the company fails to record that assignment within three months, that inventor may assign the same invention to another entity before the recordation of the first assignment document. If this happens this second entity may own the rights, and the first assignment document may be void. Accordingly, to avoid this danger of an invention being assigned to a third party, thereby voiding the first and proper assignment, it is important that assignments be recorded promptly with the United States Patent and Trademark Office. This holds true even for patent applications that have not been issued into a patent, and even includes provisional patent applications.

CHAPTER 11

Getting a Second Look by the Patent Office: Reexamination and Reissue

11.1 INTRODUCTION

Once a patent is issued, the patent owner can take a few avenues to tweak the claims of the patent or otherwise "fix" a patent. If there is a clear error of a formal type, the patent owner can file a Certificate of Correction request, asking the United States Patent and Trademark Office to issue a Certificate of Correction to correct such things as data that is erroneously entered into the system and that appears wrong on the cover sheet of the patent or typographical errors in the body of the patent. If printed prior art was not considered during the prosecution of the patent application, but is relevant to the patentability of one or more claims of the patent, a reexamination may be requested in order to get the examiner to consider this additional prior art. If the examiner determines that the prior art presents a problem, he or she may reject the claims, in which case the claims can be further narrowed to clearly get around that prior art. The claims cannot be broadened during the reexamination process.

If, during the process of prosecuting a patent application that has issued into a patent, the applicant or its attorney made an error without deceptive intent, the patent applicant can surrender the patent and file a reissue application at any time during the life of a patent. However, if a reissue application is filed within two years from the issue date, the patent owner can broaden the claims, subject to the examiner's approval. Accordingly, if the patent application discloses subject matter which, through error, was mistakenly not pursued during the prosecution of that application, the reissue process will give the patent owner another chance to present claims directed to that subject matter, which may be broader or which may cover a given alternate solution that might be adopted by a competitor.

11.2 MORE ABOUT REEXAMINATION*

A reexamination can be invoked by the patent owner, to improve/strengthen its patent, or by a third party seeking to invalidate or limit the claims of the patent.

After the business has made a determination, along with its attorney, that one of their existing or intended products or processes may infringe an existing patent, a business may, if the conditions warrant, challenge the claims of the patent with a request to the Patent and Trademark Office for reexamination of the patent. A request for reexamination may be an option if a prior art reference is found which has a bearing on the patentability of any claim of the particular patent, and which was not initially considered by the Patent and Trademark Office when granting the patent.

A reexamination proceeding is possible only if a prior art reference not initially considered by the Patent Office when the patent was granted is found to raise a substantial new question of patentability affecting any claims of the patent concerned. A request for reexamination is akin to an affirmative defense of invalidity, where, after being sued for patent infringement, the defendant effectively counterclaims by asserting that the claims of the patent are invalid. In the litigation setting, however, any prior art reference, including only those before the PTO when initially granting the patent, regardless of whether new prior art has been discovered, may be used to prove invalidity. Therefore, in an invalidity defense to infringement, the claimant may, in effect, challenge the PTO's judgement in granting the patent.

A reexamination, however, is a proceeding within the Patent Office and has a much narrower scope than asserting an invalidity defense in court. The requester of a reexamination is not challenging the PTO's judgment, but is, rather, informing the PTO of prior art that was not considered which may have a bearing on the patented claims. If the director grants the reexamination, the examiner may consider patents and publications other than those cited in the request, including patents and publications previously considered, and may raise any issues proper for reexamination, including issues previously addressed by the Office. Other issues that affect patentability, such as inequitable conduct of the patent owner, inventorship, prior public use, and on sale bar, which are available in an invalidity defense, are not open to consideration in a reexamination proceeding; only patentability issues related to prior art are considered.

It is not uncommon for new relevant prior art (not considered by the PTO) to be uncovered after a patent issues. During patent prosecution, the PTO may limit its search for prior art to U.S., European, and Japanese patents, in addition to any prior art references disclosed by the patentee. Other publications, which include published articles, shelved theses at colleges and universities, and arti-

---

*This section has been provided by Paul Gennari, Esq.

cles posted on the internet, might be difficult to find and thus not be discovered in a prior art search by the PTO.

Given these circumstances, it is not surprising that a vast majority of requests for reexamination are granted in a given year. Between 1995 and 1999, there were on average 384 requests per year, and 354 of those requests were granted (92 percent on average granted). However, viewed as a whole, these numbers are dwarfed in relation to the enormous number of patents that issue each year in the United States. For instance, between the same time period noted above, a total of 667,838 patents were issued. Thus, between 1995 and 1999, only about .05 percent of issued patents became the subject of a reexamination.[1]

In order to request a reexamination, the requesting party must, first of all, be armed with a prior art reference that was not initially considered by the PTO. Assuming that the company has such a prior art reference, other factors will have a bearing on whether the request should be made. For example, a business must weigh the costs associated with such a proceeding against the likelihood of success, and against other avenues available to invalidate a patent. Although the costs associated with the proceeding may be insignificant compared to the overall value of invalidating certain claims, the cost should be weighed against the degree of success anticipated from a reexamination proceeding. The term "degree of success" is used here because a patentee under reexamination is allowed to amend the claims to overcome the new prior art. If such amended claims are deemed patentable, the amended claims may still preclude a third party register from practicing the invention. For example, in 1994, 89 percent of the reexamination requests were granted that year, but only 5.6 percent of the reexamined patents were completely rejected with no claims remaining after reexamination.[2] Therefore, a third party requester should be prepared for less than a "knock out" victory.

These figures, however, may be misleading. They do not represent the effects recent changes in the reexamination laws and rules will have on the process and its benefits to those seeking to challenge a patent.

Although not a prerequisite, a business that may wish to request a reexamination (i.e., a third party requester) is, presumably, one that could potentially be sued for infringement if it proceeded with its products or processes without a license from the owner of the patent. In such a case, the business may have the option of filing for a declaratory judgment that patent claims are invalid. Alternatively, it may proceed with its products or processes with the expectation that it may be sued for infringement and, if eventually sued, then assert an affirmative invalidity defense. These options are typically expensive, and the latter is an undesirable defensive position. Armed with a potent prior art reference, such a situation can be avoided either through negotiations with the patent holder, or if the patent holder is not cooperative or has a different view of the prior art, a reexamination proceeding, which can be a relatively inexpensive offensive move. Because reexamination is performed by the PTO with limited input by the patentee and requester, or their counsel, a reexamination proceeding is typically not only less expensive than a legal proceeding, but is also quicker.

If a third party requester (not the patent owner) decides to file a request for reexamination, the requester must decide whether to make an ex parte request or an inter parte request. Generally, in an ex parte reexamination, the requester is not involved in the reexamination proceeding and can only make an initial reply to the patent owner's first response to the request for reexamination. In an inter parte reexamination, the requester may respond to each statement or amendment that the patent owner presents during the reexamination proceeding. Advantages and disadvantages to each type of proceeding are discussed below, but regardless of the type of request, the procedure is quite simple.

An inter parte or ex parte request may come from anyone, and the requesting party need make no showing of standing or special interest in the validity of the patent. Further, the requesting party may be the patent owner. The request must be in writing and be accompanied by a required reexamination fee. The request may be filed by an attorney or agent identifying another party on whose behalf the request is filed. Also, in an ex parte request, the requesting party may remain anonymous upon a written request to the PTO.

Both an ex parte and inter parte request for reexamination must set forth the pertinency and manner of applying cited prior art to every claim for which reexamination is requested. The request must include:

1. a statement pointing out each substantial new question of patentability based on prior art;
2. an identification for every claim for which reexamination is required and a detailed explanation of the application of the cited prior art, including, if appropriate, a demonstration of how the claims distinguish the prior art;
3. a copy of every patent or printed publication referred to as prior art accompanied by an English language translation of the pertinent portions of any non-English prior art;
4. the entire specification, claims, and drawings of the patent for which reexamination is requested in cut-and-paste form with single columns of the printed patent mounted on separate sheets; and
5. a certification that a copy of the request, if filed by a person other than the patent owner, has been served on the patent owner at the address for correspondence, which certification must indicate the name and address of the parties served.

The request should point out how any new questions of patentability are substantially different from those raised in the earlier prosecution of the patent or in any prior federal court litigation concerning the patent. If the request is made by the patent owner, a proposed amendment may be included which will be considered only if the request is granted.

Within three months following the filing date of a request for reexamination, the director will consider the request and determine whether a substantial new question of patentability affecting any claim of the patent concerned is raised by the request. The determination relates to any claim, not just those singled out by the requester, and the determination may be made with or without considering patents or publications in addition to those cited in the request. The substantial new patentability question must arise from patents or publications, not from other sources such as public use or sale, inventorship, or fraud. The examiner's determination, based on the claims in effect at the time of the determination, is placed in the official patent file, and a copy is given or mailed to the patent owner and to the person requesting reexamination. The patent owner is not entitled to respond until the PTO makes the determination that there is a substantial new patentability question. Whenever no substantial new question of patentability has been found, the requester will receive a refund of a portion of the required fee.

If the director grants a request for reexamination, the patent owner has no right to petition or request reconsideration. However, when the request is denied, the requester may seek review with the PTO by petition to the Commissioner within one month. When the request for reexamination is granted, the patent owner may file a statement on the question, including any amendment to his or her patent and new claim or claims he or she may wish to propose, for consideration in the reexamination. After the patent owner files a statement and serves it on the party who requested examination, that requesting party in an ex parte reexamination proceeding has two months to file and serve a reply to the statement, and that person must serve a copy of the reply to the patent owner.

After the statement and reply, the reexamination is conducted according to the procedures established for initial examination of the patent application. In any reexamination proceeding, the patent owner is permitted to propose any amendment to a patent in order to distinguish the invention as claimed from the prior art cited, or in response to a decision adverse to the patentability of a claim of a patent. The patent owner is not allowed to broaden the scope of any claims under reexamination. From this point forward, the requester of an ex parte reexamination proceeding is not entitled to respond to any amendments made by the patent owner.

In an inter parte request for reexamination, however, each time the patent owner files a response to an action on the merits from the PTO, the requester has one opportunity to file written comments addressing issues raised by the action of the Office or the patent owner's response. The written comments must be filed within 30 days after being served of the patent owner's response. As such, the requester of an inter parte reexamination proceeding may not remain anonymous.

The recourse available to a patent owner and a third party requester differ depending on whether an inter parte or an ex parte reexamination is requested.

In an inter parte reexamination, the patent owner may appeal to the Board of Patent Appeals, and may seek court review with respect to any decision adverse to the patentability of any original or proposed amended or new claim of the patent. The third party requester may also be a party to the appeal before the Board of Patent Appeals, but may not be a party to court review. If a determination is made in favor of the patent owner, the requester may appeal the decision to the Board of Patent Appeals, and the patent owner may be a party to such an appeal. A requester, however, may not appeal an adverse Board decision to the courts or participate in any appeal to the courts by the patentee. In an ex parte reexamination, the requester has no right to appeal a decision favorable to the patentee, either to the Board or to the courts.[3]

Given that a requester in an inter parte reexamination proceeding has far more input during the proceeding and may be party to an appeal to the Board, one would assume that an inter parte request would be the request of choice. However, the requester should temper his or he enthusiasm to use this process, since the inter parte request creates an estoppel effect against the requester if he or she loses.

An inter parte reexamination imposes two estoppels on a requester. The first is an estoppel with respect to patent claims. A requester whose request results in a PTO order for inter parte reexamination is estopped from later challenging, in a civil patent action, the validity of a claim already determined during the inter parte reexamination proceedings if the basis of the later challenge was already raised or could have been raised during the reexamination. The estoppel provision does not prevent the assertion of invalidity based on newly discovered prior art unavailable to both the requester and the PTO at the time of the inter parte reexamination.

The second is a fact estoppel. Any party who requests an inter parte reexamination is estopped from later challenging, in a civil action, any fact determined during the process of the reexamination, except that a fact can be later proved erroneous if new information is uncovered that was unavailable during the reexamination.

Another estoppel provision concerns the practice of filing serial reexamination proceedings. An inter parte reexamination proceeding provides that if the third party requester loses an inter parte reexamination or a civil suit concerning the validity of claims, (i.e., the decision favors the owner of the patent), the requester is estopped from thereafter requesting another inter parte reexamination on the previously reexamined claims on the issues that were raised in the previous reexamination.

Thus, a requester faced with this choice between inter parte and ex parte reexamination needs to balance several competing concerns, principally the enhanced opportunity to participate in inter parte reexamination against the over-reaching estoppel effects if the requester should lose and find itself in court in an infringement suit.

The other main difference between an ex parte and an inter parte reexamination is that under an inter parte reexamination request, the law explicitly provides that the patent owner may obtain a stay of any pending litigation involving an issue of patentability of any claims which are the subject of the inter parte reexamination, unless the court before which such litigation is pending determines that a stay would not serve the interest of justice. By contrast, stays in connection with ex parte reexaminations have been granted as an exercise of a court's inherent powers.

11.3 MORE ABOUT REISSUE*

A reissue is essentially a new patent application filed to correct a defect in the original patent. Unlike a normal patent application which *must* be examined by the Patent Office when the requisite fee is paid, a reissue application will only be examined if the Patent Office is convinced that the proper kind of defect in the original patent exists to justify another examination. A convincing showing must also be made that all of the other requirements for reissue have been met.

(a) Conditions for Patent Reissue

A reissue is authorized under 35 U.S.C. §251.

Whenever any patent is, through error without any deceptive intention, deemed wholly or partly inoperative or invalid, by reason of a defective specification or drawing, or by reason of the patentee claiming more or less than he had a right to claim in the patent, the Commissioner shall, on the surrender of such patent and the payment of the fee required by law, reissue the patent for the invention disclosed in the original patent, and in accordance with a new and amended application, for the unexpired part of the term of the original patent. No new matter shall be introduced into the application for reissue.

The Commissioner may issue several reissued patents for distinct and separate parts of the thing patented, upon demand of the applicant, and upon payment of the required fee for a reissue for each of such reissued patents.

The provisions of this title relating to applications for patent shall be applicable to applications for reissue of a patent, except that application for reissue may be made and sworn to by the assignee of the entire interest if the application does not seek to enlarge the scope of the claims of the original patent.

No reissued patent shall be granted enlarging the scope of the claims of the original patent unless applied for within two years from the grant of the original patent.

*This section has been provided by Paul E. White, Esquire.

The words of this statute govern when a patent may be reissued. The statute allows reissue of an issued patent when *all* of the following conditions are met:

1. There is an *error*. This includes that:
   a) The patent is "deemed" (by the Patent Office Commissioner) wholly or partly inoperative or invalid for one of a number of possible reasons;
   b) The error that led to the inoperative or invalid condition of the patent was made without deceptive intention; and
   c) The reissue is for the same invention as that disclosed in the original patent.
2. The applicant surrenders the original patent and pays a fee.
3. An application for reissue is filed, and this application follows all rules for a new application for patent, all the special rules for a reissue patent, and has a reissue declaration which meets the requirements of the rules.

The existence of an "error" is the key to reissue. If error is found, reissue examination will be granted.

(b) Qualifying Error

Error in a patent occurs as a result of accident, inadvertence, or mistake in the procurement of the patent. Any deliberate act is not an "error." Reissue is unique among Patent Office proceedings in that *conduct* must be examined, to determine whether the conduct which occurred constitutes qualifying error.

Generally, the most common "error" to be corrected is that of claiming more or less than the inventor had a right to claim in the patent. For instance, it may be found subsequent to the patent issuance that broader claims might have been possible. This can be corrected by reissue (so long as the reissue is requested within two years from the date of the grant of the original patent) by declaring in a reissue declaration that the inventor claimed less than he or she had a right to claim in the patent, that this was done by accident or mistake, and that, therefore, this error should be corrected by broadening of the claims. For example, sufficient error may be demonstrated by a patent owner in seeking reissue to add product claims to the original patent's process and product-by-process claims. (*Scripps Clinic & Research Foundation v. Genentech, Inc.,* 18 USPQ2d 1001, 18 USPQ2d 1896 (Fed. Cir. 1991)).

Conversely, if events subsequent to the patent issuing uncover better prior art than was known during prosecution, it may be found that what was claimed was more than the inventor had a right to claim and could therefore be corrected by reissue. In the latter case, this error could also be corrected by reexamination because this would involve a substantial new question of patentability.

Error is easy to establish for the purpose of narrowing the claims as long as the reason for the narrowing was not known before issuance of the patent. Discovering prior art is a sufficient error, as long as the effect of that prior art was not understood before the patent issued. If the prior art was known, the failure to bring it to the attention of the Patent Office was deliberate and not an error. Error is more difficult to establish for broadening the claims since there are not usually any new circumstances and in general, this broadening could have been done before the patent issued. The job of the patent attorney is to convince the Patent Office that there is a new reason for broadening the claims.

The satisfaction of two criteria is required to establish qualifying error. There must be an error in the patent, which means that the patent must be defective or partially inoperative because of defects in the specification or drawings or because of claiming more or less than you have a right to claim. This first part will be satisfied by any reissue application which has any changes whatsoever made to correct something which is wrong. The second criteria for establishing error, and the part that causes most of the problems, is the error in conduct, which must be through "inadvertence, accident or mistake." A mere *conclusion* of oversight in drafting does not establish inadvertence, accident, or mistake. The entire factual scenario leading to the error must be described, so that the Patent Office can determine if this constitutes error.

The most common grounds for filing a reissue are improper scope of the claims, errors in the disclosure, errors in claiming or perfecting foreign priority, or errors in referring to other applications. The following are proper grounds for filing a reissue:

1. An attorney's failure to appreciate the full scope of the invention;
2. Misjoinder of inventors;
3. Failure to file a certified copy of the original foreign application;
4. Failure to adequately claim priority in a previous application;
5. Claims too broad-based on new prior art;
6. Claims too narrow-based on better understanding of the art;
7. The desire to include narrower claims as a hedge against the possible invalidation of a broad claim. This practice is apparently acceptable to grant reissue even though it need not declare that the application claimed more nor less than you were entitled to claim.

(c) Non-Qualifying Error

It is helpful to know what you *cannot* correct. Anything else may be correctable.

1. You cannot correct, by reissue (or by any other means of correction) anything that you could not have corrected during prosecution. This includes insufficient disclosure, failure to disclose the best mode, or unpatentable subject matter.
2. The *recapture rule* prevents the patentee from securing through reissue a claim that is of the same or broader scope than those claims cancelled by

amendment during the prosecution of the original patent, based on the prior art that the Examiner applied. This is analogous to file wrapper estoppel in that it prevents recovering (i.e., claiming) the subject matter nullified by the arguments which were made during prosecution. The arguments made during prosecution, that is, those made in the "file wrapper," provide a limit on the permissible scope of the claim, and prevent a claim from being broadened to encompass that which was given up during the prosecution.

The stated rationale for the recapture rule, however, is that intentionally giving up subject matter during prosecution is not an error. When a patent applicant responds to a PTO rejection by cancelling or amending a claim, it is considered a deliberate or intentional act and not an error. The deliberate withdrawal or amendment of a claim in order to obtain a patent does not involve inadvertence, accident, or mistake. This prevents recapturing the same subject matter which was earlier cancelled, and also prevents recapture of any broader subject matter.

Mentor Corp. v. Coloplast, Inc., 27 USPQ2d 1521 (Fed. Cir. 1993) relevantly states:

> "If a patentee tries to recapture what he or she previously surrendered in order to obtain allowance of original patent claims, that deliberate withdrawal or amendment . . . cannot be said to involve the inadvertence of mistake contemplated by 35 U.S.C.251, and is not an error of the kind which will justify the granting of a reissue patent which includes the matter withdrawn."
>
> "The recapture rule bars the patentee from acquiring, through reissue, claims that are of the same or of broader scope than those claims that were cancelled from the original application."
>
> "The recapture rule does not apply where there is no evidence that amendment of the originally filed claims was in any sense an admission that the scope of that claim was not in fact patentable . . ."

Furthermore, as stated by the Federal Circuit in *Hester Industries Inc. v. Stein Inc.* 46 USPQ2d 1641, (Fed. Cir. 1998), amendment of a claim is not the only permissible predicate for establishing surrender of subject matter during prosecution because arguments made to overcome prior art can equally evidence an admission sufficient to give rise to a finding of surrender.

In the decision of *In re Clement,* 45 USPQ2d 1161, 1164 (Fed. Cir. 1997), the Federal Circuit summarized the following principles:

A. if the reissue claim is as broad as or broader than the canceled or amended claim in all aspects, the recapture rule bars the claim;

B. if it is narrower in all aspects, the recapture rule does not apply, but other rejections are possible;

C. if the reissue claim is broader in some aspects, but narrower in others, then: a) if the reissue claim is as broad as or broader in an aspect germane to a prior art rejection, but narrower in another aspect completely unrelated to the rejection, the recapture rule bars the claim; b) if the reissue claim is narrower in an aspect germane to prior art rejection, and broader in an aspect unrelated to the rejection, the recapture rule does not bar the claim, but other rejections are possible.

However, one type of broadening is possible by reissue, even though this broadening would recapture some of the given-up subject matter. The recapture rule does not bar a patentee from securing a reissue claim that is broader in a material respect than a cancelled claim when it is narrower than the cancelled claim in a way that is material to the error. The narrowing part constitutes the proper kind of error. The broadening in some other respect might not have been apparent during prosecution. An applicant may not have considered that the claim may have been rendered patentable by the addition of a different particular limitation, "hence a deliberate decision to cancel a particular claim because it is unpatentable would not necessarily constitute a deliberate judgment that a claim that is broader in some ways and narrower in others would be unpatentable."

There is another exception to the recapture doctrine when the patentee or attorney misunderstood the applied prior art, and believed it to encompass something different than it actually encompasses. This misunderstanding in itself is then an error which can be corrected by reissue.

3. Broader claims (broadened in any respect) may be obtained only if a reissue is filed within two years. A reissue filed on the two year anniversary date is considered filed within two years. A broadening reissue means that the claims are broader in any respect than the earlier patent. However, a declaration or a claim for priority can be filed after the two years, even though this does somewhat enlarge the scope of the patent. This is not considered a broadening reissue because claim language is not actually broadened.

4. The error must be an error of the applicant, (or his agent) and an error of the court is not sufficient. *In re Carr*, 187 USPQ 209 (CCPA 1975) involved a patent which had been held invalid over the prior art by the court. One basis of the holding was inequitable conduct for not calling the PTO's attention to a reference. The applicants requested a reissue to get a new patent over the reference, basing the request on the court's having committed an error in holding the patent invalid.

   The court found that this was an insufficient basis for reissue, and that the error giving rise to a reissue must be an error of the applicant not an error of the court.

5. The error must have arisen without deceptive intent. In re Carr had in-equitable conduct and therefore there was deceptive intent.
6. You cannot file a reissue to establish co-pendency for the purpose of fil-ing a divisional application to non-elected claims.

This practice has been held unacceptable for reissue on various grounds.

a) First, the error to be corrected must be an error during prosecution. In *In re Orita*, 193 U.S.P.Q. 145 (CCPA 1977), the applicants at-tempted to file a reissue to establish co-pendency in order to file a di-visional application to non-elected claims. The applicants urged that the error was the error in failing to file the divisional. The court found that reissue-type error is inadvertence or mistake in prosecution. Fail-ure to file a divisional is not the proper kind of error since it was unre-lated to the prosecution.

b) *In re Watkinson* 14 USPQ 2d 1407 (Fed. Cir. 1990) gave another rea-son. Acquiescing in the Examiner's restriction requirement is deliberate, not error. Failing to file a divisional application forecloses applicant's right to claim that subject matter since there is no error to be corrected. After *In re Watkinson*, failure to file a divisional cannot be rectified by reissue for three separate reasons: 1) it is not error during prosecution (*Orita*); 2) acquiescing in the Examiner's restriction requirement is a de-liberate act and not an error (*Watkinson*); 3) deliberately cancelling the claims in order to allow the case to issue is cancellation of claims from the original application, and therefore recapture of these claims is pro-hibited by the recapture rule. (Watkinson, interpreting Ball Corp.).

c) Error in the restriction process will not justify a divisional application to be filed by reissue. First is the fact scenario *in Ex parte Holt and Ran-dell*. This case dealt with a situation where Holt acquiesced in an im-proper rejection of a Markush claim and later wanted to recapture the scope of this claim. The court in Watkinson found that a case as Holt might be supportable because the rejection was never proper, i.e., it had no possible merits.

However, a restriction requirement is statutorily proper under 35 U.S.C. §121. The *Watkinson* court said that they would not determine if the mer-its of a particular restriction requirement were proper once acquiesced in by patentee. Acquiescing in a restriction requirement, even if this re-striction requirement is improper, therefore, is a deliberate act and not error. The action is therefore bound by the recapture rule.

d) One way in which a reissue-based divisional might be permitted is if there was evidence in the file wrapper that a divisional application was intended, but this divisional application was never filed. The intent to claim (see section 7, below) would then be found and an argument could be made that this intent to claim showed that the proper kind of error existed. Here, there would be evidence that a divisional was intended, and that there was no acquiescence in the rejection. All other ways of establishing the proper error for purposes of co-pendency to file a divisional application have failed in the courts. Accordingly, it would seem to be good practice to make a statement in any amendment where non-elected claims were cancelled that you intended to file a divisional application (if you in fact did intend so).

7. The proper kind of error to establish grounds for a reissue will be found if applicants had an intent to claim some particular subject matter, but did not do so. Reissue claims must be for the same general invention as that originally filed and this is determined by the intent to claim. The Patent Office will determine "objectively" what the patentee intended as his invention. This has been interpreted to mean that there should be something at least fairly implying that applicant intends the material now claimed to be part of the invention. "It is not enough that an invention might have been claimed in the original patent . . . it must appear from the face of the instrument that what is covered by the reissue is intended to have been covered and secured by the original."[5] A completely separate aspect of the invention, which was never emphasized at all in the originally filed application, might not be proper subject matter for reissue. However, although the intent to claim is not conclusive, "a showing that an applicant never had any such intent makes a finding of error extremely difficult if not impossible."[6] If there was intent to claim, however, and for any reason that subject matter was never claimed, this situation would be the proper kind of error, and correctable by reissue.[7] A statement that the newly added subject matter could have been claimed is sufficient, but more generally, there must be something indicating that applicant or his counsel thought of claiming it, intended claiming it, or failed to claim it only through error.

In re Weiler involved a situation where a restriction requirement was made, was acquiesced in, and a divisional application was never filed. There was nothing indicating on the record that a divisional application was intended to be filed. The court in this case found that claims which were distinct from those claims which were elected cannot be the subject of a reissue application because, "if it were not error to forego divisional applications on subject matter to which claims had been made in the original application, it cannot on the present record have been error to forego divisional applications on subject matter to which claims had never been made."[8] One test for whether claims are directed to the same invention is, could the new claim which is presented have properly been the subject of a restriction requirement if in a single application without a linking generic claim.[9]

8. A patent must be defective. The old and now repealed section 37 C.F.R. § 1.175(a)(4) allowed the Patent Office to examine a reissue application just based on new art found by the applicant, even when no unpatentability was alleged. The Patent Office would then issue an advisory action on the patentability of the claims based on this new information. This was found to be outside the scope of 35 U.S.C. 251.[10]

9. Attorney ignorance is not error. If all you had to do was say that you did know the proper standard and therefore you did not realize that what you were doing was an error, then everything could be reissued.[11] Failure to do something is not an error if the record does not show that you intended to do it. However, if you do it, but do it wrong (that is, don't do what you intended), that is error.

10. A reissue application can not be filed to remove a terminal disclaimer. The filing of a terminal disclaimer is a deliberate act, and therefore cannot be an error.[12]

11. A reissue application can not be filed for examination of an expired patent. The Patent Office has no authority to reissue a patent that has expired. *In re Morgan*, 26 USPQ2d 1392 (Fed. Cir. 1991).

(d) Issuance of the Reissue Patent

When a reissue application is finally allowed, another issue fee must be paid, and the application issues as a reissue patent. The reissue patent is reprinted with a number that begins with "RE" and has a five digit reissue patent number, such as RE-30,000. The reissue patent is printed with all added material (underlined in the application) in italics, and with brackets around the deleted material.

(e) Effect of Reissue

The reissue patent is, in many ways, treated just like the original patent.

> The surrender of the original patent shall take effect upon the issue of the reissued patent, and every reissued patent shall have the same effect and operation in law, on the trial of actions for causes thereafter arising, as if the same have been originally granted in such amended form, but in so far as the claims or the original and reissued patents are identical, such surrender shall not affect any action then pending nor abate any cause of action then existing, and the reissued patent, to the extent that its claims are identical with the original patent, shall constitute a continuation thereof and have effect continuously from the date of the original patent.
>
> No reissue patent shall abridge or affect the right of any person or his successors in business who made, purchased or used prior to the grant of a reissue anything patented by the reissued patent, to continue the use of, or to sell to others or to be used or sold, the specific thing so made, purchased or used, unless the mak-

ing, using or selling of such thing infringes a valid claim of the reissued patent which was in the original patent. The court before which such matter is in question may provide for the continued manufacture, use or sale of the thing made, purchased or used as specified, and it may also provide for the continued practice of any process, patented by the reissue, practiced, or for the practice of which substantial preparation was made prior to the grant of the reissue, to the extent and under such terms as the court deems equitable for the protection of investments made or business commenced before the grant of the reissue.[13]

The reissued patent carries with it the changes made through reissue, but is treated as continuation of the original patent. To the extent that the claims of the two patents are the same, the mere reissuance of the patent does not affect any actions which are then pending. This means that action pending on a claim 1 for U.S. Patent 7,777,777 will not be stopped just because the patent reissues as RE99,999 as long as its claim 1 is the same as claim 1 of 7,777,777. The reissue is a continuation of the original patent, and accordingly keeps the original filing date of the original patent, and has its effect continuously from the original date. For purposes of Patent Office accounting, the issue date of the original patent is also the issue date of the reissue. Therefore, the maintenance fees for the reissue are due at the same time as they would have been due on the original patent. Any rules which refer to a patent date are interpreted using the date of the original patent, not any dates of the reissue.

(f) Doctrine of Intervening Rights

Although the reissued patent takes the original dates for purposes of novelty and other matters, the date of the reissue is very important with respect to liability for infringement. The second paragraph of 35 U.S.C. § 252 governs the Doctrine of Intervening Rights in patent reissues:

> The basic situation which gives rise to intervening rights is a situation where an original patent is not infringed by party X. The patent is then broadened by reissue, and party X subsequently does infringe this reissued patent.

With respect to any specific thing that was in existence before the date of the issue of the reissue patent, the doctrine of intervening rights gives the owner of these things an absolute right to sell them. Therefore, anything that was in existence before the date of the reissue cannot constitute an infringement. An infringer has absolute intervening rights to sell products it had in inventory or had purchased by confirmed order on the date the patentee's reissue patent issued. *BIC Leisure Products v. Windsurfing International*, 27 USPQ2d 1671 (Fed. Cir. 1993). The *absolute* right does not extend to the making of additional objects.

35 U.S.C. 252 does provide a *conditional* right to make additional objects. There is the possibility of granting an equitable right "for the continued prac-

tice of any process patented by the reissue . . . for the practice of which substantial preparation was made, prior to the grant of the reissue, to the extent and under such terms as the court deems equitable for the protection of investments made . . ." In order to grant this right, the court must decide whether what has been done constitutes substantial preparation, and also must decide how to fairly recommend the defendant.

There have been very few cases on this issue since the 1952 statute was invoked. *In Seattle Box Company, Inc. v. Industrial Crating and Packing*, 225 USPQ 357 (Fed. Cir. 1985), the court looked at many considerations to determine whether substantial preparation had been made. This case finds that the following are relevant considerations to decide what is equitable:

1. If the infringer knew of the claims of the original patent, and designed around them. The court found that enabling the patent holder to recapture what it originally dedicated to the public in the original patent would be unfair, especially after the infringer relied on the scope of the original patent. The court found that, "a person should be able to make business decisions secure in the knowledge that those actions which fall outside the original patent claims are protected." *id* at 362.
2. If the infringer had existing orders for his product at the time that the reissue patent issued. The court found that prior business commitments such as previously placed orders and contracts are one good example of pre-existing investments and business that should be recouped.
3. Whether non-infringing goods could be manufactured from the inventory on hand otherwise on-hand stock would almost certainly be usable to manufacture the now-infringing products.

The court in this case allowed the infringer to recoup his investment by filling all the orders he currently had, and manufacturing products from the raw materials currently on hand.

The doctrine of intervening rights limits the amount of protection that can be recaptured by reissue. The time when a client would most want to make a reissue application would be when there is a prospective infringer, one who is infringing what you could have claimed (but did not) in your original patent. However, this will also be the time when this infringer has the strongest arguments for intervening rights. In the one case on which the Federal Circuit has spoken, the scope of the intervening rights that they awarded was fairly minimal. However, the worst case analysis is that after all the expenses and problems associated with the reissue, a court might limit the relief it will give against the infringer at whom the reissue was aimed.

The case of *Slimfold Manufacturing Company v. Kinkead Industries*, 810 F.2d 1113 USPQ2d 1563, 1567 (Fed. Cir. 1987) stated in dictum that intervening rights are only available as a "defense" to those who actually rely on the scope of the claims in the original patent.

When the claims of a reissue patent do not merely clarify but substantively change the scope of the original patent claims, the patentee is not entitled to damages for infringing acts committed before the issue date of the reissue patent. *Westvaco Corp. v. International Paper Co.*, 26 USPQ2d 1353 (Fed. Cir. 1993).

(g) Disadvantages of Applying for a Reissue

Applying for a reissue has certain disadvantages, generally associated with the reissue process. Perhaps the most serious of these dangers are the admissions that the patent owner, through his attorney, must make in order to apply for a reissue patent.

The reissue statute requires that the declaration of a reissue patent request must specify that the patent, as issued, has an error (no such error need be specified in a reexamination request). The rules specify that the declaration must specify in detail the errors relied upon, and how they arose or occurred.[14] Therefore, in the usual case when the reissue is for the purpose of the patentee claiming less than he had a right to claim, the specific insufficiency in the claims must be specified.[15] This may require the patentee to admit, on the record, that he knows of a prospective infringer, and that the infringer does not infringe the claims as they are (before reissue). This may be taken as an admission that the infringer does not infringe the patent, which may be subsequently used against the patent owner. This admission also puts the patent owner into an intervening rights situation against that prospective infringer. If the reissue patent never issues, it may also put the owner into a situation where he has already admitted that his original claims are not infringed.

A reissue also reopens the Patent Office proceedings, in an *inter parte* scenario. While the original prosection is *ex parte* before the examiner, reissue prosecution is of a public nature. During the pendency of a reissue application, the reissue files are open for inspection by the public. Each reissue, when filed, is announced by printing in the *Official Gazette*. This gives interested members of the public an opportunity to submit information to the examiner they may believe is pertinent to the patentability or anything else about the reissue application.

Part of the reissue examination includes determining whether any "deceptive intent" occurred in the error. If so, this could put an inequitable conduct cloud over the patent.

37 CFR §1.11b provides that the filing of reissue applications will be announced each week in a special section of the *Official Gazette*. The entire reissue file maintained by the PTO is also opened at all times for public inspection and copying.

The purpose of this procedure is to notify interested parties that a particular patent may be reissued. These interested parties may then submit to the examiner items of prior art and even arguments about the unpatentability of the subject matter claimed in the reissue application.[16] At least two months must elapse between the publication and the examination of the reissue[17] to allow sufficient time for these comments.

Therefore, any member of the public may contest a reissue application, including both the new scope of the claims, and the original scope of the claims. This puts examiners in an unfamiliar position. Usually, the only arguments they get are those of the patentee, and are pro-patentability. In a reissue situation they may get arguments both for and against patentability.

(h) Advantages of Reissue or Reexamination

The advantage of reissue applications is that they are treated like applications by the Patent Office, and get all the procedural advantages of an application. For instance, extensions of time for various purposes are available as a matter of right in reissue applications under Rule 136, while reexamination proceedings allow no extensions as a matter of right. Also, revival of unintentionally abandoned reissue applications can use the simplified procedures in Rule 137, while revival of a reexamination case is only available if the case meets a very high standard of unavoidability.

However, reissue allows the examiner to consider *anything* about the patent. Reexamination is narrowly focused on the new question of patentability.

11.4 SUMMARY

In summary, reissue allows a patent owner to correct an error which has occurred in a patent without deceptive intention. This error can simply be failure to claim as much as he had a right to claim. The end result of a reissue is a new patent that is free from the original error.

Endnotes
1. 1999 PTO Annual Report.
2. *Hoechst Celanse Corp. v. BP Chemicals Ltd.*, 78 F.3d 1575 (Fed.Cir. 1996), see Chisum pg. 158 cumulative supplement.
3. See pg. 11–446 in Chisum, using for as an example Syntex v. U.S. P.T.O. (1989)
4. Chisum cites at pg. 192 in supplement, PL 106-113 s 4607, 113 Stat. 1501 (Nov. 29, 1999).
5. U.S. Industrial Chemical Inc. v. Carbide and Carbon Chemicals Corp. 315 U.S. at 676, 53 USPQ at 9-10.
6. *In re Weiler* 229 USPQ 673, 676 (Fed. Cir. 1986).
7. *In re Houndsfield*, 216 USPQ 1045 (Fed. Cir. 1982).
8. Id at 677.
9. 217 USPQ 1248, 1249 (Board of Appeals 1982).
10. E.g., see *In re Bose*, 215 USPQ 1 (CCPA, 1982).
11. *In re Weiler* 229 USPQ at 677 n.4.

12. Ex parte Anthony, 230 USPQ 467 (Board of Appeals 1982).
13. 35 U.S.C. 252.
14. 37 C.F.R. § 1.175(a)(5).
15. 37 C.F.R. §1.75(a)(3).
16. 37 C.F.R. §1.291.
17. 37 C.F.R. §1.176.

CHAPTER 12

Battle for the Same Rights: Interference Proceedings

12.1 KEEPING GOOD RECORDS FOR PATENT PROTECTION*

Keeping contemporaneous and thorough records of developing inventions is essential in ensuring that an invention first developed by a company remains the property of that company. More particularly, when two competing companies develop the same invention, with or without knowledge of the other's efforts, each might file a patent application for that invention, whether it be for a new and useful article of commerce, an improvement of an old article, or a new method of manufacturing such articles. Regardless of independent inventorship, however, the U.S. Patent and Trademark Office (PTO) in Washington, D.C. will generally award only one patent per invention; oftentimes, documentation of the invention plays a significant if not critical role in the determination of which company will be awarded the patent. The company awarded the patent is then given a significant market advantage—specifically, the right to exclude all others (including the other independently developing company) from making, using, selling, offering for sale, or importing the claimed invention in the United States for the term of the patent. Due to recent changes in patent laws, the patent term for any U.S. patent that results from an application filed after June 8, 1995, commences on the date that the patent issues and terminates 20 years after the filing date of the application.

When two companies both claim patent rights to the same invention, the PTO will award the patent to the first inventor. The PTO determines first inventorship using a procedure called an interference, an administrative proceeding during which both parties claiming to be the first inventor present evidence proving that they were the first to develop the invention. In the interference, the PTO initially presumes that the first inventor to file an application (the senior party) for a patent was also the first to invent. The PTO makes this presumption because a patent application must be sufficiently descriptive to

---

*Reprinted with the permission of Jack S. Barufka, this section was originally published in the November 1996 edition of *American Biotechnology Laboratory*.

teach the ordinary artisan how to practice the invention. The application thus constitutes good evidence that the inventor had developed the subject matter described in the application at least as early as the filing date thereof. The company with a later application filing date (the junior party), however, is given an opportunity to present evidence showing that it invented the claimed subject matter first. The senior party can then also present its own evidence to show an even earlier invention date.

Documentary evidence, such as laboratory records, is normally the crux of such evidentiary contests. The extent and completeness of each party's documentation can be directly related to the earliest invention date that it might be afforded. In the best possible scenario, a company will be entitled to an invention date as early as the date it can prove that it first conceived the invention (known as the date of conception). A company will be entitled to an invention date as of the date of conception only if such conception is followed by diligence in pursuit of a working embodiment of the invention (known as actual reduction to practice) of the filing of a patent application (known as constructive reduction to practice).

An inventor conceives of an invention when he or she has completely performed the mental part of the inventive act. This means that the inventor must have in mind every feature that is set forth in the invention as claimed in the patent application. Merely suggesting that an idea is of practical utility does not constitute conception.

An actual reduction to practice generally requires that an invention be built and sufficiently tested to demonstrate that it will work for its intended purpose in its intended environment. Constructive reduction to practice occurs when the invention is disclosed in a sufficiently descriptive patent application that has been filed in the PTO. To be entitled to the conception date as the date of invention, an inventor must prove that he or she diligently worked on the invention between the time of conception and the time the invention is reduced to practice. Prior to January 1, 1996, all three elements—conception, diligence, and reduction to practice—must have taken place in the United States or, after NAFTA, in the United States, Canada, or Mexico. As of January 1, 1996, however, inventors in the more than 120 member countries of the World Trade Organization are now also able to establish invention dates based on the requisite events in those member countries, provided that the invention date does not precede the January 1, 1996, effective date.

In general, if there is insufficient evidence (documentary or otherwise) to prove conception and diligence leading to a reduction to practice, an invention date will be granted only as of the date the invention is shown to have been first reduced to practice. Thus, keeping good technical records of developing an invention is extremely important. Such records include engineering/scientific notebooks or similar written and dated records of new projects.

Records should be maintained contemporaneously in the ordinary course of business during the development of new technology and not merely after development of the invention is complete. The records should ideally include any sketches, which might help another individual understand the technology, and any data or specifications, which provide evidence of the various tests performed. They should also highlight any innovative features that the inventor considered or implemented. Record keeping should not only help establish the earliest date of an actual working model to prove reduction to practice, but should also ideally trace the inventor's thought process in order to prove the earliest date of conception. Continued documentation leading from conception to reduction to practice should also be maintained in order to prove diligence so that the earliest invention date possible is afforded.

In addition, the evidence used to show conception, diligence, and reduction to practice must be corroborated. This means that another person apart from the inventor(s) must verify by signature and recollection an understanding of the invention as described in the notebook. The verifying signature should be accompanied by a statement such as "read and understood" to confirm that the individual not only witnessed the documentation but also understood its contents. Ideally, companies should require that each page of a laboratory notebook be signed and dated by the inventor and an additional noninventor employee on a regular basis. For additional integrity of the documentation, the notebook should also be marked as confidential, permanently bound with numbered pages, written in indelible ink, and have sufficient specificity to allow another artisan to repeat the subject matter in the author's absence.

There is no published precedent in patent case law where computer-stored data have been used to establish a priority date of invention. Therefore, at this time, computer record keeping cannot be assumed to serve as a substitute for maintaining an original, permanently bound, handwritten notebook.

In conclusion, a company that invests any significant amount of research and development money in products intended for the U.S. market would be prudent to devote the relatively minimal resources necessary to develop and maintain a record-keeping program to help ensure that company reaps the benefits of such investment. Because of the recent changes to the U.S. patent laws, such advice now applies more broadly to any research and development efforts that a company conducts in any World Trade Organization country on a product intended for the U.S. market. Since the consequences can be significant and the costs of implementation are relatively minimal, inventors and company management should take the time to review their companies' record-keeping procedures to be sure that potential future earnings are not being jeopardized.

CHAPTER 13

Patents Abroad

A U.S. patent will only give a business exclusionary rights in the United States and its territories. In order to protect a technology abroad, patent applications will need to be filed in each foreign office in which protection is desired. In many countries, a separate examination must be received from each respective patent office. In some groups of countries, such as the members of the European Patent Convention, a single patentability examination can be obtained. Once the European Patent Office decides to grant a patent, the applicant then files translations in each designated European member country for which a patent is desired. See Exhibit 13.1.

There is no multi-national patent that can be obtained. If a European Patent Office (EPO) grants an EPO patent, separate patents will then be granted for each designated member country. The business still must obtain a patent in each country for which protection is desired. In some countries (such as Singapore) a patent of another country (the UK) can simply be registered without embarking on an elaborate examination process. However, by registering the patent of another country, a separate patent is still obtained in order to provide protection to the patent owner.

In order to start the process of protecting technology abroad a business must act fairly quickly. If the foreign patent protection process is started within 12 months from the original U.S. Patent application filing date, very significant benefits can be achieved. Certain international conventions treat the U.S. filing date as an effective filing date throughout their member countries for the purpose of determining whether or not claimed inventions are patentable. Therefore, if any publications are made, or if any other prior art surfaces within that 12 month period, it would not be considered prior art against the foreign patent applications and would not affect the patentability of the claims in those countries. At least one country, Taiwan, does not recognize a U.S. filing date even if the application is filed within the 12 month period. Accordingly, a Taiwanese patent application should be filed as soon as possible after a foreign filing license is obtained from the U.S. Patent and Trademark Office. Any delays could result in a loss of patent rights in Taiwan, if there is intervening prior art. See Exhibit 13.2.

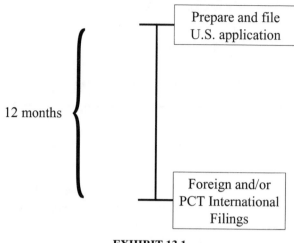

EXHIBIT 13.1

The 12 month convention priority deadline can be a very early stage for a business to make decisions as to which countries patent applications should be filed in, primarily because the costs of pursuing foreign patent protection can be very high. Just filing applications in various countries can incur costs very quickly, because, in many countries, the complete patent application will have to be translated into a foreign language.

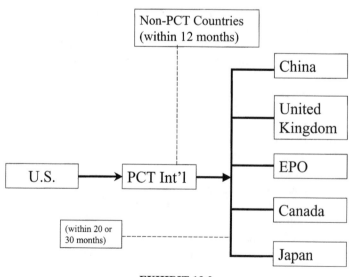

EXHIBIT 13.2

In order to allow patent applicants to postpone their decisions regarding foreign patent protection, and to give the applicants some early feedback as to their likelihood of success in obtaining protection abroad, the Patent Cooperation Treaty (PCT) was formed, and many countries have signed on to the treaty. Under the Patent Cooperation Treaty, one PCT international application can be filed within the 12 month period from the U.S. filing date, thus providing the applicant with an additional grace period before having to file patent applications in each foreign PCT-member country for which patent protection is desired. In the meantime, a PCT international search and examination may be obtained to give the applicant feedback as to the likelihood of obtaining patent protection. The filing of patent applications in each foreign-PCT member country can be delayed to either 20 or 30 months from the U.S. filing date, depending upon the type of membership of each country for which patent protection is desired, and how the applicant wishes to handle the PCT international process.

In many non-PCT countries, an individual patent application must be filed within the 12 month date from the U.S. filing date, in order to obtain an effective filing date back-dated to the U.S. filing date. In other words, the filing cannot be postponed using a PCT international application. Some non-PCT countries include Argentina and Israel.

Before deciding to apply for foreign protection, a business should make sure its foreign rights have not been lost or forfeited. Just because the patent rights were preserved in the United States does not mean the same holds true for patent rights abroad. An invention published before a patent application is filed creates an absolute bar against patentability in many foreign countries, for example, in Europe and Japan. Therefore, it is always recommended that a company not publicly disclose, use, or commercially exploit an invention until after the U.S. patent application is filed. Because international conventions give an effective filing date to foreign patent applications which is back-dated to the U.S. filing date (if the foreign applications are filed within 12 months from the U.S. filing date), any publication, public use, or commercialization after the U.S. filing date should not harm the foreign rights. However, this preservation of rights does not apply to countries which are not members of an international convention granting priority to U.S. applications, such as Taiwan. See Exhibit 13.3.

The costs of acquiring international patent protection can be many times that of acquiring a U.S. patent. A PCT international application allows postponement of much of the costs of obtaining patent protection abroad. The prosecution of a PCT international application can cost more than the entire U.S. patent prosecution process because there are government fees at different stages of the PCT international application process, as well as patent attorney charges for prosecuting the PCT international application. Aside from this process, further substantial costs are incurred by the requirement that the complete application be translated into a foreign language.

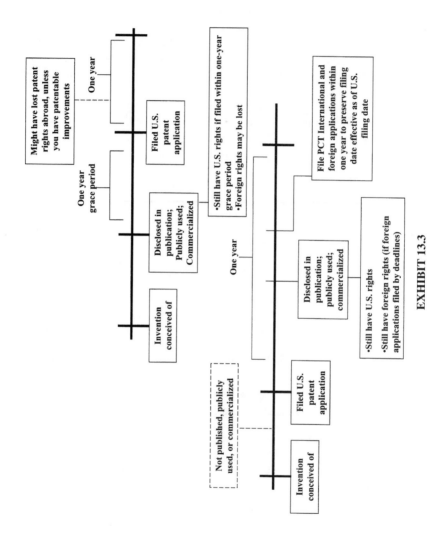

Might have lost patent rights abroad, unless you have patentable improvements

One year

Filed U.S. patent application

One year grace period

Disclosed in publication; Publicly used; Commercialized

Invention conceived of

•Still have U.S. rights if filed within one-year grace period
•Foreign rights may be lost

File PCT International and foreign applications within one year to preserve filing date effective as of U.S. filing date

One year

Disclosed in publication; publicly used; commercialized

•Still have U.S. rights
•Still have foreign rights (if foreign applications filed by deadlines)

Not published, publicly used, or commercialized

Filed U.S. patent application

Invention conceived of

EXHIBIT 13.3

The translation costs will be a significant portion (sometimes the majority) of the costs for filing a patent application in a particular country. Therefore, the costs of filing applications in Argentina and Mexico are significantly greater than the costs of filing applications in Canada and Israel. Translation costs might be reduced if the same translated application is filed in several countries that speak the same language. For example, one translation might be obtained for both Argentina and Mexico, both Spanish-speaking countries.

Once the European Patent Office grants a patent, translations need to be filed with each of the various EPO member countries for which a patent is desired, resulting in even further costs.

The entire costs for prosecuting each of the patent applications in the various foreign offices will be two to three times that of the original filing costs, although such costs can vary widely, depending upon the circumstances and the various (and frequently unpredictable) requirements that each country may have. In some foreign countries, additional prosecution costs after filing can be delayed, since the substance of an application will not be examined by the foreign office until a Request for Examination is filed. In some countries, a Request for Examination does not have to be filed for several years after the application is filed. However, patent protection does not exist until the patent is granted, which cannot occur in most foreign countries until after the patent application is examined.

The cost of foreign protection in Europe is a major contributor to the high costs of foreign patent protection.

Because of the significant costs of protecting a technology abroad, it is of critical importance to make an accurate determination of which countries are important before pursuing patent protection. Not only should the country and its market potential be considered, but the type of protection that would be obtained if a patent was granted in that country should also be considered. If the patent rights are not respected by a particular country's courts or government, any patent granted in that country could be relatively worthless. However, even in countries where patents are not well enforced, there can be advantages to having patents. For example, if a business wishes to purchase an interest in a government-owned business, it may receive preferences if it has patent rights and can demonstrate that it has significant know-how to contribute to the government-owned business and to the country's economy.

CHAPTER 14

The Risks of Patent Licensing and Enforcement

In a patent licensing or enforcement campaign, the patent owner may expose itself to significant risks, especially where the licensing or enforcement is aggressive. Once a patent owner approaches a competitor or prospective licensee to offer a license, the patent owner may find itself hauled into court for patent infringement of the competitor's or prospective licensee's patents. If a patent owner sues another for patent infringement, it could face counterclaims, a finding of invalidity on one or more of its patent claims, and retaliatory litigation filed in another court. Before any licensing or enforcement campaign is started by a business, it should try to anticipate the possible dangers, and carefully weigh the expected returns against the potential harm it may face.

For example, a pre-emptive patent suit, otherwise known as a declaratory judgment action, can be very costly to defend, and could result in a decision that a patent is invalid or not infringed. Being a defendant of a pre-emptive declaratory judgment action can present other disadvantages to the patent owner. The defendant-patent owner may not be financially or legally prepared for the sooner-than-expected litigation. In addition, the court chosen by the plaintiff (accused infringer) in bringing the pre-emptive suit is usually less favorable to the patent owner.

The following are examples of how some patent licensors or litigators have faced setbacks, and even significant harm, in exploiting their patent rights.

- In the spring of 1991, in response to Telect, Inc.'s efforts to exploit its patent rights, ADC Telecommunications, Inc. filed a pre-emptive patent suit against Telect. Telect had obtained a patent covering technology used in the DSX-3/4 digital signal cross-connect switch. ADC, with 70 percent of the market, had received a threat from Telect that Telect would file a patent infringement suit against ADC if ADC manufactured specific products that used certain modules covered by the patent. Before Telect could sue ADC, ADC sued Telect challenging the validity of Telect's patent.

Even when a company vigorously enforces its patents and wins a jury award of millions of dollars, that company still is vulnerable to having its patent invalidated on appeal.

- Collins Licensing L.P. received a $34.6 million jury award. A Texas federal district court jury found in February, 1992 that AT&T Corp. had infringed on a Collins patent in the use of a 5ESS digital switch. AT&T immediately stated that it intended to appeal the verdict. The Texas federal district court entered a judgement upholding the jury award shortly thereafter.

  Once the decision was appealed, the district court's decision that the patent was valid and infringed was overturned. In a non-published opinion on November 5, 1993, the Court of Appeals for the Federal Circuit held that the pertinent claims of the patent were invalid and reversed the lower court's damage award.

When a patent owner threatens several companies with patent litigation, the threatened companies can join forces in an attempt to invalidate the charging company's patents.

- Brooktrout Technology, Inc., an integrated voice and fax systems provider in Needham, Massachusetts, was demanding royalties and initial payments of $50,000 from other firms that provide fax response technology, and had threatened the companies with legal action if they refused to pay the royalties and licensing fees. In response to these demands by Brooktrout, the Fax Response Industry Association was formed, apparently by the companies that were approached by Brooktrout Technology, Inc.[1] The newly-formed Fax Response Industry Association filed a suit in the U.S. District Court for northern California, challenging the validity of Brooktrout's patent for fax response technology. In their suit, the association presented prior art asserting that it constituted clear and convincing evidence that the patent was invalid.

A patent owner who receives a controversial patent and then begins widespread exploitation of the patent may have its rights recalled by the U.S. Patent and Trademark Office.

- Compton's New Media obtained a patent directed to CD-ROM multimedia technology, a technology used by many CD-ROM software publishers. Once it obtained the patent, it embarked on a licensing campaign, requiring companies to consider paying royalties or entering into some relationship with Compton's. There was an uproar in the industry, with smaller companies claiming that innovation would be stifled because such a broad software patent was being asserted. Public perception was that this technology was being used for years and was not patentable, and therefore that the Compton's patent was invalid and should not have been granted. In response to the public outcry, the Commissioner of U.S. patents agreed to have the patent reexamined. Compton's is now again before the U.S. Patent & Trademark Office, and it is going to be very difficult for Compton's to salvage its broad protection.

14.1 ANTITRUST CONSIDERATIONS

In a decision dated February 17, 2000, the Federal Circuit (a U.S. Federal Appeals court) affirmed the lower court's decision to dismiss claims that Xerox Corporation violated the antitrust laws by refusing to sell patented parts and copyrighted manuals (and to license copyrighted software) to an independent service organization (ISO), CSU, LLC. *See CSU, L.L.C. v. Xerox Corp.*, Civ. Action No. MDL-1021 (D. Kan. Jan. 3, 1999) (final judgment order). The following is quoted from the Federal Circuit's published decision:

"Xerox manufactures, sells, and services high-volume copiers. Beginning in 1984, it established a policy of not selling parts unique to its series 10 copiers to independent service organizations ("ISOs"), including CSU, unless they were also end-users of the copiers. In 1987, the policy was expanded to include all new products as well as existing series 9 copiers. Enforcement of this policy was tightened in 1989, and Xerox cut off CSU's direct purchase of restricted parts. Xerox also implemented an "on-site end-user verification" procedure to confirm that the parts ordered by certain ISOs or their customers were actually for their end-user use. Initially this procedure applied to only the six most successful ISOs, which included CSU.

To maintain its existing business of servicing Xerox equipment, CSU used parts cannibalized from used Xerox equipment, parts obtained from other ISOs, and parts purchased through a limited number of its customers. For approximately one year, CSU also obtained parts from Rank Xerox, a majority-owned European affiliate of Xerox, until Xerox forced Rank Xerox to stop selling parts to CSU and other ISOs. In 1994, Xerox settled an antitrust lawsuit with a class of ISOs by which it agreed to suspend its restrictive parts policy for six and one-half years and to license its diagnostic software for four and one-half years. CSU opted out of that settlement and filed this suit alleging that Xerox violated the Sherman Act by setting the prices on its patented parts much higher for ISOs than for end-users to force ISOs to raise their prices. This would eliminate ISOs in general and CSU in particular as competitors in the relevant service markets for high speed copiers and printers.

Xerox counterclaimed for patent and copyright infringement and contested CSU's antitrust claims as relying on injury solely caused by Xerox's lawful refusal to sell or license patented parts and copyrighted software. Xerox also claimed that CSU could not assert a patent or copyright misuse defense to Xerox's infringement counterclaims based on Xerox's refusal to deal.

The district court granted summary judgment to Xerox dismissing CSU's antitrust claims and holding that if a patent or copyright is lawfully acquired, the patent or copyright holder's unilateral refusal to sell or license its patented invention or copyrighted expression is not unlawful exclusionary conduct under the antitrust laws, even if the refusal to deal impacts competition in more than one market. The court also held, in both the patent and copyright contexts, that the right holder's intent in refusing to deal and any other alleged exclusionary acts committed by the right holder are irrelevant to antitrust law. This appeal followed."

The manager should keep the following points in mind regarding the antitrust laws and patents:

- This decision is not without contradiction, as other regional circuits (particularly the Ninth Circuit) may have opinions that differ from that expressed by the Federal Circuit in this decision.
- On the one hand, intellectual property rights do not confer a privilege to violate the antitrust laws. On the other, the antitrust laws do not negate the patentee's right to exclude others from using its patented technology. To quote the Federal Circuit in another decision (*Abbott Lab. v. Brennan*, 952 F.2d 1346, 1354-55, 21 USPQ2d 1192, 1199 (Fed. Cir. 1991)), determination of whether the patentee meets the Sherman Act elements of monopolization or attempt to monopolize is governed by the rules of application of the antitrust laws to market participants, with due consideration to the exclusivity that inheres in the patent grant.
- There is no reported case in which a court has imposed antitrust liability for a unilateral refusal to sell or license a patent. In fact, the Patent Act itself provides that a patent owner shall not be denied relief or deemed guilty of misuse or *illegal extension of the patent right* by reason of his having refused to license or use any rights to the patent. 35 U.S.C. § 271(d) (1999).
- The patentee's right to exclude, however, is not without limit. For example, a patent suit may be deemed to have an anticompetitive effect (and thus subject to the antitrust laws) if the asserted patent was obtained through knowing and willful fraud per the Supreme Court's decision in *Walker Process Equipment, Inc. v. Food Machinery & Chemical Corp.*, 382 U.S. 172, 177, 86 S. Ct. 347 (1965). *See Glass Equip. Dev.*, 174 F.3d at 1343. The patent owner may have antitrust difficulties if he or she brings an infringement suit that is a mere sham "to cover what is actually no more than an attempt to interfere directly with the business relationships of a competitor."
- It is critical that businesses obtain advice from an antitrust specialist before taking any action that could be considered anticompetitive. This area

of the law is very complex. Lawyers that are not specialists are quick to seek advice from an antitrust attorney; and the general guidance provided here cannot be a substitute for an antitrust attorney.

Endnote

1. *Telecommunications Reports*, September 21, 1992.

CHAPTER 15

Choosing a Patent Attorney

Consultation with a skilled and fully qualified patent attorney is important in the patent application process and is absolutely essential to obtaining a strong and valuable patent. An inexperienced attorney or lay person can easily overlook problems that arise throughout patent prosecution, presenting great risk to the value of the patent. Even if a patent is eventually obtained, problems that have not been properly addressed during patent prosecution can hinder or even eliminate the patent's effectiveness in protecting the company's technology.

In choosing a patent attorney to guide the company through the application process, numerous factors should be considered carefully.

Most importantly, the attorney must be admitted to practice before the U.S. Patent and Trademark Office. Admission to a state bar is not sufficient for this purpose; the attorney must be a member of the patent bar and should also be technically conversant, in order to become familiar with the invention for which protection is sought.

Ideally, the attorney should participate in activities that reflect a significant attempt to keep abreast of changes in the law. This involvement is particularly vital in computer and electronics technologies, because the law regarding the patentability of computer and mathematical algorithms frequently changes and can be open to interpretation. Insight into anticipated changes in the patent law can be invaluable in ensuring the strength and breadth of a patent.

A business should ask whether the attorney has previously worked as a patent examiner in the U.S. Patent and Trademark Office. Such experience can be very helpful in understanding the inner workings of the system, although it is not critical.

The business should also consider the attorney's experience in preparing patent applications and in representing applicants before the U.S. Patent and Trademark Office. Patent prosecution is an intricate process in which the patent examiner performs a quasi-judicial role in determining patentability, and the attorney communicates with the examiner on a regular basis. The examiner may have several concerns and incentives to compromise which an inexperienced attorney may not recognize or appreciate, thereby increasing costs and delays.

Personal needs and preferences are obviously important to the business as well. Such factors may include matters as disparate as the attorney's personality, immediate access to the U.S. Patent and Trademark Office, and involvements in professional organizations, but the firm should not lose sight of two important concerns: its ability to easily communicate with and work with the attorney, and the attorney's experience in technology and the law.

Cost is always a concern in seeking legal services, and both attorney and client should take steps to minimize expenses. However, the importance of quality in the patent application process cannot be overemphasized. It is not advisable to seek lower cost at the expense of the quality of a resulting patent. Differences in quality and/or value of one patent compared to another can vary widely, and it may be very difficult for the lay person to recognize these differences, and to know if the business is being adequately represented by the patent attorney. Any deficiencies in quality or in the resulting protection obtained by a patent can render it of little value to the business.

CHAPTER 16

The U.S. Patent and Trademark Office Provides the Following Summary Description of the Provisions of the New Law

16.1 AMERICAN INVENTORS PROTECTION ACT OF 1999 IS LAW*

The American Inventors Protection Act of 1999 was signed into law (P.L. 106-113) on November 29, 1999, as part of the conference report (H. Rept. 106-479) on H.R. 3194, Consolidated Appropriations Act, Fiscal Year 2000. The text of the American Inventors Protection Act of 1999 is contained in Title IV of S. 1948, the "Intellectual Property and Communications Omnibus Reform Act of 1999." S. 1948 was enacted by reference in Division B of the conference report on H.R. 3194.

The new law presents the PTO with a number of challenges as well as opportunities. PTO staff is laboring over the preparation of the rules package to implement the substantive law changes including 18-month publication and patent extension provisions. The initial costs of setting up these new systems are likely to be substantial and may require a request to Congress for supplemental funding. The new law's recasting of PTO as a performance-based organization gives PTO substantial autonomy in managing its budget, personnel, procurement, and other administrative functions, and will permit it to run in a more businesslike manner.

---

*By Talis Dzenitis

Some key provisions of the American Inventors Protection Act of 1999, as signed into law, are as follows:

(a) The Inventors' Rights Act of 1999

This subtitle, effective 60 days after enactment, helps protect inventors against deceptive practices of certain invention promotion companies. The title requires invention promoters to disclose in writing the number of positive and negative evaluations of inventions they have given over a five-year period and their customers' success in receiving net financial profit and license agreements as a direct result of the invention promotion services.

Customers injured by failure to disclose the required information or by any material false or fraudulent representation by the invention promoter can bring a civil action to recover statutory damages up to $5,000 or actual damages. Damages of up to three times the amount awarded are available for intentional or willful violations.

The subtitle directs the Comptroller General, in consultation with the Director, to conduct a study and submit a report to Congress, within six months after enactment, on the potential risks to the U.S. biotechnology industry relating to biological deposits in support of biotechnology patents.

The Director is prohibited from entering into an agreement to provide copies of specifications and drawings of U.S. patents and applications to non-NAFTA or non-WTO member countries without the express authorization of the Secretary of Commerce. The Commissioner (see subtitle G) of Patents is required to make all complaints received by the PTO involving invention promoters publicly available, along with any responses by the invention promoters.

(b) The Patent and Trademark Fee Fairness Act of 1999

This subtitle reduces certain patent fees, effective 30 days after enactment. The Section 41(a)(1)(A) original filing fee, the Sec. 41(a)(4)(A) reissue fee, and the Sec. 41(a)(10) international application fees are each reduced from $760 to $690. The initial maintenance fee is reduced from $940 to $830.

Effective upon enactment, the Director (see subtitle G) is authorized in fiscal year 2000 to adjust trademark fees without regard to fluctuations in the CPI. The subtitle also includes language to emphasize that trademark fees can only be used for trademark-related activities.

The subtitle also requires the Director to conduct and submit to the House and Senate Judiciary Committees, within one year of enactment, a study of alternative fee structures that could be adopted by PTO to encourage maximum participation by the inventor community.

(c) The First Inventor Defense Act of 1999

Subtitle C provides a defense against charges of patent infringement for a party who had, in good faith, actually reduced the subject matter to practice at least one year before the effective filing date of the patent, and commercially used the subject matter before the effective filing date. The defense is limited to methods of "doing or conducting business."

Establishment of the defense does not invalidate the subject patent.

The subtitle is effective upon enactment but does not apply to any pending infringement action or to any subject matter for which an adjudication of infringement, including a consent judgment, has been made before the date of enactment.

(d) The Patent Term Guarantee Act of 1999

This subtitle extends the term of patents, in accordance with regulations prescribed by the Director, to compensate for certain PTO processing delays and for delays in the prosecution of applications pending more than three years. Extensions are available for delays in issuance of a patent due to interference proceedings, secrecy orders, and appellate review. Diligent applicants are guaranteed a minimum 17-year patent term.

Extension authority under this title applies only to applications filed on or after the date six months after enactment.

This subtitle also requires the Director to prescribe regulations to provide for the continued examination of an application, at the request of the applicant. The Director is authorized to establish appropriate fees for continued examination, with a 50 percent reduction for small entities. The continued examination provisions take effect six months after enactment and apply to all applications filed on or after June 8, 1995.

(e) The Domestic Publication of Foreign Filed Patent Applications Act of 1999

This subtitle provides for publication of patent applications 18 months after filing unless the applicant requests otherwise upon filing and certifies that the invention has not and will not be the subject of an application filed in a foreign country. Provisional rights are available to patentees to obtain reasonable royalties if others make, use, sell, or import the invention during the period between publication and grant.

If the foreign-filed application is less extensive than that filed with the PTO, the applicant may submit and request publication of a redacted version by the PTO.

This title also provides a prior art effect for published patent applications; requires the GAO to conduct a three-year study of applicants who file only in the United States; and requires the Director to recover the cost of early publication by charging a separate publication fee after notice of allowance is given.

The subtitle's provisions take effect one year after the date of enactment and apply to patent applications filed on or after that date.

(f) The Optional Inter Parte Reexamination Procedure Act of 1999

This subtitle establishes a reexamination alternative that expands the participation of third-party requesters by permitting those parties to submit a written response each time the patent owner files a response to the PTO. Those third-party requesters who choose to use the optional procedure, however, will not be able to appeal adverse decisions beyond the Board of Patent Appeals and Interferences. Also, they will not be able to challenge, in any later civil action, any fact determined during the process of the optional reexamination procedure.

The Director must submit to Congress within five years a report evaluating whether the optional reexamination proceedings are inequitable to any of the parties in interest and, if so, recommendations for appropriate changes.

Subtitle F takes effect on the date of enactment and its provisions apply to any patent that issues from an application filed on or after that date.

(g) The Patent and Trademark Office Efficiency Act

Subtitle G establishes the PTO as an agency within the Department of Commerce, subject to the policy direction of the Secretary of Commerce. The PTO retains responsibility for decisions regarding the management and administration of its operations and exercises independent control of its budget allocations and expenditures, personnel decisions and processes, procurements; and other administrative and management functions. The subtitle takes effect four months after the date of enactment. The subtitle requires that the patent and trademark operations shall be treated as separate operating units within the Office.

The new PTO is headed by an Under Secretary of Commerce for Intellectual Property and Director of the USPTO, appointed by the President with the advice and consent of the Senate. A Deputy Under Secretary of Commerce for Intellectual Property and Deputy Director of the USPTO is appointed by the Secretary of Commerce upon nomination by the Director.

The Secretary of Commerce appoints a Commissioner for Patents and a Commissioner for Trademarks to serve as chief operating officers for the respective units for a term of five years. The Commissioners will enter into annual performance agreements with the Secretary and will be eligible for up to 50 percent bonuses based on their performance under those agreements.

The PTO is not subject to any administratively or statutorily imposed limitation on positions or personnel.

Officers and employees of the PTO continue to be subject to the provisions of Title 5 of the United States Code relating to Federal employees.

The Secretary of Commerce appoints, within three months of enactment, nine members each to a Patent Public Advisory Committee and a Trademark Public Advisory Committee. The Committees will review and advise the Director on matters involving policies, goals, performance, budget, and user fees, and will prepare annual reports on their efforts within 60 days after the end of each fiscal year. The Federal Advisory Committee Act is not applicable to the Committees.

(h) Miscellaneous Patent Provisions

This subtitle makes a number of technical and clarifying changes to patent law and provides authority for the electronic filing, maintenance, and publication of documents.

The Director may not cease to maintain paper or microform collections of patents and trademarks for public use without providing notice and opportunity for public comment and without first submitting a report detailing such plan to the House and Senate Judiciary Committees. That report must include a description of the mechanisms in place to ensure the integrity of such collections and the data contained therein as well as to ensure prompt public access to the most current available information and a certification that the implementation of such plan will not negatively impact the public.

16.2 THE FIRST INVENTOR DEFENSE ACT*

(a) The First Inventor Defense Act (FIDA)

FIDA provides a limited defense to infringement to prior users of business methods against a subsequent inventor that files a patent application for the same business method. Successful assertion of the defense gives the prior user an unlimited right to practice the invention without invalidating the subsequent inventor's patent. The defense applies to any lawsuit filed on or after November 29, 1999, except where there has been a previous finding of infringement.

It is important to note that that the phrase "first inventor" in FIDA is a misnomer. It is really a "prior user" defense, and the choice of such language is contrary to both the actual language of the act and all legal precedent defining "first inventor." The defense requires actual reduction to practice and not merely conception of the invention. This means the defense applies both to the inventor and a third party who derived the invention from someone other than the patentee. As such, this is a "prior user defense" and not a "first inventor defense." For simplicity and technical correctness the defense provided by FIDA will be referred to as a "prior user defense."

In essence FIDA provides a defense to infringement for prior users who reduced to practice and commercially used a method of doing business before the filing of a patent application by another. The statute provides that:

---

*By Christina Patrick

> It shall be a defense to an action for infringement under [35 U.S.C.] section 271
> ... with respect to any subject matter that would otherwise infringe one or more
> claims for a *method* in the patent being asserted against a person, if such person
> had, acting in *good faith, actually reduced the subject matter to practice* at least
> 1 year before the effective filing date of such patent, and *commercially used the
> subject matter* before the effective filing date of such patent.

As evidenced by the statutory language, the prior user must meet three requirements in order to be eligible for this defense:

1. the invention must be a method;
2. the prior user must reduce the method to practice; and
3. the prior user must commercially use the method.

The latter two requirements must occur before the subsequent patentee files a patent application. The defense appears narrowly tailored, however the following discussion will show that it may have broad applicability.

(b) The invention must be for a "method."

The prior user defense is limited to method inventions. The statute defines a method as "a method of doing or conducting business." Thus, the defense does not apply when the prior user invented chemical or mechanical process, which does not otherwise qualify as a method of doing business. Congress, in effect, decided to favor one class of inventors over another. The favored class of inventors is surprisingly larger than one might think from a quick reading of FIDA. Guidance on the breadth of the definition can be found in the legislative history of FIDA, which shows that there are three reasons why FIDA applies to a large class of inventors. However, the legislative history does not provide a workable definition of business method. Instead it provides a vague definition based on the congressional intent in passing the legislation. Moreover, the statute itself is devoid of any references to the intent of the drafters.

First, the class of inventions that potentially fall under the business method definition is expansive. The Senate Section by Section Analysis of FIDA, the most persuasive form of legislative history associated with FIDA, broadly defined "method" as:

> The method that is the subject matter of the defense may be an internal method
> for doing business, such as an internal human resources management process, or
> a method for conducting business such as a preliminary or intermediate manu-
> facturing procedure, which contributes to the effectiveness of the business by
> producing a useful end result for the internal operation of the business or for ex-
> ternal sale.

Similarly, Sen. Schumer provided a comprehensive definition of "method" in his address to the President in support of the bill. He indicated that:

As used in this legislation, the term 'method' is intended to be *construed broadly.* The term 'method' is defined as a 'method of doing or conducting business.' Thus, 'method' includes any internal method of doing business, a method used in the course of doing business or conducting business, or a method for conducting business in the public marketplace. It includes a practice, process, activity, or system that is used in the design, formulation, testing, or manufacture of any product or service.

These legislative understandings of the defense show that any business method producing a "useful" end result will fall under the protective shield of FIDA.

Additionally, these liberal interpretations show that almost anything can be classified as a business method as long as it is connected to the functioning of the business. For example, the term "method" from the financial industry standpoint includes "financial instruments, financial products, financial transactions, the ordering of financial information, and any system or process that transmits or transforms information with respect to investments or other types of financial transactions." These terms, although industry specific, encompass a vast array of methods, processes, and systems. In reality, everything a business does is related to the conduct of its business. Since the legislative history shows that a broad construction of the term is desired, most of the cases involving the defense will focus on defining method. Undoubtedly, courts will have to flesh out the meaning of this amorphous definition.

Second, whether the patent holder's invention is a method is to be determined by the nature of the invention and not the type of claims.

The issue of whether [the patentee's] invention is a method is to be determined based on the underlying nature and not on the technicality of the form of the claims in the patent. For example, a method for doing or conducting business that has been claimed in a patent as a programmed machine . . . is a method for purposes of [FIDA] if the invention could have easily been claimed as a method. *Form should not rule substance.*

The defense applies to both method claims and apparatus claims containing machines or articles used to practice the method.

(c) There must be a good faith, actual reduction to practice of the business method by the prior user one year before to the effective filing date of the subsequent patentee's patent.

In order to qualify for the defense there must be a good faith, actual reduction to practice of the business method by the prior user. Good faith requires that the business method is not derived from the subsequent patentee, but it does not require that the prior user is the actual inventor of the business method. Thus, the defense applies not only to prior inventors of the same business method but also prior users that purchased or derived a secret business method from someone other than the patentee.

Reduction to practice is a term of art most often used in interference proceedings for priority purposes. Actual reduction to practice requires a physical act and "occurs when the inventor (1) constructs a product or performs a process [or method] that is within the scope of the patent claims, and (2) demonstrates the capacity of the inventive idea to achieve its intended purpose." Since method claims are to be treated like any other process claim, a method is reduced to practice when it is successfully performed.

Demonstrating successful performance of the invention may require experimentation. Whether and to what extent experimentation is required depends on the nature of the invention. For this analysis, inventions are placed into one of three categories. First, there are inventions that are so simple that no experimentation is required. Second, there are inventions that are so complex that testing under actual use is always required. Lastly, there are inventions that fall into the middle ground between simple and complex. These inventions require some testing but not stringent testing. These three classifications embody the principle that the inventor must know that an invention will work. For example, a method for conducting a survey of music listeners would likely be considered a simple invention not requiring testing. A Method for Aligning a Golf Putting Stroke would be considered a complex method requiring actual use testing, whereas a method for conducting an online auction would be somewhere in the middle and require some testing.

Reduction to practice must occur one year prior to the "effective filing date" of the patent. The phrase "effective filing date" is given its ordinary meaning in patent law. It is "the earlier of the actual filing date of the application for the patent or the filing date of any earlier United States, foreign, or international application." This definition contemplates that the prior user reduced the business method to practice one year prior to the filing of a provisional, nonprovisional, PCT, or other international patent application.

(d) The business method must be commercially used before the effective filing date of the patent.

In addition to the reduction to practice requirement, the invention must be commercially used before the effective filing date of the patent. The statute defines "commercially used" and "commercial use" as the "use of a method in the United States, so long as such use is in connection with an internal commercial use or an actual arm's length sale or other arm's length commercial transfer of a useful end result. . . ." Domestic commercialization must occur at least one day before the effective filing date of the patent. Moreover, it is irrelevant whether the use of the method is publicly accessible or known. Also, if the prior user abandoned the commercial use of the infringing business method then all activities prior to the abandonment may not be used to establish commercial use. After abandonment a prior user may resume commercial use and rely on the subsequent commercial use to meet this requirement of the defense.

There are two other important caveats to the commercial use requirement. Interestingly, premarketing regulatory review for safety or efficacy of the subject matter is considered commercial use under FIDA. The importance of this is uncertain since it is difficult to determine what type of business method would require premarketing regulatory review.

Additionally, certain activities by a nonprofit entity are considered "commercial." The use must be to benefit the public and the defense will only be available for continued use by the nonprofit entity. The defense will not apply to any subsequent commercialization or use outside of the nonprofit entity. Therefore, nonprofit entities will qualify for the defense in limited circumstances.

(e) Proofs and penalties when asserting the defense.

The prior user must meet the relatively high burden of clear and convincing evidence in order to establish the defense. To discourage abuse of the defense, FIDA provides penalties for unsuccessful assertion of the defense. If the prior user cannot show a reasonable basis for the assertion of the defense, a court will automatically find the case exceptional and award the patentee with attorney fees. However, if the prior user can demonstrate a reasonable basis for asserting the defense, even if such assertion is unsuccessful, no penalty will be imposed.

As demonstrated above, the potential beneficiaries of the defense is broader than expected and prior users must jump over many hurdles to qualify for the defense. Such hurdles are a direct result of the recent changes in the legal landscape.

It is important to understand that the defense is not a general license to the use of all claims under the patent. Instead it is a limited right extending only to the subject matter meeting the reduction to practice and commercial use requirements. However, the defense does not limit the quantity or volume of use of the business method by the prior user. The prior user is free to use and, if desired, patent any improvements that do not infringe any of the patentee's additionally claimed subject matter.

The defense is personal and "may be asserted only by the person who performed the acts necessary to establish the defense." As such, only the person who commercially used and reduced the business method to practice may assert the defense and the defense cannot be licensed, assigned, or transferred. There is one exception to the alienation prohibition. The statute provides that a third person may assert the defense when it is "an ancillary and subordinate part of a good faith assignment or transfer for other reasons of the entire enterprise or line of business to which the defense relates."

When the defense has been rightfully conveyed along with the enterprise or line of business to which it relates, there is a site limitation.

Specifically, the assignee or transferee may only claim the defense for sites where the business method was in use before the later of the effective filing date of the patent or the date of the assignment or transfer. This limitation means that a person acquiring the business cannot assert the defense for another site even if the original site is closed down and its operations are transferred to a new facility once a patent application is filed. In other words, the first or original inventor of the business method, who meets the requirements of the prior user defense, may assert the defense for every site it owns and can continue to expand its business by increasing production and adding sites indefinitely. However, a later assignee or transferee cannot expand the number of sites after a subsequent user files a patent application.

The statute also provides that when the prior user sells or otherwise disposes of a useful end product produced by the infringing business method, the patentee's rights against that third person are exhausted. As such, the patentee has no cause of action for direct or indirect infringement against the buyer or recipient of the prior user's product.

FIDA clarifies the existing prior use case law and replaces an indirect and uncertain prior user defense under 35 U.S.C. § 102(g).

Prior to the enactment of FIDA it was unclear whether a prior user of a business method held as a trade secret had a defense to infringement. Section 102(g) of the Patent Act is the only provision that addresses the overlap of patent law and trade secret law where there is a trade secret prior user and a subsequent patentee. Specifically, Section 102(g) provides that "[a] person shall be entitled to a patent unless . . . before applicant's invention thereof the invention was made in this country by another who had not abandoned, suppressed, or concealed it." By definition a trade secret is suppressed or concealed since it must be kept secret. Thus, the interpretation of "abandoned, suppressed, or concealed" determines whether a prior user is a "potential infringer" or "the source of invalidating prior art." In delineating the suppression or concealment issue, courts have drawn a line between "secret prior use" and "non-informing public use" by a prior user. Such categorization determines whether the prior use is available as prior art. If the trade secret use is available as prior art, the use invalidates the patent. If the trade secret use is not available as prior art, the use does not invalidate the patent and the prior user infringes the subsequent patent.

APPENDIX A

Sample Patents

A1 EXAMPLE BUSINESS METHOD PATENTS

No. 853,852.   PATENTED MAY 14, 1907.

E. G. ADAMS.

INSURANCE SYSTEM.

APPLICATION FILED OCT. 22, 1906.

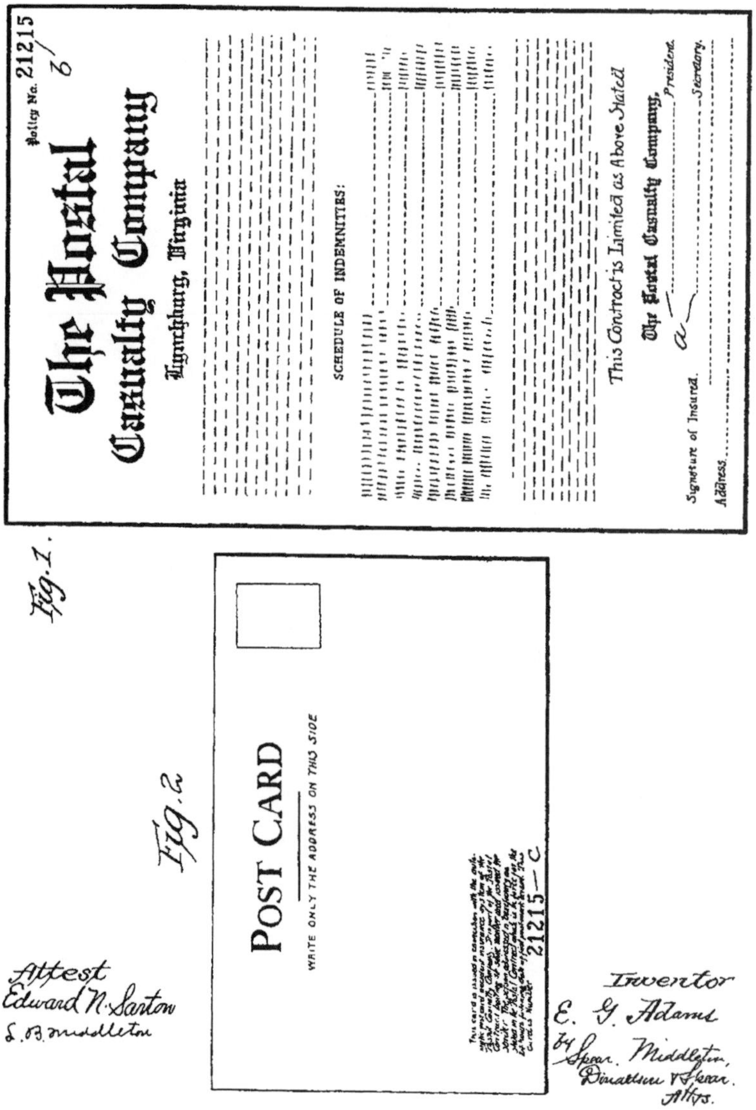

Fig. 1.

Fig. 2.

Attest
Edward N. Saxton
S. B. Middleton

Inventor
E. G. Adams
by Spear, Middleton,
Donaldson & Spear.
Attys.

UNITED STATES PATENT AND TRADEMARK OFFICE

USPTO White Paper

BACK TO APPENDIX INDEX

TEXT OF PATENT
FOR WHITE PAPER ON
BUSINESS METHODS PATENTS

UNITED STATES PATENT OFFICE.

EUGENE GRAVES ADAMS, OF LYNCHBURG, VIRGINIA, ASSIGNOR TO POSTAL INSURANCE CORPORATION, OF LYNCHBURG, VIRGINIA, A CORPORATION OF VIRGINIA.

INSURANCE SYSTEM.

No. 853,852. Specification of Letters Patent. Patented May 14,1907.

Application filed October 22,1908. Serial No. 340,110.

To all whom it may concern:

Be it known that I, EUGENE GRAVES ADAMS, a citizen of the United States, residing at Lynchburg, Virginia, have invented certain new and useful Improvements in Insurance Systems, of which the following is a specification.

My invention hereinafter described consists in the combination of an accident insurance policy, and a postal card, both specially marked or imprinted for identification, and is designed to facilitate, both for the insurer and the insured, the business of accident insurance.

It is illustrated in the accompanying drawing, in which,

Figure 1 relates to the contract part of the combination, and Fig. 2 to the postal card part.

The accident insurance policy now largely in use in railway traveling, especially involves the use of a paper or card containing an agreement on the part of the insurer, accepted by the insured, and issued on payment of a specified sum of money, and running for a specified time from the date of issue and acceptance. This contract, when purchased, is usually sent by mail to the beneficiary or agent of the insured. As such accident insurance policies are bought mainly by persons traveling and run continuously from the date of issue, they are usually purchased at a point before starting on the journey, and are practically useless to the insured during the time in which he stops at places intermediate upon his way. Further, the number of places at which policies of the ordinary form are or may be issued, is greatly limited, and is largely limited to the more important railway stations.

The particular form of contract used in connection with my invention is not material, provided it be upon a sheet or folder of paper suitable to be handled and sold, in connection with a postal card, and contain the substance of an accident insurance policy imprinted thereon, and further, a distinct mark identifying or connecting it with the postal card, of which it forms a part.

A convenient, general form is indicated in Fig. 1 of the accompanying drawing, the parts of which, not shown, are hereinafter fully described. In substance it contains agreement on the part of the insurer to pay certain specified sum or sums of money, and the condition under which such sum or sums will be paid. It contains also blank spaces indicated at *a* in Fig. 1, of suitable form and dimensions and properly located for the signature of the insurer and that of the insured, and .preferably also for the address of the latter. It contains also a mark of identification corresponding with that on the postal card with which it is to be combined and sold. This is indicated at *b* in Fig. 1.

For a more full explanation a form of contract is herein given as follows: The contract specifies the name of the company and its location and the conditions under which the owner of the contract is insured. It states the schedule of indemnities and contains blanks for the signatures of the representative of the company and of the insured. There is a reference to the host-card forming a part of the contract, stating the things necessary to be done to place it in force and how the beneficiary is to be indicated and under what conditions the insured is to be the beneficiary. There is an explanation as to the company's liability; there is also a statement under the head of general conditions and this includes the limitations to the agent and states the number of contracts one person can hold at any one time.

The postal card, indicated in Fig. 2, may be the ordinary postal card of the General Post Office, or any equivalent thereof, though preferably the common "souvenir" postal card is used by me as more salable and more suitable. It must bear a mark preferably a numeral, indicated at c Fig. 2 corresponding with that upon the contract, where by it is identified with the said contract, and made part thereof. It must also contain an explanatory statement that the card is issued in connection with the Accident Insurance System of the Postal Casualty Co., and that it is a part of the postal contract bearing the same number and issued to the sender. It also indicates that the person addressed is the beneficiary and that the contract is in force for 24 hours following the date of the first post mark thereon.

The policy and the post-card bear the same number. It will be understood that the substance and not the precise form of the imprint on either part of this combination is of the essence thereof. These parts (the card and contract) are made in form suitable for their proper combination and for sale as postal cards of the souvenir type are now so commonly sold. The purchaser buys as many as he desires, of the combined card and contract, and having signed as above explained, he directs the card to the beneficiary but need not mail it until he is about to start on his journey. He may buy one for each stage, of suitable length of time limit to cover, say, the first stage of the journey, and, having provided himself with as many as he needs, he may mail one at the beginning of each successive stage of that journey, and thus he does not pay insurance for time when it is not needed or uselessly. The mailing of the card inevitably involves the stamping thereon of the date and this is made the beginning of the term of the insurance. This also affords an opportunity of notifying his family or other beneficiary of his whereabouts and his remembrances.

The length of time for each particular contract may be 24 hours, or any other suited to the conditions.

I claim:

As an article of manufacture, a two part insurance policy consisting of a paper containing an insurance contract provided with suitably designated spaces for the signature of insurer and that of the insured combined with a postal card, both bearing a number or mark of identification, and the postal card bearing also printed reference to the contract paper and the beneficiary thereof, substantially as described.

In testimony whereof, I affix my signature in presence of two witnesses.

EUGENE GRAVES ADAMS.

Witnesses:

C. S. MORRIS,

R. H. WOOLFOLK, Jr.

US005715399A

United States Patent [19]

Bezos

[11] Patent Number: 5,715,399

[45] Date of Patent: Feb. 3, 1998

[54] SECURE METHOD AND SYSTEM FOR COMMUNICATING A LIST OF CREDIT CARD NUMBERS OVER A NON-SECURE NETWORK

[75] Inventor: **Jeffrey P. Bezos**, Bellevue, Wash.

[73] Assignee: **Amazon.Com, Inc.**, Seattle, Wash.

[21] Appl. No.: **453,273**

[22] Filed: **May 30, 1995**

Related U.S. Application Data

[63] Continuation-in-part of Ser. No. 413,242, Mar. 30, 1995.

[51] Int. Cl.[6] **G06F 17/60**; G06G 7/52

[52] U.S. Cl. **395/227**; 235/379; 235/380; 235/381; 395/239

[58] **Field of Search** .... 235/379, 380, 235/487, 381; 902/24; 364/401 R; 340/827, 825.33, 825.34, 825.35; 395/239, 240, 227

[56] **References Cited**

U.S. PATENT DOCUMENTS

5,336,870 8/1994 Huges et al. 235/379

OTHER PUBLICATIONS

Loshin, P., "Selling Online With . . . First Virtual", Chapters 3 and 4, Charles River Media, Inc., 1996.
Borenstein, N. "Perils and Pitfalls of Practical Internet Commerce (Part I)." <http://www.fv.com/company/first year1.html>. 1996.

Templeton, B., "USENIX–Race to Develop Internet Commerce," Newsbytes News Network, IAC Newsletter, Jan. 1995.
"Wells Fargo and CyberCash Team Up to Provide Secure Online Payment Systems," CyberCash News Release, Dec. 1994.
Somogyi, S., "How Would You Like to Pay for That? A Guide to Digital Cash and Carry Technology," Digital Media, v4, n7, p. 13, Dec. 1994.

Primary Examiner—Wellington Chin
Assistant Examiner—Melissa Kay Carman
Attorney, Agent, or Firm—Ronald M. Anderson

[57] **ABSTRACT**

A method and system for securely indicating to a customer one or more credit card numbers that a merchant has on file for the customer when communicating with the customer over a non-secure network. The merchant sends a message to the customer that contains only a portion of each of the credit card numbers that are on file with the merchant. The message may also contain a notation explaining which portion of each of the credit card numbers has been extracted. A computer (38) retrieves the credit card numbers on file for the customer in a database (40), constructs the message, and transits the message to a customer location (10) over the Internet network (30) or other non-secure network. The customer can then confirm in a return message that a specific one of the credit card numbers on file with the merchant should be used in charging a transaction. Since only a portion of the credit card number(s) are included in any message transmitted, a third party cannot discover the customer's complete credit card number(s).

20 Claims, 3 Drawing Sheets

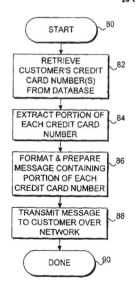

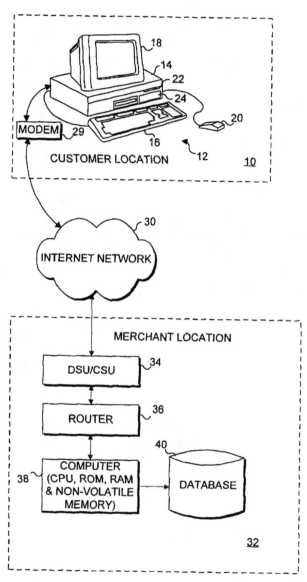

Fig. 1

TO: JOHN@CUSTOMER.COM   56
FROM: MAILBOT@MERCHANT.COM
SUBJECT: CREDIT CARD SELECTION;
               ORDER MESSAGE ID (MID) MID-JOHN-7452

[ORDER SPECIFIC INFORMATION WOULD BE INCLUDED IN
THE FIRST PARAGRAPH.]

WE ALREADY HAVE YOUR SHIPPING ADDRESS AND CREDIT
CARD INFORMATION ON FILE. PLEASE CONFIRM IN A REPLY
MESSAGE THAT THE INFORMATION LISTED BELOW IS
CORRECT BY INCLUDING THE WORDS "AS USUAL" AS THE
FIRST TWO WORDS IN THE BODY OF THE MESSAGE OR,
PROVIDE ANY CORRECTIONS TO THE INFORMATION.

YOUR SHIPPING ADDRESS WILL BE:
          JOHN W. CUSTOMER
          123 ANYSTREET
58   ANYCITY, AS 12345

WE HAVE THE FOLLOWING CREDIT CARD NUMBERS ON FILE
FOR YOU (ONLY THE LAST FIVE DIGITS ARE SHOWN FOR
SECURITY REASONS). PLEASE INDICATE THE CREDIT CARD
NUMBER THAT SHOULD BE USED TO PAY FOR THIS ORDER
BY INCLUDING THE REFERENCE LETTER OF THAT CREDIT
CARD, WHICH IS USED BELOW, IN YOUR REPLY MESSAGE.
                                          54

REF. LETTER	TYPE	LAST 5 DIGITS	EXP. DATE
A.	VISA	86543	10/98
B.	VISA	21883	04/97
C.	MC	15609	08/98

52

50

Fig. 2

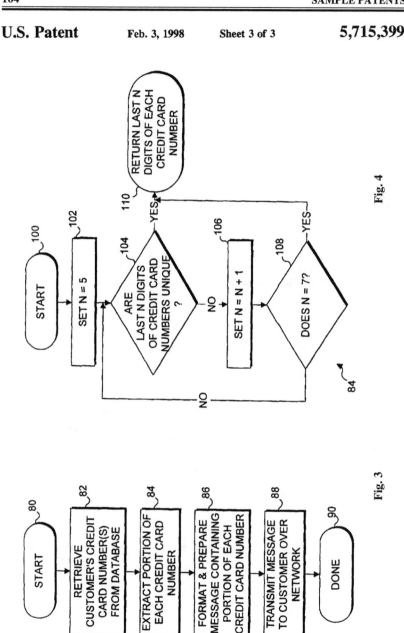

Fig. 4

Fig. 3

5,715,399

1

SECURE METHOD AND SYSTEM FOR COMMUNICATING A LIST OF CREDIT CARD NUMBERS OVER A NON-SECURE NETWORK

RELATED APPLICATIONS

This application is a continuation-in-part of prior copending application Ser. No. 08/413,242, filed Mar. 30, 1995, the benefit of the filing date of which is hereby claimed under 35 U.S.C. § 120.

FIELD OF THE INVENTION

The present invention generally relates to a method and system for communicating confidential information over a non-secure network, and more specifically, for communicating credit card data over the non-secure network.

BACKGROUND OF THE INVENTION

Catalog shopping represents an increasing part of the economy. The growth in its popularity can in part be explained because consumers have learned that goods purchased from a catalog are often much less expensive than if purchased through a normal retail store. In addition, because a customer can shop without leaving the comfort of home or office, placing an order for merchandise from a catalog makes much more efficient use of the customer's time.

Shopping for goods and services using a personal computer to place an order on a network is a natural extension to the more traditional catalog shopping, since the customer enjoys these same benefits. The COMPUSERVE™ network and other private networks have long offered members the opportunity to browse through on-line "Electronic Shopping Malls" and place orders for goods shown and described therein. New opportunities for shopping via personal computers arise than as more people gain access to the Internet network, with its interconnectivity and easy access to locations throughout the world via the World Wide Web or E-mail.

A credit card facilitates making purchases via telephone or over the network. However, users are justifiably concerned about their credit card numbers being transmitted over networks such as the Internet, for example, via E-mail, because of the lack of secure communications.

Security on public networks at the present time is virtually non-existent, making it relatively easy for an unauthorized third party to gain access to credit card data transmitted over the network. Once a dishonest person has another person's credit card number, thousands of dollars can be improperly charged to that credit card account.

Currently, most transactions occurring over networks such as the Internet are done in two parts. The majority of the order information, such as customer name and shipping address, is transmitted over the network. In the second step, the customer places a telephone call to the merchant to provide credit card information for billing purposes. Alternatively, the customer may fax the credit card information to the merchant.

Regardless of the method used by the customer to convey the credit card information to the merchant, after the information has once been conveyed, it can remain "on file" with the merchant in a customer database. For subsequent purchases, the customer need not communicate a credit card number to the merchant. The customer need only provide his or her name to the merchant, and so long as the shipping address provided by the customer matches that on file, the

2

merchant will use the credit card number the customer previously gave to the merchant to charge the order placed. If the shipping address is different than that on file with the merchant, the transaction can still be completed if the customer confirms his or her identity, possibly by providing an account ID and/or password established at the time the credit card number was initially conveyed.

Leaving a credit card number on file with the merchant is advantageous to the customer, because it eliminates the need to communicate the credit card information when making subsequent purchases. Providing the credit card information each time that a purchase is made is inconvenient to a customer. Furthermore, each time that the credit card information is communicated to a merchant, another opportunity is presented for an unauthorized third party to gain access to the credit card data.

Credit cards are so convenient to use and easy to obtain that most people have several general purpose credit cards of different types. As a result, a problem can arise when placing orders with a merchant that maintains credit card information from previous orders for each customer. Since a substantial period of time may elapse between orders placed with a particular merchant, it is possible that the customer may forget which credit card number (or numbers) were left on file with a merchant. The specific credit card number on file with the merchant may be important to the customer for any number of reasons, including the possibility that the credit card to which the merchant may charge the transaction is at its credit limit and should therefore not be charged for the current purchase.

As noted above, it is also possible that the customer may have more than one credit card number on file with the merchant and may prefer to charge the current transaction to a specific credit card account. If the customer is to choose between multiple credit card numbers on file with the merchant, it would be advantageous if the merchant could present to the customer, at the time the order is placed, a list of the credit card numbers the merchant has on file for that customer.

The merchant could send the list of credit card numbers on file to the customer over the Internet or other non-secure network, by straightforward means, such as by displaying to the customer a World Wide Web page containing the credit card numbers or by sending an E-mail message containing the credit card numbers to the customer. However, sending the credit card numbers in this manner would jeopardize the security of the numbers, possibly placing the customer at risk.

Alternatively, the credit card numbers could be encrypted at the merchant's location using any of several techniques (including public key encryption) before being transmitted to the customer location, where they would be unencrypted and then viewed by the customer. However, applying encryption techniques when transmitting a list of credit card numbers requires that the customer have access to the proper decryption software. The widespread dissemination of such software will likely not occur for some time.

A new method for a merchant to convey a list of credit card numbers on file for a customer to the customer over a non-secure network is needed that does not jeopardize the security of the customer's credit card information. The present invention provides a solution to this problem that is relatively efficient and foolproof.

SUMMARY OF THE INVENTION

In accordance with the present invention, a method is defined for enabling a merchant to indicate to a customer, by

5,715,399

3

a communication over a non-secure network, the customer's credit card number that will be charged for a transaction; the indication occurs without risk that a third party will discover the customer's credit card number. The credit card number is maintained in a database by the merchant. As used throughout this specification and in the claims that follow, the term "credit card" is intended to encompass debit cards and any other form of credit or debit used to make a purchase by providing a reference number that uniquely identifies a purchaser's account from which funds to pay a seller for goods or services will be transferred. The method includes the step of retrieving the credit card number of the customer from the database. A portion of the credit card number that is substantially smaller than the complete credit card number is then extracted from the credit card number retrieved. Next, a message containing the portion of the credit card number is constructed and the message is transmitted to the customer over the non-secure network.

The message also preferably includes a notation indicating the portion of the credit card number that has been included in the message. Also, in the preferred embodiment, the portion comprises the last N digits of the credit card number, where N is an integer. In the preferred embodiment, the message may comprise either an E-mail message addressed to the customer or a World Wide Web page.

In addition, the method also deals with the condition where the merchant maintains a plurality of credit card numbers of the customer in the database. In this case, each of the plurality of the credit card numbers of the customer that are in the database are retrieved and portions of each of the plurality of credit card numbers of the customer are extracted. The message is constructed so that it contains the portions of each of the plurality of the credit card numbers of the customer.

If the portions of the plurality of the credit card numbers of the customer do not all differ from each other, the size of the portion of each of said plurality of the credit card numbers extracted is successively increased (up to some predefined limit) to form a larger portion, until the larger portions of the credit card numbers all differ from each other. Then, the message is constructed to include the larger portions of the plurality of the credit card numbers. In addition, the method preferably further comprises the step of indicating in the message to the customer a credit card expiration date associated with each of the portions of the credit card numbers listed. The portions of two credit card numbers then differ from each other if the credit card expiration dates associated with the portions of the two credit card numbers are different, even though the portions of the two credit card numbers are numerically equal. Similarly, the message can indicate a credit card expiration date associated with each of the portions of the credit card numbers listed. Then, the portions of two credit card numbers will be found to differ from each other if the credit card expiration dates associated with the portions of the two credit card numbers are different, even though the portions of the two credit card numbers are numerically equal.

When the database includes multiple credit cards for the customer, the customer is requested to indicate a specific one of the plurality of the credit card numbers of the customer that should be used in a transaction with the merchant. This response can be provided to the merchant in a return message from the customer to the merchant.

Another aspect of the present invention is directed to a system for constructing and transmitting a message from a merchant to a customer using a non-secure transmission

4

method. The message indicates a credit card number (or numbers) of the customer that is maintained by the merchant in a database. The system includes a computer for use in constructing and transmitting the messages, and the computer has a central processor that executes instructions. A memory in the computer stores the instructions to be executed, and non-volatile storage stores the database and the messages. The instructions stored in the memory of the computer cause the central processor to perform functions that are generally consistent with the steps of the method described above.

BRIEF DESCRIPTION OF THE DRAWING FIGURES

The foregoing aspects and many of the attendant advantages of this invention will become more readily appreciated as the same becomes better understood by reference to the following detailed description, when taken in conjunction with the accompanying drawings, wherein:

FIG. 1 is a block diagram illustrating the components involved in the communication between a merchant location and a customer location, over a non-secure network, in accord with the present invention;

FIG. 2 illustrates an exemplary E-mail message transmitted from a merchant to a customer that includes portions of credit card numbers indicating the credit card information that the merchant is maintaining for the customer;

FIG. 3 is a flow chart showing the steps for conveying to a customer an indication of the customer's credit card numbers that are on file by the merchant, in accord with the present invention; and

FIG. 4 is a flow chart illustrating the steps implemented when extracting a portion of each of the credit card numbers for inclusion in a message transmitted to the customer by the merchant.

DESCRIPTION OF THE PREFERRED EMBODIMENT

With reference to FIG. 1, the principal components used to implement the present invention are illustrated in a block diagram. At the top of the Figure, a dash line defines a customer location 10, which in many cases will be the customer's home or place of business. At customer location 10, a personal computer 12 is employed to receive and transmit E-mail or to receive and transmit data over the World Wide Web or to receive and transmit messages by some other means. Personal computer 12 is generally conventional in design, comprising a processor chassis 14 within which are disposed a central processing unit (CPU) and supporting integrated circuitry. Coupled to processor chassis 14 is a keyboard 16 and a monitor 18. Personal computer 12 is controlled by the customer using keyboard 16 and a mouse 20 (optional) or other pointing device that controls a cursor that is moved about on the screen of the monitor to make selections in programs executing on the personal computer. In the front panel of the processor chassis are mounted a floppy drive 22 and a hard drive 24.

Although a desktop type of personal computer is illustrated in FIG. 1, it will be understood that a laptop or other type of portable computer, a "dumb" terminal, or a personal digital assistant can also be used in connection with the present invention, for receiving and transmitting messages over a non-secure network. In addition, a workstation on a local area network at the customer location can be used instead of personal computer 12 for receiving and transmit-

5,715,399

5

ting messages over the non-secure network. Accordingly, it should be apparent that the details of personal computer 12 are not particularly relevant to the present invention. Personal computer 12 simply serves as a convenient interface for receiving and transmitting messages over the non-secure network.

While the present invention is applicable to private networks such as COMPUSERVE™, PRODIGY™, and AMERICA ONLINE™, in FIG. 1, personal computer 12 is shown connected to an Internet network 30. The connection between personal computer 12 and the Internet can be through a modem and telephone line via a private network service provider that is directly connected to the Internet network, through an Internet service provider that is directly connected, or via a direct high-speed data connection. The details of the type of connection to the Internet (or other) network are of no consequence in the present invention.

Internet network 30 is depicted in FIG. 1 as an amorphous shape to indicate that it is a complex system, which can involve many thousands of nodes and components, conveying signals by land lines, satellite, and/or optical fibers. The details of the Internet network are, however, not important in the present invention.

The present invention is likely to find application when a customer is placing or has placed an order with an on-line merchant for a service or merchandise via the Internet (or other non-secure network). The present, invention is applicable in those cases where the customer has previously placed one or more orders with the merchant and has provided the merchant with one or more credit card numbers, which the merchant has maintained in a customer file. To complete a current transaction with the customer, the merchant will need for the customer to confirm that a credit card previously provided should be charged for the transaction. If more than one credit card number appears in the file for the customer, it will also be necessary for the customer to indicate the specific credit card number that should be charged. When a merchant needs to transmit information indicating the credit card numbers that a customer has on file with the merchant, a message containing this information can be transmitted over the Internet network from a merchant location 32 to the appropriate customer location 10, using the present invention, without compromising the confidentiality and security of the customer's credit card number(s).

In FIG. 1, merchant location 32 is indicated by a dash line surrounding the components, including a computer 38, that the merchant uses to communicate with customers through messages conveyed over the Internet. Preferably, computer 38 comprises a SUN SPARC5™ minicomputer, which includes a CPU, RAM, ROM, and a non-volatile storage device (a high-speed hard drive—not separately shown) for use in storing a database 40. Computer 38 is coupled to a router 36, such as a Livingston PORTMASTER™, which is connected to a digital service unit/customer service unit (DSU/CSU) 34, such as an ADC KENTROX D-SERV™. The DSU/CSU is connected to high-speed data lines that access Internet network 30. In the memory of computer 38 are stored application programs that execute on the CPU. Among these programs, for use in the present invention, are an ORACLE™ database management system and custom software. The programs or software comprise machine instructions that instruct the CPU within computer 38 to implement the steps of the present invention, generally as explained below.

Credit card numbers for customers are stored in database 40 by the merchant. Each credit card number is associated

6

with one of the customers who has previously transacted business with the merchant and with other data for the customers, such as names, addresses, and telephone numbers.

As discussed above in the Background of the Invention, public networks such as Internet network 30 are notoriously lacking in security for transmission of sensitive and confidential data, such as credit card numbers. Sending a message containing a complete credit card number from merchant location 32 to customer location 10 over Internet network 30 would jeopardize the security of the credit card number. However, a merchant can safely employ the present invention to convey a message to a customer indicating the credit card number(s) that the customer has on file with the merchant; the message can be conveyed over the Internet network from merchant location 32 to customer location 10, without risk that the customer's credit card number(s) might be discovered by a third party.

An exemplary E-mail message 50 that indicates a customer's credit card numbers on file by a merchant is shown in FIG. 2. A message heading 56 includes an E-mail address, indicates the merchant who is sending the message, provides an order message ID (MID) number that identifies the current transaction to be charged to the customer's credit card account, and notes that the subject of the message is credit card selection.

In the body of the message, an explanation is provided that indicates the response required of the customer. Although not shown in this exemplary message, the merchant may also include language in the message soliciting the customer to make a particular or additional purchases. More importantly, the customer is asked to reply to the E-mail message by confirming or correcting a customer address 58 and indicating a specific one of the credit card numbers in a list 52 that is to be charged for the current transaction. If a customer has only a single credit card number on file with the merchant, the message will ask the customer to confirm that the credit card number on file should be charged for the current transaction.

The message sent by the merchant indicates only a portion of each of the credit card numbers that the customer has on file with the merchant. In this example, a heading 54 notes that ONLY the last five digits of the entire twelve to sixteen digits in the typical credit card number are included in the message, in list 52. Although in this example, the last five digits of the complete credit card number are displayed in the message, it will be appreciated that either fewer or more than five digits of the credit card number can instead be displayed in list 52.

Alternatively, the message might display the first n digits of the credit card numbers; however, this alternative is less likely, because the first few digits are the same for a large number of credit cards. This detail is relatively unimportant, so long as the message displays only a relatively small subset of the entire credit card number.

Further details of the process for indicating to the customer the credit card numbers that the customer has on file with the merchant are illustrated in the flow chart shown in FIG. 3, beginning at a start block 80. In a block 82, computer 38 retrieves from database 40 all of the credit card numbers on file for a specific customer, who is at customer location 10. In a block 84, computer 38 extracts a portion of each of the credit card numbers retrieved in block 82. In a block 86, computer 38 constructs a message (E-mail, World Wide Web page, or other type of message) containing the portion(s) of the credit card number(s) extracted in block 84. In a block

5,715,399

7

88, computer 38 transmits the message prepared in block 86 from merchant location 32 to customer location 10 over Internet network 30. In a block 90, the process is concluded.

In the preferred embodiment, the step of extracting a portion of each credit card number, which is referenced in block 84, is described in detail in FIG. 4, beginning at a start block 100. In a block 102, a variable N is set equal to 5. In a decision block 104, the numbers represented by the last N digits of each credit card number are examined for uniqueness. (The last N digits of a credit card number referred to as a "tail" in the following discussion.) If the tails of the customer's credit card numbers are all different or unique within the set of tails, the extraction process concludes in a block 110, by returning the last N digits or tail of each credit card number. If the tails of all of the customer's credit card numbers are not unique within the set, the value of N is incremented by 1 in a block 106. Although not specifically indicated within the flow chart, uniqueness of a tail also depends upon the type of credit card, and may depend upon other data on the credit card, such as the expiration date. Thus, a customer's VISA™ credit card expiring on 5/97 would be uniquely identified relative the customer's DIS-COVER™ credit card expiring on 8/96, even though both cards were indicated by the same last N digits or tails, because the two credit cards are of different type and/or have different expiration dates.

In a decision block 108, the variable N is examined to determine if it is equal 7. If so, the extraction process again concludes in block 110, by returning the last N digits as the tails of the customer's credit card numbers. Returning to decision block 108, if N does not equal 7, processing loops back to decision block 104, where the N digits comprising the tails of the customer's credit card numbers are again examined for uniqueness within the set. Regardless of the path taken, the logic eventually reaches block 110, from which point processing continues with block 86 in FIG. 3.

Although the present invention has been described in connection with the preferred form of practicing it, those of ordinary skill in the art will understand that many modifications can be made thereto within the scope of the claims that follow. Accordingly, it is not intended that the scope of the invention in any way be limited by the above description, but instead be determined entirely by reference to the claims that follow.

The invention in which an exclusive fight is claimed is defined by the following:

1. A method enabling a merchant to indicate to a customer by a communication over a non-secure network, a credit card number of the customer that is maintained in a database by the merchant, said method comprising the steps of:

   (a) retrieving the credit card number of the customer from the database;

   (b) extracting a portion of the credit card number, said portion being substantially smaller than the complete credit card number;

   (c) constructing a message containing the portion of the credit card number; and

   (d) transmitting the message to the customer over the non-secure network.

2. The method of claim 1, wherein the message also includes a notation indicating the portion of the credit card number that has been included in the message.

3. The method of claim 1, wherein the portion comprises the last N digits of the credit card number, where N is an integer.

4. The method of claim 1, wherein the message comprises an E-mail message addressed to the customer.

8

5. The method of claim 1, wherein the message comprises a World Wide Web page.

6. The method of claim 1, wherein the merchant maintains a plurality of credit card numbers of the customer in the database, further comprising the steps of repeating steps (a) and (b) for each of the plurality of the credit card numbers of the customer that are in the database to obtain portions of each of the plurality of credit card numbers of the customer; and constructing the message so that the message contains the portions of each of the plurality of the credit card numbers of the customer.

7. The method of claim 6, further comprising the steps of determining if the portions of the plurality of the credit card numbers of the customer all differ from each other, and if not, successively increasing a size of the portion of each of said plurality of the credit card numbers extracted to form a larger portion, until said larger portions all differ from each other; and then constructing the message to include the larger portions of said plurality of the credit card numbers.

8. The method of claim 7, further comprising the step of indicating in the message a type of credit card for each of the portions of the credit card numbers listed, wherein the portions of two credit card numbers differ from each other f the portions of said two credit card numbers are from different types of credit cards, even though the portions of said two credit card numbers are numerically equal.

9. The method of claim 7, further comprising the step of indicating in the message a credit card expiration date associated with each of the portions of the credit card numbers listed, wherein the portions of two credit card numbers differ from each other if the credit card expiration dates associated with the portions of said two credit card numbers are different, even though the portions of said two credit card numbers are numerically equal.

10. The method of claim 7, further comprising the step of requesting the customer to indicate a specific one of the plurality of the credit card numbers of the customer that should be used in a transaction with the merchant in a return message.

11. A system for constructing and transmitting a message from a merchant to a customer using a non-secure transmission method, said message indicating a credit card number of the customer that is maintained by the merchant in a database, comprising:

   (a) a computer for use in constructing and transmitting said messages, said computer having a central processor that executes instructions, a memory for storing the instructions to be executed, and non-volatile storage for storing the database and the messages; and

   (b) said instructions stored in the memory of the computer causing the central processor to:

      (i) retrieve the credit card number of the customer from the database stored in the non-volatile storage;

      (ii) extract a portion of said credit card number, said portion being substantially smaller than the complete credit card number;

      (iii) construct a message including the portion of the credit card number; and

      (iv) transmit the message to the customer using the nonsecure transmission method.

12. The system of claim 11, wherein the instructions cause the central processor to include in the message a notation indicating the portion of the credit card number that has been included in the message.

13. The system of claim 11, wherein the instructions cause the central processor to extract the last N digits of the credit card number for use as said portion, where N is an integer.

5,715,399

9

14. The system of claim 11, wherein the instructions cause the central processor to construct the message as an E-mail message.

15. The system of claim 11, wherein the instructions cause the central processor to construct the message as a World Wide Web page.

16. The system of claim 11, wherein the merchant maintains a plurality of credit card numbers for the customer in the database, and wherein the instructions cause the central processor to:

(a) retrieve all of said plurality of the credit card numbers from the database;

(b) extract portions of the plurality of the credit card numbers; and

(c) construct the message so that the message includes said portions of said plurality of credit card numbers.

17. The system of claim 16, wherein the instructions further cause the central processor to:

determine if the portions of the plurality of the credit card numbers of the customer that are extracted all differ from each other, and if not:

(a) successively increase a size of said portions to form larger portions of said plurality of credit card numbers until said larger portions all differ from each other; and

10

(b) construct the message so that the message includes the larger portions.

18. The system of claim 17, wherein the instructions cause the central processor to indicate in the message a type of credit card associated with each portion of the credit card numbers listed; and to determine that the portions of the credit card numbers differ from each other if the portions of said two credit card numbers are for different types of credit cards, although the portions of said two credit card numbers are numerically equal.

19. The system of claim 17, wherein the instructions cause the central processor to indicate in the message a credit expiration date associated with each of the portions of the credit card numbers listed; and to determine that the portions of two credit card numbers differ from each other if the portions of said two credit card numbers are associated with different credit card expiration dates, although the portions of said two credit card numbers are numerically equal.

20. The system of claim 11, wherein the instructions cause the central processor to construct the message to include a request that the customer indicate a specific one of the plurality of the credit card numbers of the customer that should be used in a transaction with the merchant, in a return message.

* * * * *

UNITED STATES PATENT AND TRADEMARK OFFICE
CERTIFICATE OF CORRECTION

PATENT NO. : 5,715,399

DATED   : February 3, 1998

INVENTOR(S) : Jeffrey P. Bezos

It is certified that error appears in the above-indentified patent and that said Letters Patent is hereby corrected as shown below:

On the Title page, item [57]:

In the Abstract:	"transits" should read --transmits--
Column 4, Line 61	"other," should read --other--
Column 5, Line 27	"present," should read --present--
Column 6, Line 33	"E-mall" should read --E-mail--
Column 7, Line 14	"tall" should read --tail--
Column 7, Line 18	"tall" should read --tail--
Column 7, Line 45	"fight" should read --right--
Column 7, Line 55 (Claim 1)	"number;," should read --number;--
Column 8, Line 24 (Claim 8)	"f" should read --if--

Signed and Sealed this

Seventh Day of July, 1998

Attest:

BRUCE LEHMAN

Attesting Officer   *Commissioner of Patents and Trademarks*

A2 EXAMPLES OF PATENTS DRAFTED BY THE AUTHOR

US005790828A

United States Patent [19]

Jost

[11] **Patent Number:**   **5,790,828**

[45] **Date of Patent:**   **Aug. 4, 1998**

[54] **DISK MESHING AND FLEXIBLE STORAGE MAPPING WITH ENHANCED FLEXIBLE CACHING**

[75] Inventor: **Larry Thomas Jost**, St. Louis, Mo.

[73] Assignee: **Southwestern Bell Technology Resources, Inc.**, Austin, Tex.

[21] Appl. No.: **724,149**

[22] Filed: **Sep. 30, 1996**

Related U.S. Application Data

[63] Continuation of Ser. No. 53,655, Apr. 29, 1993, abandoned.

[51] Int. Cl.^{6} **G06F 12/02**; G06F 12/10; G06F 13/16

[52] U.S. Cl. **395/404**; 395/440; 395/441; 395/464; 395/412

[58] Field of Search 395/441, 440, 395/464, 404, 412

[56]   **References Cited**

U.S. PATENT DOCUMENTS

4,399,503	8/1983	Hawley	395/440
4,433,374	2/1984	Hanson et al.	395/465
4,530,055	7/1985	Hamstra et al.	395/463
4,811,203	3/1989	Hamstra	395/469
5,146,578	9/1992	Zangenehpour	395/464
5,241,666	8/1993	Idleman et al.	395/872

5,315,602	5/1994	Noya et al.	371/40.4
5,410,667	4/1995	Belsan et al.	395/441
5,423,046	6/1995	Nunnelley et al.	395/441
5,530,845	6/1996	Hiatt et al.	395/500

FOREIGN PATENT DOCUMENTS

0586117	3/1994	European Pat. Off. .
1231570	5/1971	United Kingdom .
1310467	3/1973	United Kingdom .
89/09468	10/1989	WIPO .

Primary Examiner—Eddie P. Chan
Assistant Examiner—Reginald G. Bragdon
Attorney, Agent, or Firm—Greenblum & Bernstein P.L.C.

[57]   **ABSTRACT**

A data processing system which includes a processor having a processor memory and a mechanism for specifying an address that corresponds to a processor-requested data block located within another memory to be accessed by the processor. A hierarchical memory system is provided, which includes a cache and a long-term storage. An address of a requested data block is translated to a second addressing scheme, and is meshed, so that proximate data blocks are placed on different physical target disks within the long-term storage. A user-configuration mechanism is provided, which allows the user to define one or more user-configurable parameters which will control the access to the cache, and the transfer of data between the processor and the cache, and between the cache and the long-term storage.

18 Claims, 25 Drawing Sheets

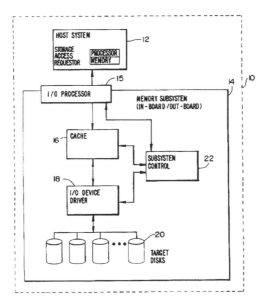

US005671385A

United States Patent [19]

Jost

[11] **Patent Number:**   **5,671,385**

[45] **Date of Patent:**   **Sep. 23, 1997**

[54] **MEMORY SUBSYSTEM WITH DISK MESHING, CONTROLLER MESHING, AND EFFICIENT CACHE BUFFER LOOKUP**

[75] Inventor: **Larry T. Jost**, St. Louis, Mo.

[73] Assignee: **Southwestern Bell Technology Resources, Inc.**, Austin, Tex.

[21] Appl. No.: **235,714**

[22] Filed: **Apr. 29, 1994**

Related U.S. Application Data

[63] Continuation-in-part of Ser. No. 53,655, Apr. 29, 1993, abandoned.

[51] Int. Cl.⁶ **G06F 12/06**; G06F 12/10
[52] U.S. Cl. **395/404**; 395/441; 395/412
[58] **Field of Search** 395/404, 440, 395/441, 412, 416

[56]   **References Cited**

U.S. PATENT DOCUMENTS

4,145,745	3/1979	De Bijl et al.	395/404
4,399,503	8/1983	Hawley	395/440
4,433,374	2/1984	Hanson et al.	395/465
4,489,378	12/1984	Dixon et al.	395/853
4,530,055	7/1985	Hamstra et al.	395/463
4,811,203	3/1989	Hanstra	395/469
5,018,095	5/1991	Nissimov	395/404
5,193,184	3/1993	Belsan et al.	395/404
5,241,666	8/1993	Idleman et al.	395/872
5,315,602	5/1994	Noya et al.	371/40.4
5,379,391	1/1995	Belsan et al.	395/441
5,519,844	5/1996	Stallmo	395/404

FOREIGN PATENT DOCUMENTS

0586117	3/1994	European Pat. Off. .
1231570	5/1971	United Kingdom .
1310467	3/1973	United Kingdom .
89/09468	10/1989	WIPO .

OTHER PUBLICATIONS

"Logical Addressing Extension for Multiple Disk Drive Units", IBM TDB vol. 32, No. 8A, Jan. 1990: 231–232 Jan. 1990.
Olson, Thomas M. "Disk Array Performance in a Random IO Environment" Computer Architecture News vol. 17, No. 5, Sep. 1989: 71–77 Sep. 1989.
APS 7800 Software Release Documentation Revision 7.7 (Apr. 14, 1994).
"A Discussion of Raid Technology" 1992 Dyna tek Automation System, Inc., 1991 Integra Technologies Inc.

Primary Examiner—Eddie P. Chan
Assistant Examiner—Reginald G. Bragdon
Attorney, Agent, or Firm—Greenblum & Bernstein P.L.C.

[57]   **ABSTRACT**

In a data processing system, source block addresses are linearly mapped to virtual linear target disks equal in size to actual physical disks comprised by the long-term storage. Blocks of the virtual linear target disks are then assigned to disk-meshed disks equal in size to the actual physical disks whereby each block within a set of adjacently addressed linear target disk blocks is assigned to a separate disk-meshed disk. Controller meshing may be performed by assigning each disk-meshed disk to a controller-meshed disk which will comprise the actual physical disk, whereby respective sets of blocks within respective disk-meshed disks, all having the same disk controller, are assigned to equal-sized controller-meshed disks located on different disk controllers. Additional mechanisms that may be provided in the data processing system include efficient cache buffer lookup linked lists, and a mechanism for accelerating processing performed by an ancillary processing mechanism by ignoring a delay time.

7 Claims, 20 Drawing Sheets

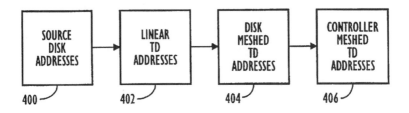

Fig. 1

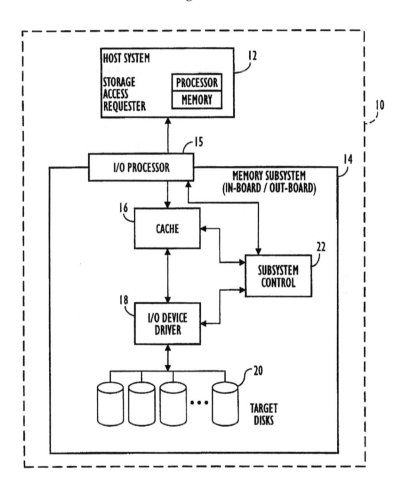

Fig. 2

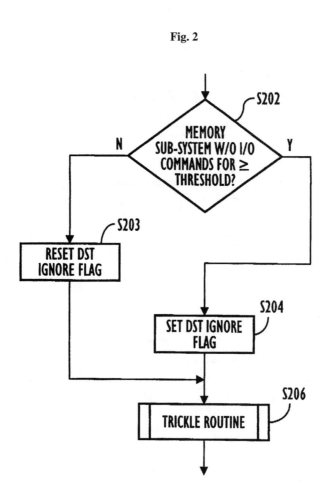

US005835684A

United States Patent [19]

Bourne et al.

[11] **Patent Number:** **5,835,684**

[45] **Date of Patent:** **Nov. 10, 1998**

[54] **METHOD FOR PLANNING/CONTROLLING ROBOT MOTION**

[75] Inventors: **David Alan Bourne**, Pittsburgh, Pa.; **Sivaraj Sivarama Krishnan**, Bangalore, India

[73] Assignees: **Amada Company, Ltd.**, Kanagawa, Japan; **Amada America, Inc.**, Calif.

[21] Appl. No.: **338,115**

[22] Filed: **Nov. 9, 1994**

[51] Int. Cl.^{6} **G06F 15/20**
[52] U.S. Cl. **395/90**; 364/461; 364/474.2
[58] Field of Search 395/90; 364/461, 364/474.2

[56] **References Cited**

U.S. PATENT DOCUMENTS

4,745,812	5/1988	Amazeen et al.	73/777
4,942,767	7/1990	Haritonidis et al.	73/705
4,949,277	8/1990	Trovato et al.	395/90
5,005,394	4/1991	Sartorio et al.	72/10
5,047,916	9/1991	Kondo	395/90
5,058,406	10/1991	Sartorio et al.	72/9
5,083,256	1/1992	Trovato et al.	364/461
5,092,645	3/1992	Okada	294/86.4
5,307,282	4/1994	Conradson et al.	364/468
5,513,299	4/1996	Terasaki et al.	395/90

FOREIGN PATENT DOCUMENTS

0301527	2/1989	European Pat. Off. .
0335314	10/1989	European Pat. Off. .
0355454	2/1990	European Pat. Off. .
3110018	5/1991	Japan .
3110022	5/1991	Japan .
4309414	11/1992	Japan .
9109696	7/1991	WIPO .
9503901	2/1995	WIPO .

OTHER PUBLICATIONS

Patent Abstracts of Japan, vol. 017, No. 126, Mar. 17, 1993, & JP–A–04 309 414.
Patent Abstracts of Japan, vol. 015, No. 298, Jul. 29, 1991, & JP–A–03 110 022.

Patent Abstracts of Japan, vol. 015, No. 298, Jul. 29, 1991, & JP–A–03 110 018.
Patent Abstracts of Japan, vol. 018, No. 239, May 9, 1994, & JP–A–06 031 345.
Patent Abstracts of Japan, vol. 015, No. 325, Aug. 19, 1991, & JP–A–03 124 318.
Ichikawa et al., Y., "A Heuristic Planner and an Executive for Mobile Robor Control", *IEEE Transactions on Systems, Man and Cybernetics*, vol. SMC–15, No. 4, pp. 558–563, New York, U.S.A. (Jul./Aug. 1985).

(List continued on next page.)

Primary Examiner—George B. Davis
Attorney, Agent, or Firm—Greenblum & Bernstein P.L.C.

[57] **ABSTRACT**

A computerized method/system is provided for planning motion of a robot within a free space confined by obstacles, from an initial position to a goal position. In executing the method/system, a plan is generated so that the robot can hold and maneuver a workpiece throughout a sequence of bending operations to be performed by a bending apparatus. A plurality of proposed movements to be made by the robot are proposed for an mth movement within a sequence of movements, and at least a portion of the robot and the obstacles that confine the free space are modeled. A determination is made as to whether a collision will occur between the robot and an obstacle for each proposed movement, and a plan is generated including the sequence of movements by choosing for each movement in the sequence of movements, a proposed movement that will not result in a collision and that will bring the robot closer to the goal position. In choosing proposed movements, an estimated cost associated with each proposed movement may be taken into account. The estimated cost may be based upon a euclidian distance to the goal position from the position of the robot after the particular proposed movement is made as the mth movement, and/or the estimated cost may be determined as a function of the robot travel time from an (m−1)th movement to the mth movement. Different methods are provided for performing fine motion planning and gross motion planning.

66 Claims, 33 Drawing Sheets

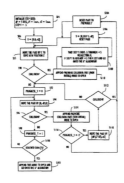

5,835,684

Page 2

OTHER PUBLICATIONS

Zussman et al., E., "A Planning Approach for Robot–Assisted Multiple–Bent Profile Handling", *Robotics and Computer–Integrated Manufacturing,* vol. 11, No. 1 pp. 35–40, Kidlington, Oxford, GB (March 1994).

Huang et al., H., "Time–Optimal Control for a Robotic Contour Follwing Problem", *IEEE Journal of Robotics and Automation,* vol. 4, No. 2, pp. 140–149, New York, U.S.A. (Apri. 1988).

Hoermann, K., "A Cartesian Approach to Findpath for Industrial Robots", *Nato ASI Series,* vol. F29, pp. 425–450, Springler–Verlag Berlin Heidelberg, DE (1987).

Fink et al., B., "Schnelle Bahnplanung Fuer Industrieroboter Mit Veraenderlichem Arbeitsraum", *Automatisierungstechinik–At,* vol. 39, No. 6, pp. 197–200, 201–204, Munich, DE (Jun. 1991).

Shaffer et al., C.A., "A Real–Time Robot Arm Collision Avoidance System", *IEEE Transactions on Robotics and Automation,* vol. 8, No. 2, pp. 149–160, New York, U.S.A. (Apr. 1992).

Lee et al., C.T. "A Divided–And–Conquer Approach With Heuristics of Motion Planning for a Cartesian Manipulator", *IEEE Transactions on Systems, Man and Cybernetics,* vol. 22, No. 5, pp. 929–944, New York U.S.A. (Sep./Oct. 1992).

O'Donnell et al., P.A., "Deadlock–Free and Collision–Free Coordination of Two Robot manipulators", *Proceedings of the 1989 IEEE International Conference on Robotics and Automation,* vol. 1, pp. 484–489, Scottsdale, AZ (May 1989).

Weule et al., V.H., "Rechnerintergrierte Fertigung Von Abkantteilen"*V.A.I.–Zeitschrift,* vol. 130, No. 9 pp. 101–106, Dusseldorf, W. Germany (Sep. 1988).

Reissner, V.J., "Innovationsschub Bei Rechnerintegrierten Umformsystemen", *Technische Rundschau,* vol. 85 No. 5, pp. 20–25, Bern, CH (Feb. 5, 1993).

Geiger et al., M., "Inferenzmaschine Fuer Ein Biegestadienplanungssystem", *Zwf Cim Zeitschrift Fur Wirtschaftliche Fertigung Und Automatisierung,* vol. 87, No. 5, pp. 261–264, Munich, DE (May 1992).

Database Dialog, Information Access Co., file 621, Access No. 0134529, *Communigraphics Inc;* "LVD Introduces New CNC/DNC/CAD/CAM Control System for Press Brakes at IMTS'86", & New Product Announcements, No. 0134529, Plainville, CT, U.S.A. (Jul. 1996).

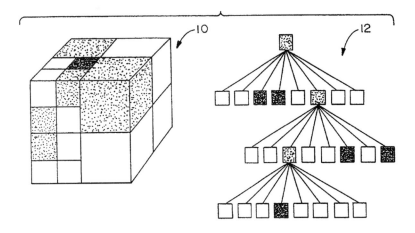

FIG. I

PRIOR ART

APPENDIX B

Data on Patent Activity: Issuances, Technology, and Litigations

Law suits filed in 1994, asserting a certain type of computer-related patents (Class 395)

Year of Patent Grant	Title
1990	Label Generation Apparatus
1993	System and Method for Disk Mapping and Data Retrieval
	Network Adapter Using Status Inlines and Data Lines for Bi-Directionally Transferring Data between LAN and Standard P.C. Parallel Port
1992	Geometric Inference Engine
1986	Hierarchical Knowledge System
1994	Network Adapter Using Status Inlines and Data Lines for Bi-Directionally Transferring Data between LAN and Standard P.C. Parallel Port
1994	Network Adapter Using Status Inlines and Data Lines for Bi-Directionally Transferring Data between LAN and Standard P.C. Parallel Port
1993	System and Method for Disk Mapping and Data Retrieval
1994	System and Methods for Intelligent Movement on Computer Displays
1992	Method and Apparatus for Generating Program Code Files
1993	Mass Data Storage Library

Lawsuits filed in 1994, asserting a certain type of computer-related patents (Class 395)

Year of Patent Grant	Title
1992	Geometric Inference Engine
1986	Hierarchical Knowledge System
1994	Network Adapter Using Status Inlines and Data Lines for Bi-Directionally Transferring Data between LAN and Standard P.C. Parallel Port
1994	Network Adapter Using Status Inlines and Data Lines for Bi-Directionally Transferring Data between LAN and Standard P.C. Parallel Port
1993	System and Method for Disk Mapping and Data Retrieval
1994	System and Methods for Intelligent Movement on Computer Displays
1992	Method and Apparatus for Generating Program Code
1993	Mass Data Storage Library
1994	Network Adapter Using Status Inlines and Data Lines for Bi-Directionally Transferring Data between LAN and Standard P.C. Parallel Port
1991	User Interface With Multiple Workspace for Sharing Display System Objects
1993	Video Image Creation System Which Proportionally Mixes Previously Created Image Pixel Data with Currently Created Data

Class 395, filed 1995

Year of Patent Grant	Title
1995	Electronic Spreadsheet System and Methods for Compiling a Formula Stored in a Spreadsheet into Native Machine Code for Execution by a Floating-Point Unit upon Spreadsheet Recalculation
1986	Multiple Configuration Memory Circuit
1994	Virtual Printer
1995	Real-Time Operating System and Virtual Digital Signal Processor for the Control of a Computer
1991	Portable Data Storage and Editing Device
1995	Electronic Spreadsheet System and Methods for Compiling a Formula Stored in a Spreadsheet into Native Machine Code for Execution by a Floating-Point Unit upon Spreadsheet Recalculation
1986	Multiple Configuration Memory Circuit
1992	Computer Bus Interconnection Device
1995	Real-Time Operating System and Virtual Digital Signal Processor for the Control of a Computer
1993	Apparatus and Method for Communicating Textual and Image Information between a Host Computer and a Remote Display Terminal

Year of Patent Grant	Title
1994	Network Adapter Using Status Inlines and Data Lines for Bi-Directionally Transferring Data between LAN and Standard PC Parallel Port
1995	Real-Time Operating System and Virtual Digital Signal Processor for the Control of a Computer
1994	Flash File System
1992	Backup Computer Program for Networks
1994	Network Adapter Using Status Inlines and Data Lines for Bi-Directionally Transferring Data between LAN and Standard PC Parallel Port
1993	Process and Apparatus for Reducing Power Usage Microprocessor Devices Operating from Stored Energy Sources
1994	Method for Inserting New Machine Instructions into Preexisting Machine Code to Monitor Preexisting Machine Access to Memory
1994	Virtual Printer
1994	Network Adapter Using Status Inlines and Data Lines for Bi-Directionally Transferring Data between LAN and Standard PC Parallel Port

Class 395, filed 1996

Year of Patent Grant	Title
1980	Generating Timing Signals
1993	Texture Range Controls for Improved Texture
1981	Data Processing System and Apparatus for Color
1996	A Disk Storage Subsystem for Interfacing with a Parallel Path, a Nonvolatile Storage Medium
1994	Method and Apparatus for Assigning Signatures to Identify Members of a Set of Mass
1990	Label Generation Apparatus
1994	Method for Inserting New Machine Instructions into Preexisting Machine Code to Monitor Preexisting Machine Access to Memory
1990	Method for Canonical Ordering of Binary Data For Portable Operating Systems
1987	Secure Data Processing System Architecture with Formal Control
1983	Process and Apparatus for Converting a Source Program into an Object Program
1995	Method and Apparatus for Generating and Displaying Multiple Simultaneously-Active Windows
1980	Generating Timing Signals
1994	Method and Apparatus for Storing and Retrieving Multi-Dimensional Data in Computer Memory
1987	Secure Data Processing System Architecture with Formal Control

Year of Patent Grant	Title
1993	Apparatus and Method for Communicating Textual and Image Information between a Host Computer and a Remote Display Terminal
1993	Video Image Creating System Which Proportionally Mixes Previously Created Image Pixel Data with Currently Created Data

Class 395, filed 1997

Year of Patent Grant	Title
1989	Computer System User Interface
1997	Method for Manipulating Disk Partitions
1997	Microprocessor with Externally Controllable Power
1997	Method for Manipulating Disk Partitions
1997	Method for Manipulating Disk Partitions
1996	IDE-ATA CD Drive Controller Having a Digital Signal; Processor Interface, Dynamic Random Access Memory, Data Error Detection and Correction and a Host Interface
1993	System for Storing Data in Backup Tape Device
1981	Data Processing System and Apparatus for Color Graphics Display
1981	Data Processing System and Apparatus for Color
1997	Method for Manipulating Disk Partitions
1995	Override Timing Control Circuitry and Method for Terminating Program and Erase Sequence in a Flash Memory
1992	Method of Formatting Data from a Mouse
1997	Method for Manipulating Disk Partitions
1996	Case-Based Reasoning System
1996	Dynamic Non-Volatile Memory Update in a Computer
1994	In Transit Detection of Computer Virus with Safeguard
1994	In Transit Detection of Computer Virus with Safeguard
1996	Method and Apparatus for Computer Program Usage Monitoring
1996	Picture Frame with Associated Audio Message
1982	Industrial Communications Network with Mastership Determined by Need
1995	Method of Reorganizing an Index File Without Storing by Changing the Physical Order of Pages to Match the Logical Order Determined from the Index Structure
1995	Audio Recording and Distance Measuring System
1996	Method and Apparatus for Computer Program Usage Monitoring
1993	Addressable Computer Tape Drive Activation System
1997	Direct View Interactive Photo and Image Forming Process for Same

Year of Patent Grant	Title
1997	Direct View Interactive Photo Kiosk and Image Forming Process for Same
1988	Apparatus and Method for Providing a Cache Memory Unit with a Write Operation Utilizing Two Systems Clock Cycles
1997	Virus Detection and Removal Apparatus for Computer Networks
1997	Microprocessor with Externally Controllable Power Management
1995	Variable Rate Vocoder
1995	Method to Reorganize an Index File Without Sorting by Changing the Physical Order of Pages to Match the Logical Order Determined from the Index Structure
1997	Method and System for the Arrangement of Vocoder Data for the Making of Transmission Channel Induced Errors
1996	Distributed Computer Network Including Hierarchical Resource Information Structure and Related Method of Distributing Resources
1984	Virtual Storage System and Method
1984	Virtual Storage System Method
1996	Relational Database Access System Using Semantically Dynamic Objects
1997	Programmable Hand Held Labeler
1989	Computer System User Interface
1989	Surface Detail Mapping System

Class 395, filed 1998

Year of Patent Grant	Title
1992	Method and Apparatus for Fast Surface Detail Application to an Image
1992	Method and Apparatus for Automatic Memory Configuration by a Computer
1997	Console Simulator, Multi-Console Management System and Console Management Distribution System
1998	Enhanced DRAM with Single Row SRAM Cache for All Device Read Operations
1990	Method and Apparatus for Generating Aesthetically Alterable Character Designs
1989	Surface Detail Mapping System
1989	Surface Detail Mapping System
1997	Method for Selecting Assignments
1998	Host Signal Processing Modem Using a Software Simulation of a UART
1998	Texture Compositing Apparatus and Method

Year of Patent Grant	Title
1998	Server and Web Browser Terminal Emulator for Persistent Connection to a Legacy Host System and Method of Operation
1998	Server and Web Browser Terminal Emulator for Persistent Connection to a Legacy Host System and Method Operation
1986	Electronic Security System for Externally Powered Devices
1997	Audio-Video Transceiver Provided with a Device for Reconfiguration of Incompatibly Received - Transmitted Video and Audio Information
1998	Method and Apparatus for Extending the Signal Path of a Peripheral Component Interconnect Bus to a Remote Location
1998	Universal Electronic Resource Denotation, Request, and Delivery System
1994	Graphical Method for Programming a Virtual Instrument
1996	Method and System Detecting Intrusion into a Misuse of Data Processing System
1997	Apparatus Systems and Methods for Controlling Graphics and Video Data in Multi-Media Data Processing and Display Systems
1981	Arrangement for Deleting Trailing Message Portions
1996	RISC Architecture Computer Configured for Emulation of the Instruction Set of a Target Computer
1986	Highlighting and Classifying Segments on a CRT Display
1994	Graphical Language Methodology for Information Display
1997	Console Stimulator Multi-Console Management System and Console Management Distribution System
1994	General Purpose Parallel Port Interface
1994	General Purpose Parallel Port Interface
1987	Touchscreen Two-Dimensional Emulation of Three-Dimensional Objects
1986	Highlighting and Classifying Segments on a CRT Display
1998	Apparatus and Method for Integrating Texture Memory and Interpolation Logic in a Computer System
1997	Flash Eeprom System
1998	Interconnection System for Viewing and Controlling Remotely Connected Computers with On-Screen Video Overlay for Controlling of the Interconnection Switch
1991	Data Processing System and Apparatus for Color Graphics Display
1997	Direct View Interactive Photo Kiosk and Image Forming Process for Same
1997	Method and Apparatus for Synchronizing, Displaying, and Manipulating Text and Image Documents
1993	Multimedia Search System Using a Plurality of Entry Path Means Which Indicate Interrelatedness
1997	Computer Memory Product with Preemptive Multithreading Software
1984	Virtual Storage System and Method

APPENDIX C

Preserving Trade Secret Rights and Avoiding Liability for Violating Those of Others

It is important for all company personnel to remember their obligations to keep confidential and refrain from using anyone else's "proprietary information."[1] This could be the proprietary information of a former employer, or perhaps of another company for which the company is performing work.

Please be aware that even the appearance of an improper receipt, use, or disclosure of another's proprietary information could expose the company, as well as those involved individuals, to costly litigation, and possibly damaging liability if a court rules a violation occurred. The use or disclosure of another's proprietary information, even within the company, might jeopardize the company's legitimate ownership of or right to use technologies.

The company's goal, therefore, should be to reduce the risk of litigation and to help the company retain all ownership and use rights in its own legitimate discoveries and developments. Accordingly, it is imperative that all the company's employees, consultants, and representatives are cautious and follow the following mandatory Rules for Treatment of Third Party Proprietary Information.

(a) Rules for Treatment of Third Party Proprietary Information

The company should take steps to make sure all its employees and consultants are aware that the improper receipt, use, or disclosure of the proprietary information of others could have serious consequences for the company. Significant intellectual property and use rights can be inadvertently lost by careless use or misappropriation of confidential information. Such conduct by an employee or consultant could subject the company, and the individual(s) personally, to legal liability. Accordingly, all company personnel need to take the following precautionary steps:

- Do not receive, use, or disclose another's proprietary information, except to the extent specifically authorized and required by a contract signed by the information's rightful owner.
- Whenever an individual has had or has access to the proprietary information of others, that individual must not discuss even remotely related business matters with any other company employees that do not have the same access.
- Even where one company employee, consultant, or representative is communicating with another working on the same project pursuant to the same consulting agreement, the client's proprietary information should be discussed only as necessary; (i.e., such information should be shared only on a need-to-know basis).

Do not disclose or use for the benefit of the company any non-public information considered by another entity to be proprietary, without first obtaining approval from the management or its intellectual property counsel.

Endnote

1. "Proprietary information" may comprise any information or knowledge in which the person or company developing or disclosing it has ownership rights. Such rights are usually created and/or protected by contract (sometimes "implied", i.e., not in writing), and usually are defined to include "trade secrets." As defined in the Uniform Trade Secrets Act (with 1985 Amendments), a "trade secret" is "information, including a formula, pattern, compilation, program, device, method, technique, or process, that:

    (i) derives independent economic value, actual or potential, from not being generally known to, and not being readily ascertainable by proper means by, other persons who can obtain economic value from its disclosure or use, and

    (ii) is the subject of efforts that are reasonable under the circumstances to maintain its secrecy."

APPENDIX D

Select Sections of the Patent Laws [Excerpted from the February 2000 Edition of the Manual of Patent Examining Procedure (MPEP)]

Appendix L Patent Laws

United States Code Title 35 - Patents

Editor's Note: Appendix L reflects the law in force on the date of publication. Several additional changes to the laws will become effective in the ensuing months as a result of Public Law 106-113.

In the laws as reproduced herein, references to the "Director" should be construed as references to the "Commissioner of Patents and Trademarks," and references to the "Commissioner of Patents" should be construed as references to the "Assistant Commissioner for Patents."

PART I — PATENT AND TRADEMARK OFFICE

CHAPTER 1 — ESTABLISHMENT, OFFICERS, FUNCTIONS

CHAPTER 2 — PROCEEDINGS IN THE PATENTS AND TRADEMARK OFFICE

CHAPTER 3 — PRACTICE BEFORE PATENT AND TRADEMARK OFFICE

CHAPTER 4 — PATENT FEES; FUNDING; SEARCH SYSTEMS

PART II — PATENTABILITY OF INVENTIONS AND GRANT OF PATENTS

CHAPTER 10 — PATENTABILITY OF INVENTIONS

CHAPTER 11 — APPLICATION FOR PATENT

CHAPTER 12 — EXAMINATION OF APPLICATION

CHAPTER 13 — REVIEW OF PATENT AND TRADEMARK OFFICE DECISION

MANUAL OF PATENT EXAMINING PROCEDURE

PATENT LAWS

MANUAL OF PATENT EXAMINING PROCEDURE

PART II — PATENTABILITY OF INVENTIONS AND GRANT OF PATENTS

CHAPTER 10 — PATENTABILITY OF INVENTIONS

35 U.S.C. 100   Definitions.

When used in this title unless the context otherwise indicates -

(a)   The term "invention" means invention or discovery.

(b)   The term "process" means process, art, or method, and includes a new use of a known process, machine, manufacture, composition of matter, or material.

(c)   The terms "United States" and "this country" mean the United States of America, its territories and possessions.

(d)   The word "patentee" includes not only the patentee to whom the patent was issued but also the successors in title to the patentee.

(e)   The term "third-party requester" means a person requesting ex parte reexamination under section 302 or inter partes reexamination under section 311 who is not the patent owner.

(Subsection (e) added Nov. 29, 1999, Public Law 106-113, sec. 1000(a)(9), S. 1948 sec. 4603, 113 Stat. 1501.)

35 U.S.C. 101   Inventions patentable.

Whoever invents or discovers any new and useful process, machine, manufacture, or composition of matter, or any new and useful improvement thereof, may obtain a patent therefor, subject to the conditions and requirements of this title.

35 U.S.C. 102   Conditions for patentability; novelty and loss of right to patent.

A person shall be entitled to a patent unless —

(a)   the invention was known or used by others in this country, or patented or described in a printed publication in this or a foreign country, before the invention thereof by the applicant for patent, or

PATENT LAWS

(b)   the invention was patented or described in a printed publication in this or a foreign country or in public use or on sale in this country, more than one year prior to the date of the application for patent in the United States, or

(c)   he has abandoned the invention, or

(d)   the invention was first patented or caused to be patented, or was the subject of an inventor's certificate, by the applicant or his legal representatives or assigns in a foreign country prior to the date of the application for patent in this country on an application for patent or inventor's certificate filed more than twelve months before the filing of the application in the United States, or

(e)   the invention was described in a patent granted on an application for patent by another filed in the United States before the invention thereof by the applicant for patent, or on an international application by another who has fulfilled the requirements of paragraphs (1), (2), and (4) of section 371(c) of this title before the invention thereof by applicant for patent, or

(f)   he did not himself invent the subject matter sought to be patented, or

(g)(1) during the course of an interference conducted under section 135 or section 291, another inventor involved therein establishes, to the extent permitted in section 104, that before such person's invention thereof the invention was made by such other inventor and not abandoned, suppressed, or concealed, or (2) before such person's invention thereof, the invention was made in this country by another inventor who had not abandoned, suppressed, or concealed it. In determining priority of invention under this subsection, there shall be considered not only the respective dates of conception and reduction to practice of the invention, but also the reasonable diligence of one who was first to conceive and last to reduce to practice, from a time prior to conception by the other.

(Amended July 28, 1972, Public Law 92-358, sec. 2, 86 Stat. 501; Nov. 14, 1975, Public Law 94-131, sec. 3, 89 Stat. 691.)

(Subsection (g) amended Nov. 29, 1999, Public Law 106-113, sec. 1000(a)(9), S. 1948 sec. 4806, 113 Stat. 1501.)

35 U.S.C. 103   Conditions for patentability; non-obvious subject matter.

(a)   A patent may not be obtained though the invention is not identically disclosed or described as set forth in section 102 of this title, if the differences between the subject matter sought to be patented and the prior art are such that the subject matter as a whole would have been obvious at the time the invention was made to a person having ordinary skill in the art to which said subject matter pertains. Patentability shall not be negatived by the manner in which the invention was made.

(b)(1) Notwithstanding subsection (a), and upon timely election by the applicant for patent to proceed under this subsection, a biotechnological process using or resulting in a composition of matter that is novel under section 102 and nonobvious under subsection (a) of this section shall be considered nonobvious if-

(A)   claims to the process and the composition of matter are contained in either the same application for patent or in separate applications having the same effective filing date; and

(B)   the composition of matter, and the process at the time it was invented, were owned by the same person or subject to an obligation of assignment to the same person.

(2)   A patent issued on a process under paragraph (1)-

(A)   shall also contain the claims to the composition of matter used in or made by that process, or

(B)   shall, if such composition of matter is claimed in another patent, be set to expire on the same date as such other patent, notwithstanding section 154.

(3)   For purposes of paragraph (1), the term "biotechnological process" means-

(A)   a process of genetically altering or otherwise inducing a single- or multi-celled organism to-

(i)   express an exogenous nucleotide sequence,

(ii)   inhibit, eliminate, augment, or alter expression of an endogenous nucleotide sequence, or

(iii)   express a specific physiological characteristic not naturally associated with said organism;

(B)   cell fusion procedures yielding a cell line that expresses a specific protein, such as a monoclonal antibody; and

(C)   a method of using a product produced by a process defined by subparagraph (A) or (B), or a combination of subparagraphs (A) and (B).

(c)   Subject matter developed by another person, which qualifies as prior art only under one or more of subsections (e), (f), and (g) of section 102 of this title, shall not preclude patentability under this section where the subject matter and the claimed invention were, at the time the invention was made, owned by the same person or subject to an obligation of assignment to the same person.

(Amended Nov. 8, 1984, Public Law 98-622, sec. 103, 98 Stat. 3384; Nov. 1, 1995, Public Law 104-41, sec.1, 109 Stat. 351; Nov. 29, 1999, Public Law 106-113, sec. 1000(a)(9), S. 1948 sec. 4807, 113 Stat. 1501.)

35 U.S.C. 104   Invention made abroad.

(a)   IN GENERAL.—

(1)   PROCEEDINGS.—In proceedings in the Patent and Trademark Office, in the courts, and before any other competent authority, an applicant for a patent, or a patentee, may not establish a date of invention by reference

MANUAL OF PATENT EXAMINING PROCEDURE

to knowledge or use thereof, or other activity with respect thereto, in a foreign country other than a NAFTA country or a WTO member country, except as provided in sections 119 and 365 of this title.

(2)   RIGHTS.—If an invention was made by a person, civil or military—

(A)   while domiciled in the United States, and serving in any other country in connection with operations by or on behalf of the United States,

(B)   while domiciled in a NAFTA country and serving in another country in connection with operations by or on behalf of that NAFTA country, or

(C)   while domiciled in a WTO member country and serving in another country in connection with operations by or on behalf of that WTO member country, that person shall be entitled to the same rights of priority in the United States with respect to such invention as if such invention had been made in the United States, that NAFTA country, or that WTO member country, as the case may be.

(3)   USE OF INFORMATION.—To the extent that any information in a NAFTA country or a WTO member country concerning knowledge, use, or other activity relevant to proving or disproving a date of invention has not been made available for use in a proceeding in the Patent and Trademark Office, a court, or any other competent authority to the same extent as such information could be made available in the United States, the Commissioner, court, or such other authority shall draw appropriate inferences, or take other action permitted by statute, rule, or regulation, in favor of the party that requested the information in the proceeding.

(b)   DEFINITIONS.—As used in this section—

(1)   The term "NAFTA country" has the meaning given that term in section 2(4) of the North American Free Trade Agreement Implementation Act; and

(2)   The term "WTO member country" has the meaning given that term in section 2(10) of the Uruguay Round Agreements Act.

(Amended Jan. 2, 1975, Public Law 93-596, sec. 1, 88 Stat. 1949; Nov. 14, 1975, Public Law 94-131, sec. 6, 89 Stat. 691; Nov. 8, 1984, Public Law 98-622, sec. 403(a), 98 Stat. 3392; Dec. 8, 1993, Public Law 103-182, sec. 331, 107 Stat. 2113; Dec. 8, 1994, Public Law 103-465, sec. 531(a), 108 Stat. 4982.)

35 U.S.C. 105   Inventions in outer space.

(a)   Any invention made, used, or sold in outer space on a space object or component thereof under the jurisdiction or control of the United States shall be considered to be made, used or sold within the United States for the purposes of this title, except with respect to any space object or component thereof that is specifically identified and otherwise provided for by an international agreement to which the United States is a party, or with respect to any space object or component thereof that is carried on the registry of a foreign state in accordance with the Convention on Registration of Objects Launched into Outer Space.

(b)   Any invention made, used, or sold in outer space on a space object or component thereof that is carried on the registry of a foreign state in accordance with the Convention on Registration of Objects Launched into Outer Space, shall be considered to be made, used, or sold within the United States for the purposes of this title if specifically so agreed in an international agreement between the United States and the state of registry.

(Added Nov. 15, 1990, Public Law 101-580, sec. 1(a), 104 Stat. 2863.)

CHAPTER 11 — APPLICATION FOR PATENT

Sec.
111   Application.
112   Specification.
113   Drawings.
114   Models, specimens.
115   Oath of applicant.
116   Inventors.
117   Death or incapacity of inventor.
118   Filing by other than inventor.
119   Benefit of earlier filing date; right of priority.
120   Benefit of earlier filing date in the United States.
121   Divisional applications.
122   Confidential status of applications.

35 U.S.C. 111   Application.

(a)   IN GENERAL.—

(1)   WRITTEN APPLICATION.—An application for patent shall be made, or authorized to be made, by the inventor, except as otherwise provided in this title, in writing to the Commissioner.

(2)   CONTENTS.—Such application shall include—

(A)   a specification as prescribed by section 112 of this title;

(B)   a drawing as prescribed by section 113 of this title; and

(C)   an oath by the applicant as prescribed by section 115 of this title.

(3)   FEE AND OATH.—The application must be accompanied by the fee required by law. The fee and oath may be submitted after the specification and any required drawing are submitted, within such period and under such conditions, including the payment of a surcharge, as may be prescribed by the Commissioner.

(4)   FAILURE TO SUBMIT.—Upon failure to submit the fee and oath within such prescribed period, the application shall be regarded as abandoned, unless it is

shown to the satisfaction of the Commissioner that the delay in submitting the fee and oath was unavoidable or unintentional. The filing date of an application shall be the date on which the specification and any required drawing are received in the Patent and Trademark Office.

(b) PROVISIONAL APPLICATION.—

(1) AUTHORIZATION.—A provisional application for patent shall be made or authorized to be made by the inventor, except as otherwise provided in this title, in writing to the Commissioner. Such application shall include—

(A) a specification as prescribed by the first paragraph of section 112 of this title; and

(B) a drawing as prescribed by section 113 of this title.

(2) CLAIM.—A claim, as required by the second through fifth paragraphs of section 112, shall not be required in a provisional application.

(3) FEE.—

(A) The application must be accompanied by the fee required by law.

(B) The fee may be submitted after the specification and any required drawing are submitted, within such period and under such conditions, including the payment of a surcharge, as may be prescribed by the Commissioner.

(C) Upon failure to submit the fee within such prescribed period, the application shall be regarded as abandoned, unless it is shown to the satisfaction of the Commissioner that the delay in submitting the fee was unavoidable or unintentional.

(4) FILING DATE.—The filing date of a provisional application shall be the date on which the specification and any required drawing are received in the Patent and Trademark Office.

(5) ABANDONMENT.—Notwithstanding the absence of a claim, upon timely request and as prescribed by the Director, a provisional application may be treated as an application filed under subsection (a). Subject to section 119(e)(3) of this title, if no such request is made, the provisional application shall be regarded as abandoned 12 months after the filing date of such application and shall not be subject to revival after such 12-month period.

(6) OTHER BASIS FOR PROVISIONAL APPLICATION.—Subject to all the conditions in this subsection and section 119(e) of this title, and as prescribed by the Commissioner, an application for patent filed under subsection (a) may be treated as a provisional application for patent.

(7) NO RIGHT OF PRIORITY OR BENEFIT OF EARLIEST FILING DATE.—A provisional application shall not be entitled to the right of priority of any other application under section 119 or 365(a) of this title or to the

benefit of an earlier filing date in the United States under section 120, 121, or 365(c) of this title.

(8) APPLICABLE PROVISIONS.—The provisions of this title relating to applications for patent shall apply to provisional applications for patent, except as otherwise provided, and except that provisional applications for patent shall not be subject to sections 115, 131, 135, and 157 of this title.

(Amended Aug. 27, 1982, Public Law 97-247, sec. 5, 96 Stat. 319; Dec. 8, 1994, Public Law 103-465, sec. 532(b)(3), 108 Stat. 4986; Nov. 29, 1999, Public Law 106-113, sec. 1000(a)(9), S. 1948 sec. 4801(a), 113 Stat. 1501.)

35 U.S.C. 112   Specification.

The specification shall contain a written description of the invention, and of the manner and process of making and using it, in such full, clear, concise, and exact terms as to enable any person skilled in the art to which it pertains, or with which it is most nearly connected, to make and use the same, and shall set forth the best mode contemplated by the inventor of carrying out his invention.

The specification shall conclude with one or more claims particularly pointing out and distinctly claiming the subject matter which the applicant regards as his invention.

A claim may be written in independent or, if the nature of the case admits, in dependent or multiple dependent form.

Subject to the following paragraph, a claim in dependent form shall contain a reference to a claim previously set forth and then specify a further limitation of the subject matter claimed. A claim in dependent form shall be construed to incorporate by reference all the limitations of the claim to which it refers.

A claim in multiple dependent form shall contain a reference, in the alternative only, to more than one claim previously set forth and then specify a further limitation of the subject matter claimed. A multiple dependent claim shall not serve as a basis for any other multiple dependent claim. A multiple dependent claim shall be construed to incorporate by reference all the limitations of the particular claim in relation to which it is being considered.

An element in a claim for a combination may be expressed as a means or step for performing a specified function without the recital of structure, material, or acts in support thereof, and such claim shall be construed to cover the corresponding structure, material, or acts described in the specification and equivalents thereof.

(Amended July 24, 1965, Public Law 89-83, sec. 9, 79 Stat. 261; Nov. 14, 1975, Public Law 94-131, sec. 7, 89 Stat. 691.)

35 U.S.C. 113   Drawings.

The applicant shall furnish a drawing where necessary for the understanding of the subject matter sought to be patented. When the nature of such subject matter admits of illustration by a drawing and the applicant has not furnished such a drawing, the Commissioner may require its submission within a time period of not less than two months from the sending of a notice thereof. Drawings submitted after the filing date of the application may not be used (i) to overcome any insufficiency of the specification due to lack of an enabling disclosure or otherwise inadequate disclosure therein, or (ii) to supplement the original disclosure thereof for the purpose of interpretation of the scope of any claim.

(Amended Nov. 14, 1975, Public Law 94-131, sec. 8, 89 Stat. 691.)

35 U.S.C. 114   Models, specimens.

The Commissioner may require the applicant to furnish a model of convenient size to exhibit advantageously the several parts of his invention.

When the invention relates to a composition of matter, the Commissioner may require the applicant to furnish specimens or ingredients for the purpose of inspection or experiment.

35 U.S.C. 115   Oath of applicant.

The applicant shall make oath that he believes himself to be the original and first inventor of the process, machine, manufacture, or composition of matter, or improvement thereof, for which he solicits a patent; and shall state of what country he is a citizen. Such oath may be made before any person within the United States authorized by law to administer oaths, or, when made in a foreign country, before any diplomatic or consular officer of the United States authorized to administer oaths, or before any officer having an official seal and authorized to administer oaths in the foreign country in which the applicant may be, whose authority is proved by certificate of a diplomatic or consular officer of the United States, or apostille of an official designated by a foreign country which, by treaty or convention, accords like effect to apostilles of designated officials in the United States. Such oath is valid if it complies with the laws of the state or country where made. When the application is made as provided in this title by a person other than the inventor, the oath may be so varied in form that it can be made by him.

(Amended Aug. 27, 1982, Public Law 97-247, sec. 14(a), 96 Stat. 321.)

35 U.S.C. 116   Inventors.

When an invention is made by two or more persons jointly, they shall apply for patent jointly and each make the required oath, except as otherwise provided in this title. Inventors may apply for a patent jointly even though (1) they did not physically work together or at the same time, (2) each did not make the same type or amount of contribu-

tion, or (3) each did not make a contribution to the subject matter of every claim of the patent.

If a joint inventor refuses to join in an application for patent or cannot be found or reached after diligent effort, the application may be made by the other inventor on behalf of himself and the omitted inventor. The Commissioner, on proof of the pertinent facts and after such notice to the omitted inventor as he prescribes, may grant a patent to the inventor making the application, subject to the same rights which the omitted inventor would have had if he had been joined. The omitted inventor may subsequently join in the application.

Whenever through error a person is named in an application for patent as the inventor, or through an error an inventor is not named in an application, and such error arose without any deceptive intention on his part, the Commissioner may permit the application to be amended accordingly, under such terms as he prescribes.

(Amended Aug. 27, 1982, Public Law 97-247, sec. 6(a), 96 Stat. 320; Nov. 8, 1984, Public Law 98-622, sec. 104(a), 98 Stat. 3384.)

35 U.S.C. 117   Death or incapacity of inventor.

Legal representatives of deceased inventors and of those under legal incapacity may make application for patent upon compliance with the requirements and on the same terms and conditions applicable to the inventor.

35 U.S.C. 118   Filing by other than inventor.

Whenever an inventor refuses to execute an application for patent, or cannot be found or reached after diligent effort, a person to whom the inventor has assigned or agreed in writing to assign the invention or who otherwise shows sufficient proprietary interest in the matter justifying such action, may make application for patent on behalf of and as agent for the inventor on proof of the pertinent facts and a showing that such action is necessary to preserve the rights of the parties or to prevent irreparable damage; and the Commissioner may grant a patent to such inventor upon such notice to him as the Commissioner deems sufficient, and on compliance with such regulations as he prescribes.

35 U.S.C. 119   Benefit of earlier filing date; right of priority.

(a)   An application for patent for an invention filed in this country by any person who has, or whose legal representatives or assigns have, previously regularly filed an application for a patent for the same invention in a foreign country which affords similar privileges in the case of applications filed in the United States or to citizens of the United States, or in a WTO member country, shall have the same effect as the same application would have if filed in this country on the date on which the application for patent for the same invention was first filed in such foreign coun-

PATENT LAWS

try, if the application in this country is filed within twelve months from the earliest date on which such foreign application was filed; but no patent shall be granted on any application for patent for an invention which had been patented or described in a printed publication in any country more than one year before the date of the actual filing of the application in this country, or which had been in public use or on sale in this country more than one year prior to such filing.

(b)   No application for patent shall be entitled to this right of priority unless a claim therefor and a certified copy of the original foreign application, specification, and drawings upon which it is based are filed in the Patent and Trademark Office before the patent is granted, or at such time during the pendency of the application as required by the Commissioner not earlier than six months after the filing of the application in this country. Such certification shall be made by the patent office of the foreign country in which filed and show the date of the application and of the filing of the specification and other papers. The Commissioner may require a translation of the papers filed if not in the English language and such other information as he deems necessary.

(c)   In like manner and subject to the same conditions and requirements, the right provided in this section may be based upon a subsequent regularly filed application in the same foreign country instead of the first filed foreign application, provided that any foreign application filed prior to such subsequent application has been withdrawn, abandoned, or otherwise disposed of, without having been laid open to public inspection and without leaving any rights outstanding, and has not served, nor thereafter shall serve, as a basis for claiming a right of priority.

(d)   Applications for inventors' certificates filed in a foreign country in which applicants have a right to apply, at their discretion, either for a patent or for an inventor's certificate shall be treated in this country in the same manner and have the same effect for purpose of the right of priority under this section as applications for patents, subject to the same conditions and requirements of this section as apply to applications for patents, provided such applicants are entitled to the benefits of the Stockholm Revision of the Paris Convention at the time of such filing.

(e)(1) An application for patent filed under section 111(a) or section 363 of this title for an invention disclosed in the manner provided by the first paragraph of section 112 of this title in a provisional application filed under section 111(b) of this title, by an inventor or inventors named in the provisional application, shall have the same effect, as to such invention, as though filed on the date of the provisional application filed under section 111(b) of this title, if the application for patent filed under section 111(a) or sec-

tion 363 of this title is filed not later than 12 months after the date on which the provisional application was filed and if it contains or is amended to contain a specific reference to the provisional application.

(2)   A provisional application filed under section 111(b) of this title may not be relied upon in any proceeding in the Patent and Trademark Office unless the fee set forth in subparagraph (A) or (C) of section 41(a)(1) of this title has been paid.

(3)   If the day that is 12 months after the filing date of a provisional application falls on a Saturday, Sunday, or Federal holiday within the District of Columbia, the period of pendency of the provisional application shall be extended to the next succeeding secular or business day.

(f)   Applications for plant breeder's rights filed in a WTO member country (or in a foreign UPOV Contracting Party) shall have the same effect for the purpose of the right of priority under subsections (a) through (c) of this section as applications for patents, subject to the same conditions and requirements of this section as apply to applications for patents.

(g)   As used in this section—

(1)   the term " WTO member country" has the same meaning as the term is defined in section 104(b)(2) of this title; and

(2)   the term " UPOV Contracting Party" means a member of the International Convention for the Protection of New Varieties of Plants.

(Amended Oct. 3, 1961, Public Law 87-333, sec. 1, 75 Stat. 748; July 28, 1972, Public Law 92-358, sec. 1, 86 Stat. 501; Jan. 2, 1975, Public Law 93-596, sec. 1, 88 Stat. 1949; Dec. 8, 1994, Public Law 103-465, sec. 532(b)(1), 108 Stat. 4985; Nov. 29, 1999, Public Law 106-113, sec. 1000(a)(9), S. 1948 secs. 4801, 4802, 113 Stat. 1501.)

35 U.S.C. 120   Benefit of earlier filing date in the United States.

An application for patent for an invention disclosed in the manner provided by the first paragraph of section 112 of this title in an application previously filed in the United States, or as provided by section 363 of this title, which is filed by an inventor or inventors named in the previously filed application shall have the same effect, as to such invention, as though filed on the date of the prior application, if filed before the patenting or abandonment of or termination of proceedings on the first application or on an application similarly entitled to the benefit of the filing date of the first application and if it contains or is amended to contain a specific reference to the earlier filed application.

(Amended Nov. 14, 1975, Public Law 94-131, sec. 9, 89 Stat. 691; Nov. 8, 1984, Public Law 98-622, sec. 104(b), 98 Stat. 3385.)

35 U.S.C. 121   Divisional applications.

MANUAL OF PATENT EXAMINING PROCEDURE

If two or more independent and distinct inventions are claimed in one application, the Commissioner may require the application to be restricted to one of the inventions. If the other invention is made the subject of a divisional application which complies with the requirements of section 120 of this title it shall be entitled to the benefit of the filing date of the original application. A patent issuing on an application with respect to which a requirement for restriction under this section has been made, or on an application filed as a result of such a requirement, shall not be used as a reference either in the Patent and Trademark Office or in the courts against a divisional application or against the original application or any patent issued on either of them, if the divisional application is filed before the issuance of the patent on the other application. If a divisional application is directed solely to subject matter described and claimed in the original application as filed, the Commissioner may dispense with signing and execution by the inventor. The validity of a patent shall not be questioned for failure of the Commissioner to require the application to be restricted to one invention.

(Amended Jan. 2, 1975, Public Law 93-596, sec. 1, 88 Stat. 1949.)

35 U.S.C. 122　Confidential status of applications.

Applications for patents shall be kept in confidence by the Patent and Trademark Office and no information concerning the same given without authority of the applicant or owner unless necessary to carry out the provisions of any Act of Congress or in such special circumstances as may be determined by the Commissioner.

(Amended Jan. 2, 1975, Public Law 93-596, sec. 1, 88 Stat. 1949.)

CHAPTER 12 — EXAMINATION OF
APPLICATION

Sec.
131　Examination of application.
132　Notice of rejection; reexamination.
133　Time for prosecuting application.
134　Appeal to the Board of Patent Appeals and Interferences.
135　Interferences.

35 U.S.C. 131　Examination of application.

The Commissioner shall cause an examination to be made of the application and the alleged new invention; and if on such examination it appears that the applicant is entitled to a patent under the law, the Commissioner shall issue a patent therefor.

35 U.S.C. 132　Notice of rejection; reexamination.

Whenever, on examination, any claim for a patent is rejected, or any objection or requirement made, the Commissioner shall notify the applicant thereof, stating the reasons for such rejection, or objection or requirement, together with such information and references as may be useful in judging of the propriety of continuing the prosecution of his application; and if after receiving such notice, the applicant persists in his claim for a patent, with or without amendment, the application shall be reexamined. No amendment shall introduce new matter into the disclosure of the invention.

35 U.S.C. 133　Time for prosecuting application.

Upon failure of the applicant to prosecute the application within six months after any action therein, of which notice has been given or mailed to the applicant, or within such shorter time, not less than thirty days, as fixed by the Commissioner in such action, the application shall be regarded as abandoned by the parties thereto, unless it be shown to the satisfaction of the Commissioner that such delay was unavoidable.

35 U.S.C. 134　Appeal to the Board of Patent Appeals and Interferences.

(a)　PATENT APPLICANT.— An applicant for a patent, any of whose claims has been twice rejected, may appeal from the decision of the administrative patent judge to the Board of Patent Appeals and Interferences, having once paid the fee for such appeal.

(b)　PATENT OWNER.— A patent owner in any reexamination proceeding may appeal from the final rejection of any claim by the administrative patent judge to the Board of Patent Appeals and Interferences, having once paid the fee for such appeal.

(c)　THIRD-PARTY.— A third-party requester in an inter partes proceeding may appeal to the Board of Patent Appeals and Interferences from the final decision of the administrative patent judge favorable to the patentability of any original or proposed amended or new claim of a patent, having once paid the fee for such appeal. The third-party requester may not appeal the decision of the Board of Patent Appeals and Interferences.

(Amended Nov. 8, 1984, Public Law 98-622, sec. 204(b)(1), 98 Stat. 3388; Nov. 29, 1999, Public Law 106-113, sec. 1000(a)(9), S. 1948 sec. 4605(b), 113 Stat. 1501.)

35 U.S.C. 135　Interferences.

(a)　Whenever an application is made for a patent which, in the opinion of the Commissioner, would interfere with any pending application, or with any unexpired patent, an interference may be declared and the Commissioner shall give notice of such declaration to the applicants, or applicant and patentee, as the case may be. The Board of Patent Appeals and Interferences shall determine questions

PATENT LAWS

of priority of the inventions and may determine questions of patentability. Any final decision, if adverse to the claim of an applicant, shall constitute the final refusal by the Patent and Trademark Office of the claims involved, and the Commissioner may issue a patent to the applicant who is adjudged the prior inventor. A final judgment adverse to a patentee from which no appeal or other review has been or can be taken or had shall constitute cancellation of the claims involved in the patent, and notice of such cancellation shall be endorsed on copies of the patent distributed after such cancellation by the Patent and Trademark Office.

(b)   A claim which is the same as, or for the same or substantially the same subject matter as, a claim of an issued patent may not be made in any application unless such a claim is made prior to one year from the date on which the patent was granted.

(c)   Any agreement or understanding between parties to an interference, including any collateral agreements referred to therein, made in connection with or in contemplation of the termination of the interference, shall be in writing and a true copy thereof filed in the Patent and Trademark Office before the termination of the interference as between the said parties to the agreement or understanding. If any party filing the same so requests, the copy shall be kept separate from the file of the interference, and made available only to Government agencies on written request, or to any person on a showing of good cause. Failure to file the copy of such agreement or understanding shall render permanently unenforceable such agreement or understanding and any patent of such parties involved in the interference or any patent subsequently issued on any application of such parties so involved. The Commissioner may, however, on a showing of good cause for failure to file within the time prescribed, permit the filing of the agreement or understanding during the six-month period subsequent to the termination of the interference as between the parties to the agreement or understanding.

The Commissioner shall give notice to the parties or their attorneys of record, a reasonable time prior to said termination, of the filing requirement of this section. If the Commissioner gives such notice at a later time, irrespective of the right to file such agreement or understanding within the six-month period on a showing of good cause, the parties may file such agreement or understanding within sixty days of the receipt of such notice.

Any discretionary action of the Commissioner under this subsection shall be reviewable under section 10 of the Administrative Procedure Act.

(d)   Parties to a patent interference, within such time as may be specified by the Commissioner by regulation, may determine such contest or any aspect thereof by arbitration. Such arbitration shall be governed by the provisions

of title 9 to the extent such title is not inconsistent with this section. The parties shall give notice of any arbitration award to the Commissioner, and such award shall, as between the parties to the arbitration, be dispositive of the issues to which it relates. The arbitration award shall be unenforceable until such notice is given. Nothing in this subsection shall preclude the Commissioner from determining patentability of the invention involved in the interference.

(Subsection (c) added Oct. 15, 1962, Public Law 87-831, 76 Stat. 958.)

(Subsections (a) and (c) amended, Jan. 2, 1975, Public Law 93-596, sec. 1, 88 Stat. 1949.)

(Subsection (a) amended Nov. 8, 1984, Public Law 98-622, sec. 202, 98 Stat. 3386.)

(Subsection (d) added Nov. 8, 1984, Public Law 98-622, sec. 105, 98 Stat. 3385.)

CHAPTER 13 — REVIEW OF PATENT AND TRADEMARK OFFICE DECISION

Sec.
141   Appeal to Court of Appeals for the Federal Circuit.
142   Notice of appeal.
143   Proceedings on appeal.
144   Decision on appeal.
145   Civil action to obtain patent.
146   Civil action in case of interference.

35 U.S.C. 141   Appeal to the Court of Appeals for the Federal Circuit.

An applicant dissatisfied with the decision in an appeal to the Board of Patent Appeals and Interferences under section 134 of this title may appeal the decision to the United States Court of Appeals for the Federal Circuit. By filing such an appeal the applicant waives his or her right to proceed under section 145 of this title. A patent owner in any reexamination proceeding dissatisfied with the final decision in an appeal to the Board of Patent Appeals and Interferences under section 134 may appeal the decision only to the United States Court of Appeals for the Federal Circuit. A party to an interference dissatisfied with the decision of the Board of Patent Appeals and Interferences on the interference may appeal the decision to the United States Court of Appeals for the Federal Circuit, but such appeal shall be dismissed if any adverse party to such interference, within twenty days after the appellant has filed notice of appeal in accordance with section 142 of this title, files notice with the Commissioner that the party elects to have all further proceedings conducted as provided in section 146 of this title. If the appellant does not, within thirty days after filing of such notice by the adverse party, file a civil action under

MANUAL OF PATENT EXAMINING PROCEDURE

section 146, the decision appealed from shall govern the further proceedings in the case.

(Amended Apr. 2, 1982, Public Law 97-164, sec. 163(a)(7), (b)(2), 96 Stat. 49, 50; Nov. 8, 1984, Public Law 98-622, sec. 203(a), 98 Stat. 3387; Nov. 29, 1999, Public Law 106-113, sec. 1000(a)(9), S. 1948 sec. 4605(c), 113 Stat. 1501.)

35 U.S.C. 142   Notice of appeal.

When an appeal is taken to the United States Court of Appeals for the Federal Circuit, the appellant shall file in the Patent and Trademark Office a written notice of appeal directed to the Commissioner, within such time after the date of the decision from which the appeal is taken as the Commissioner prescribes, but in no case less than 60 days after that date.

(Amended Jan. 2, 1975, Public Law 93-596, sec. 1, 88 Stat. 1949; Apr. 2, 1982, Public Law 97-164, sec. 163(a)(7), 96 Stat. 49; Nov. 8, 1984, Public Law 98-620, sec. 414(a), 98 Stat. 3363.)

35 U.S.C. 143   Proceedings on appeal.

With respect to an appeal described in section 142 of this title, the Commissioner shall transmit to the United States Court of Appeals for the Federal Circuit a certified list of the documents comprising the record in the Patent and Trademark Office. The court may request that the Commissioner forward the original or certified copies of such documents during the pendency of the appeal. In any reexamination case, the Director shall submit to the court in writing the grounds for the decision of the Patent and Trademark Office, addressing all the issues involved in the appeal. The court shall, before hearing an appeal, give notice of the time and place of the hearing to the Commissioner and the parties in the appeal.

(Amended Jan. 2, 1975, Public Law 93-596, sec. 1, 88 Stat. 1949; Apr. 2, 1982, Public Law 97-164, sec. 163(a)(7), 96 Stat. 49; Nov. 8, 1984, Public Law 98-620, sec. 414(a), 98 Stat. 3363; Nov. 29, 1999, Public Law 106-113, sec. 1000(a)(9), S. 1948 sec. 4605(d), 113 Stat. 1501.)

35 U.S.C. 144   Decision on appeal.

The United States Court of Appeals for the Federal Circuit shall review the decision from which an appeal is taken on the record before the Patent and Trademark Office. Upon its determination the court shall issue its mandate and opinion, which shall be entered of record in the Patent and Trademark Office and shall govern the further proceedings in the case.

(Amended Jan. 2, 1975, Public Law 93-596, sec. 1, 88 Stat. 1949; Apr. 2, 1982, Public Law 97-164, sec. 163(a)(7), 96 Stat. 49; Nov. 8, 1984, Public Law 98-620, sec. 414(a), 98 Stat. 3363.)

35 U.S.C. 145   Civil action to obtain patent.

An applicant dissatisfied with the decision of the Board of Patent Appeals and Interferences in an appeal under sec-

tion 134(a) of this title may, unless appeal has been taken to the United States Court of Appeals for the Federal Circuit, have remedy by civil action against the Commissioner in the United States District Court for the District of Columbia if commenced within such time after such decision, not less than sixty days, as the Commissioner appoints. The court may adjudge that such applicant is entitled to receive a patent for his invention, as specified in any of his claims involved in the decision of the Board of Patent Appeals and Interferences, as the facts in the case may appear, and such adjudication shall authorize the Commissioner to issue such patent on compliance with the requirements of law. All the expenses of the proceedings shall be paid by the applicant.

(Amended Apr. 2, 1982, Public Law 97-164, sec. 163(a)(7), 96 Stat. 49; Nov. 8, 1984, Public Law 98-620, sec. 203(b), 98 Stat. 3387; Nov. 29, 1999, Public Law 106-113, sec. 1000(a)(9), S. 1948 sec. 4605(e), 113 Stat. 1501.)

35 U.S.C. 146   Civil action in case of interference.

Any party to an interference dissatisfied with the decision of the Board of Patent Appeals and Interferences may have remedy by civil action, if commenced within such time after such decision, not less than sixty days, as the Commissioner appoints or as provided in section 141 of this title, unless he has appealed to the United States Court of Appeals for the Federal Circuit, and such appeal is pending or has been decided. In such suits the record in the Patent and Trademark Office shall be admitted on motion of either party upon the terms and conditions as to costs, expenses, and the further cross-examination of the witnesses as the court imposes, without prejudice to the right of the parties to take further testimony. The testimony and exhibits of the record in the Patent and Trademark Office when admitted shall have the same effect as if originally taken and produced in the suit.

Such suit may be instituted against the party in interest as shown by the records of the Patent and Trademark Office at the time of the decision complained of, but any party in interest may become a party to the action. If there be adverse parties residing in a plurality of districts not embraced within the same state, or an adverse party residing in a foreign country, the United States District Court for the District of Columbia shall have jurisdiction and may issue summons against the adverse parties directed to the marshal of any district in which any adverse party resides. Summons against adverse parties residing in foreign countries may be served by publication or otherwise as the court directs. The Commissioner shall not be a necessary party but he shall be notified of the filing of the suit by the clerk of the court in which it is filed and shall have the right to intervene. Judgment of the court in favor of the right of an applicant to a patent shall authorize the Commissioner to

PATENT LAWS

issue such patent on the filing in the Patent and Trademark Office of a certified copy of the judgment and on compliance with the requirements of law.

(Amended Jan. 2, 1975, Public Law 93-596, sec. 1, 88 Stat. 1949; Apr. 2, 1982, Public Law 97-164, sec. 163(a)(7), 96 Stat. 49; Nov. 8, 1984, Public Law 98-622, sec. 203(c), 98 Stat. 3387.)

CHAPTER 14 — ISSUE OF PATENT

Sec.

35 U.S.C. 151   Issue of patent.

If it appears that applicant is entitled to a patent under the law, a written notice of allowance of the application shall be given or mailed to the applicant. The notice shall specify a sum, constituting the issue fee or a portion thereof, which shall be paid within three months thereafter.

Upon payment of this sum the patent shall issue, but if payment is not timely made, the application shall be regarded as abandoned.

Any remaining balance of the issue fee shall be paid within three months from the sending of a notice thereof, and, if not paid, the patent shall lapse at the termination of this three-month period. In calculating the amount of a remaining balance, charges for a page or less may be disregarded.

If any payment required by this section is not timely made, but is submitted with the fee for delayed payment and the delay in payment is shown to have been unavoidable, it may be accepted by the Commissioner as though no abandonment or lapse had ever occurred.

(Amended July 24, 1965, Public Law 89-83, sec. 4, 79 Stat. 260; Jan. 2, 1975, Public Law 93-601, sec. 3, 88 Stat. 1956.)

35 U.S.C. 152   Issue of patent to assignee.

Patents may be granted to the assignee of the inventor of record in the Patent and Trademark Office, upon the application made and the specification sworn to by the inventor, except as otherwise provided in this title.

(Amended Jan. 2, 1975, Public Law 93-596, sec. 1, 88 Stat. 1949.)

35 U.S.C. 153   How issued.

Patents shall be issued in the name of the United States of America, under the seal of the Patent and Trademark Office, and shall be signed by the Commissioner or have his signature placed thereon and attested by an officer of the Patent and Trademark Office designated by the Commissioner, and shall be recorded in the Patent and Trademark Office.

(Amended Jan. 2, 1975, Public Law 93-596, sec. 1, 88 Stat. 1949.)

35 U.S.C. 154   Contents and term of patent.

(a)   IN GENERAL.—

(1)   CONTENTS.—Every patent shall contain a short title of the invention and a grant to the patentee, his heirs or assigns, of the right to exclude others from making, using, offering for sale, or selling the invention throughout the United States or importing the invention into the United States, and, if the invention is a process, of the right to exclude others from using, offering for sale or selling throughout the United States, or importing into the United States, products made by that process, referring to the specification for the particulars thereof.

(2)   TERM.—Subject to the payment of fees under this title, such grant shall be for a term beginning on the date on which the patent issues and ending 20 years from the date on which the application for the patent was filed in the United States or, if the application contains a specific reference to an earlier filed application or applications under section 120, 121, or 365(c) of this title, from the date on which the earliest such application was filed.

(3)   PRIORITY.—Priority under section 119, 365(a), or 365(b) of this title shall not be taken into account in determining the term of a patent.

(4)   SPECIFICATION AND DRAWING.—A copy of the specification and drawing shall be annexed to the patent and be a part of such patent.

(b)   TERM EXTENSION.—

(1)   INTERFERENCE DELAY OR SECRECY ORDERS.—If the issue of an original patent is delayed due to a proceeding under section 135(a) of this title, or because the application for patent is placed under an order pursuant to section 181 of this title, the term of the patent shall be extended for the period of delay, but in no case more than 5 years.

(2)   EXTENSION FOR APPELLATE REVIEW. —If the issue of a patent is delayed due to appellate review by the Board of Patent Appeals and Interferences or by a Federal court and the patent is issued pursuant to a decision in the review reversing an adverse determination of patentability, the term of the patent shall be extended for a period of time but in no case more than 5 years. A patent shall not be eligible for extension under this paragraph if it is subject to a terminal disclaimer due to the issue of another patent claiming subject matter that is not patentably distinct from that under appellate review.

MANUAL OF PATENT EXAMINING PROCEDURE

(3) LIMITATIONS.—The period of extension referred to in paragraph (2)—

(A) shall include any period beginning on the date on which an appeal is filed under section 134 or 141 of this title, or on which an action is commenced under section 145 of this title, and ending on the date of a final decision in favor of the applicant;

(B) shall be reduced by any time attributable to appellate review before the expiration of 3 years from the filing date of the application for patent; and

(C) shall be reduced for the period of time during which the applicant for patent did not act with due diligence, as determined by the Commissioner.

(4) LENGTH OF EXTENSION.—The total duration of all extensions of a patent under this subsection shall not exceed 5 years.

(c) CONTINUATION.—

(1) DETERMINATION.—The term of a patent that is in force on or that results from an application filed before the date that is 6 months after the date of the enactment of the Uruguay Round Agreements Act shall be the greater of the 20-year term as provided in subsection (a), or 17 years from grant, subject to any terminal disclaimers.

(2) REMEDIES.—The remedies of sections 283, 284, and 285 of this title shall not apply to acts which —

(A) were commenced or for which substantial investment was made before the date that is 6 months after the date of the enactment of the Uruguay Round Agreements Act; and

(B) became infringing by reason of paragraph (1).

(3) REMUNERATION.—The acts referred to in paragraph (2) may be continued only upon the payment of an equitable remuneration to the patentee that is determined in an action brought under chapter 28 and chapter 29 (other than those provisions excluded by paragraph (2)) of this title.

(Amended July 24, 1965, Public Law 89-83, sec. 5, 79 Stat. 261; Dec. 12, 1980, Public Law 96-517, sec. 4, 94 Stat. 3018; Aug. 23, 1988, Public Law 100-418, sec. 9002, 102 Stat. 1563; Dec 8, 1994, Public Law 103-465, sec. 532 (a)(1), 108 Stat. 4983; Oct. 11, 1996, Public Law 104-295, sec. 20(e)(1), 110 Stat. 3529.)

35 U.S.C. 155 Patent term extension.

Notwithstanding the provisions of section 154, the term of a patent which encompasses within its scope a composition of matter or a process for using such composition shall be extended if such composition or process has been subjected to a regulatory review by the Federal Food and Drug Administration pursuant to the Federal Food, Drug and Cosmetic Act leading to the publication of regulation permitting the interstate distribution and sale of such composition or process and for which there has thereafter been a stay of regulation of approval imposed pursuant to section 409 of the Federal Food, Drug and Cosmetic Act, which stay was in effect on January 1, 1981, by a length of time to be measured from the date such stay of regulation of approval was imposed until such proceedings are finally resolved and commercial marketing permitted. The patentee, his heirs, successors, or assigns shall notify the Commissioner of Patents and Trademarks within 90 days of the date of enactment of this section or the date the stay of regulation of approval has been removed, whichever is later, of the number of the patent to be extended and the date the stay was imposed and the date commercial marketing was permitted. On receipt of such notice, the Commissioner shall promptly issue to the owner of record of the patent a certificate of extension, under seal, stating the fact and length of the extension and identifying the composition of matter or process for using such composition to which such extension is applicable. Such certificate shall be recorded in the official file of each patent extended and such certificate shall be considered as part of the original patent, and an appropriate notice shall be published in the Official Gazette of the Patent and Trademark Office.

(Added Jan. 4, 1983, Public Law 97-414, sec. 11(a), 96 Stat. 2065.)

35 U.S.C. 155A Patent term restoration.

(a) Notwithstanding section 154 of this title, the term of each of the following patents shall be extended in accordance with this section:

(1) Any patent which encompasses within its scope a composition of matter which is a new drug product, if during the regulatory review of the product by the Federal Food and Drug Administration —

(A) the Federal Food and Drug Administration notified the patentee, by letter dated February 20, 1976, that such product's new drug application was not approvable under section 505(b)(1) of the Federal Food, Drug and Cosmetic Act;

(B) in 1977 the patentee submitted to the Federal Food and Drug Administration the results of a health effects test to evaluate the carcinogenic potential of such product;

(C) the Federal Food and Drug Administration approved, by letter dated December 18, 1979, the new drug application for such application; and

(D) the Federal Food and Drug Administration approved, by letter dated May 26, 1981, a supplementary application covering the facility for the production of such product.

(2) Any patent which encompasses within its scope a process for using the composition described in paragraph (1).

PATENT LAWS

(b)   The term of any patent described in subsection (a) shall be extended for a period equal to the period beginning February 20, 1976, and ending May 26, 1981, and such patent shall have the effect as if originally issued with such extended term.

(c)   The patentee of any patent described in subsection (a) of this section shall, within ninety days after the date of enactment of this section, notify the Commissioner of Patents and Trademarks of the number of any patent so extended. On receipt of such notice, the Commissioner shall confirm such extension by placing a notice thereof in the official file of such patent and publishing an appropriate notice of such extension in the *Official Gazette* of the Patent and Trademark Office.

(Added Oct. 13, 1983, Public Law 98-127, sec. 4(a), 97 Stat. 832.)

35 U.S.C. 156   Extension of patent term.

(a)   The term of a patent which claims a product, a method of using a product, or a method of manufacturing a product shall be extended in accordance with this section from the original expiration date of the patent if —

(1)   the term of the patent has not expired before an application is submitted under subsection (d)(1) for its extension;

(2)   the term of the patent has never been extended under subsection (e)(1) of this section;

(3)   an application for extension is submitted by the owner of record of the patent or its agent and in accordance with the requirements of paragraphs (1) through (4) of subsection (d);

(4)   the product has been subject to a regulatory review period before its commercial marketing or use;

(5)(A)except as provided in subparagraph (B) or (C), the permission for the commercial marketing or use of the product after such regulatory review period is the first permitted commercial marketing or use of the product under the provision of law under which such regulatory review period occurred;

(B)   in the case of a patent which claims a method of manufacturing the product which primarily uses recombinant DNA technology in the manufacture of the product, the permission for the commercial marketing or use of the product after such regulatory period is the first permitted commercial marketing or use of a product manufactured under the process claimed in the patent; or

(C)   for purposes of subparagraph (A), in the case of a patent which -

(i)   claims a new animal drug or a veterinary biological product which (I) is not covered by the claims in any other patent which has been extended, and (II) has received permission for the commercial marketing or use in non-food-producing animals and in food-producing animals, and

(ii)   was not extended on the basis of the regulatory review period for use in non-food-producing animals, the permission for the commercial marketing or use of the drug or product after the regulatory review period for use in food-producing animals is the first permitted commercial marketing or use of the drug or product for administration to a food-producing animal.

The product referred to in paragraphs (4) and (5) is hereinafter in this section referred to as the "approved product."

(b)   Except as provided in subsection (d)(5)(F), the rights derived from any patent the term of which is extended under this section shall during the period during which the term of the patent is extended —

(1)   in the case of a patent which claims a product, be limited to any use approved for the product —

(A)   before the expiration of the term of the patent —

(i)   under the provision of law under which the applicable regulatory review occurred, or

(ii)   under the provision of law under which any regulatory review described in paragraph (1), (4), or (5) of subsection (g) occurred, and

(B)   on or after the expiration of the regulatory review period upon which the extension of the patent was based;

(2)   in the case of a patent which claims a method of using a product, be limited to any use claimed by the patent and approved for the product —

(A)   before the expiration of the term of the patent -

(i)   under any provision of law under which an applicable regulatory review occurred, and

(ii)   under the provision of law under which any regulatory review described in paragraph (1), (4), or (5) of subsection (g) occurred, and

(B)   on or after the expiration of the regulatory review period upon which the extension of the patent was based; and

(3)   in the case of a patent which claims a method of manufacturing a product, be limited to the method of manufacturing as used to make —

(A)   the approved product, or

(B)   the product if it has been subject to a regulatory review period described in paragraphs (1), (4), or (5) of subsection (g).

As used in this subsection, the term "product" includes an approved product.

(c)   The term of a patent eligible for extension under subsection (a) shall be extended by the time equal to the regulatory review period for the approved product which period occurs after the date the patent is issued, except that—

    (1) each period of the regulatory review period shall be reduced by any period determined under subsection (d)(2)(B) during which the applicant for the patent extension did not act with due diligence during such period of the regulatory review period;

    (2) after any reduction required by paragraph (1), the period of extension shall include only one-half of the time remaining in the periods described in paragraphs (1)(B)(i), (2)(B)(i), (3)(B)(i), (4)(B)(i), and (5)(B)(i) of subsection (g);

    (3) if the period remaining in the term of a patent after the date of the approval of the approved product under the provision of law under which such regulatory review occurred when added to the regulatory review period as revised under paragraphs (1) and (2) exceeds fourteen years, the period of extension shall be reduced so that the total of both such periods does not exceed fourteen years, and

    (4) in no event shall more than one patent be extended under subsection (e)(i) for the same regulatory review period for any product.

    (d)(1) To obtain an extension of the term of a patent under this section, the owner of record of the patent or its agent shall submit an application to the Commissioner. Except as provided in paragraph (5), such an application may only be submitted within the sixty-day period beginning on the date the product received permission under the provision of law under which the applicable regulatory review period occurred for commercial marketing or use. The application shall contain —

    (A) the identity of the approved product and the Federal statute under which regulatory review occurred;

    (B) the identity of the patent for which an extension is being sought and the identity of each claim of such patent;

    (C) information to enable the Commissioner to determine under subsections (a) and (b) the eligibility of a patent for extension and the rights that will be derived from the extension and information to enable the Commissioner and the Secretary of Health and Human Services or the Secretary of Agriculture to determine the period of the extension under subsection (g);

    (D) a brief description of the activities undertaken by the applicant during the applicable regulatory review period with respect to the approved product and the significant dates applicable to such activities; and

    (E) such patent or other information as the Commissioner may require.

    (2)(A) Within 60 days of the submittal of an application for extension of the term of a patent under paragraph (1), the Commissioner shall notify —

    (i) the Secretary of Agriculture if the patent claims a drug product or a method of using or manufacturing a drug product and the drug product is subject to the Virus-Serum-Toxin Act, and

    (ii) the Secretary of Health and Human Services if the patent claims any other drug product, a medical device, or a food additive or color additive or a method of using or manufacturing such a product, device, or additive and if the product, device, and additive are subject to the Federal Food, Drug and Cosmetic Act, of the extension application and shall submit to the Secretary who is so notified a copy of the application. Not later than 30 days after the receipt of an application from the Commissioner, the Secretary reviewing the application shall review the dates contained in the application pursuant to paragraph (1)(C) and determine the applicable regulatory review period, shall notify the Commissioner of the determination, and shall publish in the Federal Register a notice of such determination.

    (B)(i) If a petition is submitted to the Secretary making the determination under subparagraph (A), not later than 180 days after the publication of the determination under subparagraph (A), upon which it may reasonably be determined that the applicant did not act with due diligence during the applicable regulatory review period, the Secretary making the determination shall, in accordance with regulations promulgated by the Secretary, determine if the applicant acted with due diligence during the applicable regulatory review period. The Secretary making the determination shall make such determination not later than 90 days after the receipt of such a petition. For a drug product, device, or additive subject to the Federal Food, Drug, and Cosmetic Act or the Public Health Service Act, the Secretary may not delegate the authority to make the determination prescribed by this clause to an office below the Office of the Commissioner of Food and Drugs. For a product subject to the Virus-Serum-Toxin Act, the Secretary of Agriculture may not delegate the authority to make the determination prescribed by this clause to an office below the office of the Assistant Secretary for Marketing and Inspection Services.

    (ii) The Secretary making a determination under clause (i) shall notify the Commissioner of the determination and shall publish in the Federal Register a notice of such determination together with the factual and legal basis for such determination. Any interested person may request, within the 60-day period beginning on the publication of a determination, the Secretary making the determination to hold an informal hearing on the determination. If

PATENT LAWS

such a request is made within such period, such Secretary shall hold such hearing not later than 30 days after the date of the request, or at the request of the person making the request, not later than 60 days after such date. The Secretary who is holding the hearing shall provide notice of the hearing to the owner of the patent involved and to any interested person and provide the owner and any interested person an opportunity to participate in the hearing. Within 30 days after the completion of the hearing, such Secretary shall affirm or revise the determination which was the subject of the hearing and notify the Commissioner of any revision of the determination and shall publish any such revision in the Federal Register.

(3)   For the purposes of paragraph (2)(B), the term "due diligence" means that degree of attention, continuous directed effort, and timeliness as may reasonably be expected from, and are ordinarily exercised by, a person during a regulatory review period.

(4)   An application for the extension of the term of a patent is subject to the disclosure requirements prescribed by the Commissioner.

(5)(A)If the owner of record of the patent or its agent reasonably expects that the applicable regulatory review period described in paragraphs (1)(B)(ii), (2)(B)(ii), (3)(B)(ii), (4)(B)(ii), or (5)(B)(ii) of subsection (g) that began for a product that is the subject of such patent may extend beyond the expiration of the patent term in effect, the owner or its agent may submit an application to the Commissioner for an interim extension during the period beginning 6 months, and ending 15 days before such term is due to expire. The application shall contain—

(i)   the identity of the product subject to regulating review and the Federal statute under which such review is occurring;

(ii)   the identity of the patent for which interim extension is being sought and the identity of each claim of such patent which claims the product under regulatory review or a method of using or manufacturing the product;

(iii)   information to enable the Commissioner to determine under subsection (a)(1), (2), and (3) the eligibility of a patent for extension;

(iv)   a brief description of the activities undertaken by the applicant during the applicable regulatory review period to date with respect to the product under review and the significant dates applicable to such activities; and

(v)   such patent or other information as the Commissioner may require.

(B)   If the Commissioner determines that, except for permission to market or use the product commercially, the patent would be eligible for an extension of the patent term under this section, the Commissioner shall publish in the Federal Register a notice of such determination, including the identity of the product under regulatory review, and shall issue to the applicant a certificate of interim extension for a period of not more than 1 year.

(C)   The owner of record of a patent, or its agent, for which an interim extension has been granted under subparagraph (B), may apply for not more than 4 subsequent interim extensions under this paragraph, except that, in the case of a patent subject to subsection (g)(6)(C), the owner of record of the patent, or its agent, may apply for only 1 subsequent interim extension under this paragraph. Each such subsequent application shall be made during the period beginning 60 days before, and ending 30 days before, the expiration of the preceding interim extension.

(D)   Each certificate of interim extension under this paragraph shall be recorded in the official file of the patent and shall be considered part of the original patent.

(E)   Any interim extension granted under this paragraph shall terminate at the end of the 60-day period beginning on the day on which the product involved receives permission for commercial marketing or use, except that, if within that 60-day period, the applicant notifies the Commissioner of such permission and submits any additional information under paragraph (1) of this subsection not previously contained in the application for interim extension, the patent shall be further extended, in accordance with the provisions of this section—

(i)   for not to exceed 5 years from the date of expiration of the original patent term; or

(ii)   if the patent is subject to subsection (g)(6)(C), from the date on which the product involved receives approval for commercial marketing or use.

(F)   The rights derived from any patent the term of which is extended under this paragraph shall, during the period of interim extension—

(i)   in the case of a patent which claims a product, be limited to any use then under regulatory review;

(ii)   in the case of a patent which claims a method of using a product, be limited to any use claimed by the patent then under regulatory review; and

(iii)   in the case of a patent which claims a method of manufacturing a product, be limited to the method of manufacturing as used to make the product then under regulatory review.

(e)(1) A determination that a patent is eligible for extension may be made by the Commissioner solely on the basis of the representations contained in the application for the extension. If the Commissioner determines that a patent is eligible for extension under subsection (a) and that the requirements of paragraphs (1) through (4) of subsection

MANUAL OF PATENT EXAMINING PROCEDURE

(d) have been complied with, the Commissioner shall issue to the applicant for the extension of the term of the patent a certificate of extension, under seal, for the period prescribed by subsection (c). Such certificate shall be recorded in the official file of the patent and shall be considered as part of the original patent.

(2)   If the term of a patent for which an application has been submitted under subsection (d)(1) would expire before a certificate of extension is issued or denied under paragraph (1) respecting the application, the Commissioner shall extend, until such determination is made, the term of the patent for periods of up to one year if he determines that the patent is eligible for extension.

(f)   For purposes of this section:

(1)   The term "product" means:

(A)   A drug product.

(B)   Any medical device, food additive, or color additive subject to regulation under the Federal Food, Drug, and Cosmetic Act.

(2)   The term "drug product" means the active ingredient of—

(A)   a new drug, antibiotic drug, or human biological product (as those terms are used in the Federal Food, Drug, and Cosmetic Act and the Public Health Service Act) or

(B)   a new animal drug or veterinary biological product (as those terms are used in the Federal Food, Drug, and Cosmetic Act and the Virus-Serum-Toxin Act) which is not primarily manufactured using recombinant DNA, recombinant RNA, hybridoma technology, or other processes involving site specific genetic manipulation techniques, including any salt or ester of the active ingredient, as a single entity or in combination with another active ingredient.

(3)   The term "major health or environmental effects test" means a test which is reasonably related to the evaluation of the health or environmental effects of a product, which requires at least six months to conduct, and the data from which is submitted to receive permission for commercial marketing or use. Periods of analysis or evaluation of test results are not to be included in determining if the conduct of a test required at least six months.

(4)(A)Any reference to section 351 is a reference to section 351 of the Public Health Service Act.

(B)   Any reference to section 503, 505, 507, 512, or 515 is a reference to section 503, 505, 507, 512, or 515 of the Federal Food, Drug and Cosmetic Act.

(C)   Any reference to the Virus-Serum-Toxin Act is a reference to the Act of March 4, 1913 (21 U.S.C. 151 - 158).

(5)   The term "informal hearing" has the meaning prescribed for such term by section 201(y) of the Federal Food, Drug and Cosmetic Act.

(6)   The term "patent" means a patent issued by the United States Patent and Trademark Office.

(7)   The term "date of enactment" as used in this section means September 24, 1984, for human drug product, a medical device, food additive, or color additive.

(8)   The term "date of enactment" as used in this section means the date of enactment of the Generic Animal Drug and Patent Term Restoration Act for an animal drug or a veterinary biological product.

(g)   For purposes of this section, the term "regulatory review period" has the following meanings:

(1)(A)In the case of a product which is a new drug, antibiotic drug, or human biological product, the term means the period described in subparagraph (B) to which the limitation described in paragraph (6) applies.

(B)   The regulatory review period for a new drug, antibiotic drug, or human biological product is the sum of -

(i)   the period beginning on the date an exemption under subsection (i) of section 505 or subsection (d) of section 507 became effective for the approved product and ending on the date an application was initially submitted for such drug product under section 351, 505, or 507, and

(ii)   the period beginning on the date the application was initially submitted for the approved product under section 351, subsection (b) of section 505, or section 507 and ending on the date such application was approved under such section.

(2)(A)In the case of a product which is a food additive or color additive, the term means the period described in subparagraph (B) to which the limitation described in paragraph (6) applies.

(B)   The regulatory review period for a food or color additive is the sum of —

(i)   the period beginning on the date a major health or environmental effects test on the additive was initiated and ending on the date a petition was initially submitted with respect to the product under the Federal Food, Drug, and Cosmetic Act requesting the issuance of a regulation for use of the product, and

(ii)   the period beginning on the date a petition was initially submitted with respect to the product under the Federal Food, Drug, and Cosmetic Act requesting the issuance of a regulation for use of the product, and ending on the date such regulation became effective or, if objections were filed to such regulation, ending on the date such objections were resolved and commercial marketing was permitted or, if commercial marketing was permitted

PATENT LAWS

and later revoked pending further proceedings as a result of such objections, ending on the date such proceedings were finally resolved and commercial marketing was permitted.

(3)(A)In the case of a product which is a medical device, the term means the period described in subparagraph (B) to which the limitation described in paragraph (6) applies.

(B) The regulatory review period for a medical device is the sum of —

(i) the period beginning on the date a clinical investigation on humans involving the device was begun and ending on the date an application was initially submitted with respect to the device under section 515, and

(ii) the period beginning on the date an application was initially submitted with respect to the device under section 515 and ending on the date such application was approved under such Act or the period beginning on the date a notice of completion of a product development protocol was initially submitted under section 515(f)(5) and ending on the date the protocol was declared completed under section 515(f)(6).

(4)(A)In the case of a product which is a new animal drug, the term means the period described in subparagraph (B) to which the limitation described in paragraph (6) applies.

(B) The regulatory review period for a new animal drug product is the sum of —

(i) the period beginning on the earlier of the date a major health or environmental effects test on the drug was initiated or the date an exemption under subsection (j) of section 512 became effective for the approved new animal drug product and ending on the date an application was initially submitted for such animal drug product under section 512, and

(ii) the period beginning on the date the application was initially submitted for the approved animal drug product under subsection (b) of section 512 and ending on the date such application was approved under such section.

(5)(A)In the case of a product which is a veterinary biological product, the term means the period described in subparagraph (B) to which the limitation described in paragraph (6) applies.

(B) The regulatory period for a veterinary biological product is the sum of —

(i) the period beginning on the date the authority to prepare an experimental biological product under the Virus- Serum-Toxin Act became effective and ending on the date an application for a license was submitted under the Virus-Serum-Toxin Act, and

(ii) the period beginning on the date an application for a license was initially submitted for

approval under the Virus-Serum-Toxin Act and ending on the date such license was issued.

(6) A period determined under any of the preceding paragraphs is subject to the following limitations:

(A) If the patent involved was issued after the date of the enactment of this section, the period of extension determined on the basis of the regulatory review period determined under any such paragraph may not exceed five years.

(B) If the patent involved was issued before the date of the enactment of this section and —

(i) no request for an exemption described in paragraph (1)(B) or (4)(B) was submitted and no request for the authority described in paragraph (5)(B) was submitted,

(ii) no major health or environment effects test described in paragraph (2)(B) or (4)(B) was initiated and no petition for a regulation or application for registration described in such paragraph was submitted, or

(iii) no clinical investigation described in paragraph (3) was begun or product development protocol described in such paragraph was submitted, before such date for the approved product the period of extension determined on the basis of the regulatory review period determined under any such paragraph may not exceed five years.

(C) If the patent involved was issued before the date of the enactment of this section and if an action described in subparagraph (B) was taken before the date of enactment of this section with respect to the approved product and the commercial marketing or use of the product has not been approved before such date, the period of extension determined on the basis of the regulatory review period determined under such paragraph may not exceed two years or in the case of an approved product which is a new animal drug or veterinary biological product (as those terms are used in the Federal Food, Drug, and Cosmetic Act or the Virus-Serum-Toxin Act), three years.

(h) The Commissioner may establish such fees as the Commissioner determines appropriate to cover the costs to the Office of receiving and acting upon applications under this section.

(Added Sept. 24, 1984, Public Law 98-417, sec. 201(a), 98 Stat. 1598; amended Nov. 16, 1988, Public Law 100-670, sec. 201(a)-(h), 102 Stat. 3984; Dec. 3, 1993, Public Law 103-179, secs. 5, 6, 107 Stat. 2040, 2042; Dec 8, 1994, Public Law 103-465, sec. 532(c)(1), 108 Stat. 4987.)

35 U.S.C. 157   Statutory invention registration.

(a) Notwithstanding any other provision of this title, the Commissioner is authorized to publish a statutory invention registration containing the specification and drawings of a regularly filed application for a patent without examination if the applicant —

MANUAL OF PATENT EXAMINING PROCEDURE

(1)   meets the requirements of section 112 of this title;

(2)   has complied with the requirements for printing, as set forth in regulations of the Commissioner;

(3)   waives the right to receive a patent on the invention within such period as may be prescribed by the Commissioner; and

(4)   pays application, publication, and other processing fees established by the Commissioner.

If an interference is declared with respect to such an application, a statutory invention registration may not be published unless the issue of priority of invention is finally determined in favor of the applicant.

(b)   The waiver under subsection (a)(3) of this section by an applicant shall take effect upon publication of the statutory invention registration.

(c)   A statutory invention registration published pursuant to this section shall have all of the attributes specified for patents in this title except those specified in section 183 and sections 271 through 289 of this title. A statutory invention registration shall not have any of the attributes specified for patents in any other provision of law other than this title. A statutory invention registration published pursuant to this section shall give appropriate notice to the public, pursuant to regulations which the Commissioner shall issue, of the preceding provisions of this subsection. The invention with respect to which a statutory invention certificate is published is not a patented invention for purposes of section 292 of this title.

(d)   The Secretary of Commerce shall report to the Congress annually on the use of statutory invention registrations. Such report shall include an assessment of the degree to which agencies of the federal government are making use of the statutory invention registration system, the degree to which it aids the management of federally developed technology, and an assessment of the cost savings to the Federal Government of the uses of such procedures.

(Added Nov. 8, 1984, Public Law 98-662, sec. 102(a), 98 Stat. 3383.)

CHAPTER 15 — PLANT PATENTS

Sec.
161   Patents for plants.
162   Description, claim.
163   Grant.
164   Assistance of the Department of Agriculture.

35 U.S.C. 161   Patents for plants.

Whoever invents or discovers and asexually reproduces any distinct and new variety of plant, including cultivated sports, mutants, hybrids, and newly found seedlings, other than a tuber propagated plant or a plant found in an uncultivated state, may obtain a patent therefor, subject to the conditions and requirements of this title.

The provisions of this title relating to patents for inventions shall apply to patents for plants, except as otherwise provided.

(Amended Sept. 3, 1954, 68 Stat. 1190.)

35 U.S.C. 162   Description, claim.

No plant patent shall be declared invalid for noncompliance with section 112 of this title if the description is as complete as is reasonably possible.

The claim in the specification shall be in formal terms to the plant shown and described.

35 U.S.C. 163   Grant.

In the case of a plant patent, the grant shall include the right to exclude others from asexually reproducing the plant, and from using, offering for sale, or selling the plant so reproduced, or any of its parts, throughout the United States, or from importing the plant so reproduced, or any parts thereof, into the United States.

(Amended Oct. 27, 1998, Public Law 105-289, sec. 3, 112 Stat. 2781.)

35 U.S.C. 164   Assistance of the Department of Agriculture.

The President may by Executive order direct the Secretary of Agriculture, in accordance with the requests of the Commissioner, for the purpose of carrying into effect the provisions of this title with respect to plants (1) to furnish available information of the Department of Agriculture, (2) to conduct through the appropriate bureau or division of the Department research upon special problems, or (3) to detail to the Commissioner officers and employees of the Department.

CHAPTER 16 — DESIGNS

Sec.
171   Patents for designs.
172   Right of priority.
173   Term of design patent.

35 U.S.C. 171   Patents for designs.

Whoever invents any new, original, and ornamental design for an article of manufacture may obtain a patent therefor, subject to the conditions and requirements of this title.

The provisions of this title relating to patents for inventions shall apply to patents for designs, except as otherwise provided.

35 U.S.C. 172   Right of priority.

The right of priority provided for by subsections (a) through (d) of section 119 of this title and the time specified in section 102(d) shall be six months in the case of designs. The right of priority provided for by section 119(e) of this title shall not apply to designs.

(Amended Dec. 8, 1994, Public Law 103-465, sec. 532(c)(2), 108 Stat. 4987.)

35 U.S.C. 173   Term of design patent.

Patents for designs shall be granted for the term of fourteen years from the date of grant.

(Amended Aug. 27, 1982, Public Law 97-247, sec. 16, 96 Stat. 321; Dec. 8, 1994, Public Law 103-465, sec. 532(c)(3), 108 Stat. 4987.)

CHAPTER 17 — SECRECY OF CERTAIN INVENTIONS AND FILING APPLICATIONS IN FOREIGN COUNTRIES

Sec.
181   Secrecy of certain inventions and withholding of patent.
182   Abandonment of invention for unauthorized disclosure.
183   Right to compensation.
184   Filing of application in foreign country.
185   Patent barred for filing without license.
186   Penalty.
187   Nonapplicability to certain persons.
188   Rules and regulations, delegation of power.

35 U.S.C. 181   Secrecy of certain inventions and withholding of patent.

Whenever publication or disclosure by the grant of a patent on an invention in which the Government has a property interest might, in the opinion of the head of the interested Government agency, be detrimental to the national security, the Commissioner upon being so notified shall order that the invention be kept secret and shall withhold the grant of a patent therefor under the conditions set forth hereinafter.

Whenever the publication or disclosure of an invention by the granting of a patent, in which the Government does not have a property interest, might, in the opinion of the Commissioner, be detrimental to the national security, he shall make the application for patent in which such invention is disclosed available for inspection to the Atomic Energy Commission, the Secretary of Defense, and the chief officer of any other department or agency of the Government designated by the President as a defense agency of the United States.

Each individual to whom the application is disclosed shall sign a dated acknowledgment thereof, which acknowledgment shall be entered in the file of the applica-

tion. If, in the opinion of the Atomic Energy Commission, the Secretary of a Defense Department, or the chief officer of another department or agency so designated, the publication or disclosure of the invention by the granting of a patent therefor would be detrimental to the national security, the Atomic Energy Commission, the Secretary of a Defense Department, or such other chief officer shall notify the Commissioner and the Commissioner shall order that the invention be kept secret and shall withhold the grant of a patent for such period as the national interest requires, and notify the applicant thereof. Upon proper showing by the head of the department or agency who caused the secrecy order to be issued that the examination of the application might jeopardize the national interest, the Commissioner shall thereupon maintain the application in a sealed condition and notify the applicant thereof. The owner of an application which has been placed under a secrecy order shall have a right to appeal from the order to the Secretary of Commerce under rules prescribed by him.

An invention shall not be ordered kept secret and the grant of a patent withheld for a period of more than one year. The Commissioner shall renew the order at the end thereof, or at the end of any renewal period, for additional periods of one year upon notification by the head of the department or the chief officer of the agency who caused the order to be issued that an affirmative determination has been made that the national interest continues to so require. An order in effect, or issued, during a time when the United States is at war, shall remain in effect for the duration of hostilities and one year following cessation of hostilities. An order in effect, or issued, during a national emergency declared by the President shall remain in effect for the duration of the national emergency and six months thereafter. The Commissioner may rescind any order upon notification by the heads of the departments and the chief officers of the agencies who caused the order to be issued that the publication or disclosure of the invention is no longer deemed detrimental to the national security.

35 U.S.C. 182   Abandonment of invention for unauthorized disclosure.

The invention disclosed in an application for patent subject to an order made pursuant to section 181 of this title may be held abandoned upon its being established by the Commissioner that in violation of said order the invention has been published or disclosed or that an application for a patent therefor has been filed in a foreign country by the inventor, his successors, assigns, or legal representatives, or anyone in privity with him or them, without the consent of the Commissioner. The abandonment shall be held to have occurred as of the time of violation. The consent of the Commissioner shall not be given without the concurrence of the heads of the departments and the chief officers of the

MANUAL OF PATENT EXAMINING PROCEDURE

agencies who caused the order to be issued. A holding of abandonment shall constitute forfeiture by the applicant, his successors, assigns, or legal representatives, or anyone in privity with him or them, of all claims against the United States based upon such invention.

35 U.S.C. 183   Right to compensation.

An applicant, his successors, assigns, or legal representatives, whose patent is withheld as herein provided, shall have the right, beginning at the date the applicant is notified that, except for such order, his application is otherwise in condition for allowance, or February 1, 1952, whichever is later, and ending six years after a patent is issued thereon, to apply to the head of any department or agency who caused the order to be issued for compensation for the damage caused by the order of secrecy and/or for the use of the invention by the Government, resulting from his disclosure. The right to compensation for use shall begin on the date of the first use of the invention by the Government. The head of the department or agency is authorized, upon the presentation of a claim, to enter into an agreement with the applicant, his successors, assigns, or legal representatives, in full settlement for the damage and/or use. This settlement agreement shall be conclusive for all purposes notwithstanding any other provision of law to the contrary. If full settlement of the claim cannot be effected, the head of the department or agency may award and pay to such applicant, his successors, assigns, or legal representatives, a sum not exceeding 75 per centum of the sum which the head of the department or agency considers just compensation for the damage and/or use. A claimant may bring suit against the United States in the United States Court of Federal Claims or in the District Court of the United States for the district in which such claimant is a resident for an amount which when added to the award shall constitute just compensation for the damage and/or use of the invention by the Government. The owner of any patent issued upon an application that was subject to a secrecy order issued pursuant to section 181 of this title, who did not apply for compensation as above provided, shall have the right, after the date of issuance of such patent, to bring suit in the United States Court of Federal Claims for just compensation for the damage caused by reason of the order of secrecy and/or use by the Government of the invention resulting from his disclosure. The right to compensation for use shall begin on the date of the first use of the invention by the Government. In a suit under the provisions of this section the United States may avail itself of all defenses it may plead in an action under section 1498 of title 28. This section shall not confer a right of action on anyone or his successors, assigns, or legal representatives who, while in the full-time employment or service of the United States, discovered, invented, or developed the invention on which the claim is based.

(Amended Apr. 2, 1982, Public Law 97-164, sec. 160(a)(12), 96 Stat. 48; Oct. 29, 1992, Public Law 102-572, sec. 902 (b)(1), 106 Stat. 4516.)

35 U.S.C. 184   Filing of application in foreign country.

Except when authorized by a license obtained from the Commissioner a person shall not file or cause or authorize to be filed in any foreign country prior to six months after filing in the United States an application for patent or for the registration of a utility model, industrial design, or model in respect of an invention made in this country. A license shall not be granted with respect to an invention subject to an order issued by the Commissioner pursuant to section 181 of this title without the concurrence of the head of the departments and the chief officers of the agencies who caused the order to be issued. The license may be granted retroactively where an application has been filed abroad through error and without deceptive intent and the application does not disclose an invention within the scope of section 181 of this title.

The term "application" when used in this chapter includes applications and any modifications, amendments, or supplements thereto, or divisions thereof.

The scope of a license shall permit subsequent modifications, amendments, and supplements containing additional subject matter if the application upon which the request for the license is based is not, or was not, required to be made available for inspection under section 181 of this title and if such modifications, amendments, and supplements do not change the general nature of the invention in a manner which would require such application to be made available for inspection under such section 181. In any case in which a license is not, or was not, required in order to file an application in any foreign country, such subsequent modifications, amendments, and supplements may be made, without a license, to the application filed in the foreign country if the United States application was not required to be made available for inspection under section 181 and if such modifications, amendments, and supplements do not, or did not, change the general nature of the invention in a manner which would require the United States application to have been made available for inspection under such section 181.

(Amended Aug. 23, 1988, Public Law 100-418, sec. 9101(b)(1), 102 Stat. 1567.)

35 U.S.C. 185   Patent barred for filing without license.

Notwithstanding any other provisions of law any person, and his successors, assigns, or legal representatives, shall not receive a United States patent for an invention if that person, or his successors, assigns, or legal representatives shall, without procuring the license prescribed in section 184 of this title, have made, or consented to or assisted another's making, application in a foreign country for a patent or for the registration of a utility model, industrial

PATENT LAWS

design, or model in respect of the invention. A United States patent issued to such person, his successors, assigns, or legal representatives shall be invalid, unless the failure to procure such license was through error and without deceptive intent, and the patent does not disclose subject matter within the scope of section 181 of this title.

(Amended Aug. 23, 1988, Public Law 100-418, sec. 9101(b)(2), 102 Stat. 1568.)

35 U.S.C. 186   Penalty.

Whoever, during the period or periods of time an invention has been ordered to be kept secret and the grant of a patent thereon withheld pursuant to section 181 of this title, shall, with knowledge of such order and without due authorization, willfully publish or disclose or authorize or cause to be published or disclosed the invention, or material information with respect thereto, or whoever willfully, in violation of the provisions of section 184 of this title, shall file or cause or authorize to be filed in any foreign country an application for patent or for the registration of a utility model, industrial design, or model in respect of any invention made in the United States, shall, upon conviction, be fined not more than $10,000 or imprisoned for not more than two years, or both.

(Amended Aug. 23, 1988, Public Law 100-418, sec. 9101(b)(3), 102 Stat. 1568.)

35 U.S.C. 187   Nonapplicability to certain persons.

The prohibitions and penalties of this chapter shall not apply to any officer or agent of the United States acting within the scope of his authority, nor to any person acting upon his written instructions or permission.

35 U.S.C. 188   Rules and regulations, delegation of power.

The Atomic Energy Commission, the Secretary of a defense department, the chief officer of any other department or agency of the Government designated by the President as a defense agency of the United States, and the Secretary of Commerce, may separately issue rules and regulations to enable the respective department or agency to carry out the provisions of this chapter, and may delegate any power conferred by this chapter.

CHAPTER [18] 38 — PATENT RIGHTS IN
INVENTIONS MADE WITH FEDERAL
ASSISTANCE

Sec.

35 U.S.C. 200   Policy and objective.

It is the policy and objective of the Congress to use the patent system to promote the utilization of inventions arising from federally supported research or development; to encourage maximum participation of small business firms in federally supported research and development efforts; to promote collaboration between commercial concerns and nonprofit organizations, including universities; to ensure that inventions made by nonprofit organizations and small business firms are used in a manner to promote free competition and enterprise; to promote the commercialization and public availability of inventions made in the United States by United States industry and labor; to ensure that the Government obtains sufficient rights in federally supported inventions to meet the needs of the Government and protect the public against nonuse or unreasonable use of inventions; and to minimize the costs of administering policies in this area.

(Added Dec. 12, 1980, Public Law 96-517, sec. 6(a), 94 Stat. 3018.)

35 U.S.C. 201   Definitions.

As used in this chapter —

(a)   The term "Federal agency" means any executive agency as defined in section 105 of title 5, United States Code, and the military departments as defined by section 102 of title 5, United States Code.

(b)   The term "funding agreement" means any contract, grant, or cooperative agreement entered into between any Federal agency, other than the Tennessee Valley Authority, and any contractor for the performance of experimental, developmental, or research work funded in whole or in part by the Federal Government. Such term includes any assignment, substitution of parties, or subcontract of any type entered into for the performance of experimental, developmental, or research work under a funding agreement as herein defined.

(c)   The term "contractor" means any person, small business firm, or nonprofit organization that is a party to a funding agreement.

(d)   The term "invention" means any invention or discovery which is or may be patentable or otherwise pro-

MANUAL OF PATENT EXAMINING PROCEDURE

tectable under this title or any novel variety of plant which is or may be protectable under the Plant Variety Protection Act (7 U.S.C. 2321, et seq.).

(e) The term "subject invention" means any invention of the contractor conceived or first actually reduced to practice in the performance of work under a funding agreement: *Provided,* That in the case of a variety of plant, the date of determination (as defined in section 41(d) of the Plant Variety Protection Act (7 U.S.C. 2401(d)) must also occur during the period of contract performance.

(f) The term "practical application" means to manufacture in the case of a composition or product, to practice in the case of a process or method, or to operate in the case of a machine or system; and, in each case, under such conditions as to establish that the invention is being utilized and that its benefits are to the extent permitted by law or Government regulations available to the public on reasonable terms.

(g) The term "made" when used in relation to any invention means the conception or first actual reduction to practice of such invention.

(h) The term "small business firm" means a small business concern as defined at section 2 of Public Law 85-536 (15 U.S.C. 632) and implementing regulations of the Administrator of the Small Business Administration.

(i) The term "nonprofit organization" means universities and other institutions of higher education or an organization of the type described in section 501(c)(3) of the Internal Revenue Code of 1986 (26 U.S.C. 501(c)) and exempt from taxation under section 501(a) of the Internal Revenue Code (26 U.S.C. 501(a)) or any nonprofit scientific or educational organization qualified under a State nonprofit organization statute.

(Subsection (i) added Dec. 12, 1980, Public Law 96-517, sec. 6(a), 94 Stat. 3019.)

(Subsection (d) amended Nov. 8, 1984, Public Law 98-620, sec. 501(1), 98 Stat. 3364.)

(Subsection (e) amended Nov. 8, 1984, Public Law 98-620, sec. 501(2), 98 Stat. 3364.)

(Subsection (i) amended Oct. 22, 1986, Public Law 99-514, sec. 2, 100 Stat. 2095.)

35 U.S.C. 202 Disposition of rights.

(a) Each nonprofit organization or small business firm may, within a reasonable time after disclosure as required by paragraph (c)(1) of this section, elect to retain title to any subject invention: *Provided, however,* That a funding agreement may provide otherwise (i) when the contractor is not located in the United States or does not have a place of business located in the United States or is subject to the control of a foreign government, (ii) in exceptional circumstances when it is determined by the agency

that restriction or elimination of the right to retain title to any subject invention will better promote the policy and objectives of this chapter, (iii) when it is determined by a Government authority which is authorized by statute or Executive order to conduct foreign intelligence or counter-intelligence activities that the restriction or elimination of the right to retain title to any subject invention is necessary to protect the security of such activities, or (iv) when the funding agreement includes the operation of a Government-owned, contractor-operated facility of the Department of Energy primarily dedicated to that Department's naval nuclear propulsion or weapons related programs and all funding agreement limitations under this subparagraph on the contractor's right to elect title to a subject invention are limited to inventions occurring under the above two programs of the Department of Energy. The rights of the nonprofit organization or small business firm shall be subject to the provisions of paragraph (c) of this section and the other provisions of this chapter.

(b)(1) The rights of the Government under subsection (a) shall not be exercised by a Federal agency unless it first determines that at least one of the conditions identified in clauses (i) through (iii) of subsection (a) exists. Except in the case of subsection (a)(iii), the agency shall file with the Secretary of Commerce, within thirty days after the award of the applicable funding agreement, a copy of such determination. In the case of a determination under subsection (a)(ii), the statement shall include an analysis justifying the determination. In the case of determinations applicable to funding agreements with small business firms, copies shall also be sent to the Chief Counsel for Advocacy of the Small Business Administration. If the Secretary of Commerce believes that any individual determination or pattern of determinations is contrary to the policies and objectives of this chapter or otherwise not in conformance with this chapter, the Secretary shall so advise the head of the agency concerned and the Administrator of the Office of Federal Procurement Policy, and recommend corrective actions.

(2) Whenever the Administrator of the Office of Federal Procurement Policy has determined that one or more Federal agencies are utilizing the authority of clause (i) or (ii) of subsection (a) of this section in a manner that is contrary to the policies and objectives of this chapter the Administrator is authorized to issue regulations describing classes of situations in which agencies may not exercise the authorities of those clauses.

(3) At least once every 5 years, the Comptroller General shall transmit a report to the Committees on the Judiciary of the Senate and House of Representatives on the manner in which this chapter is being implemented by the agencies and on such other aspects of Government patent policies and practices with respect to federally

PATENT LAWS

funded inventions as the Comptroller General believes appropriate.

(4)   If the contractor believes that a determination is contrary to the policies and objectives of this chapter or constitutes an abuse of discretion by the agency, the determination shall be subject to the last paragraph of section 203(2).

(c)   Each funding agreement with a small business firm or nonprofit organization shall contain appropriate provisions to effectuate the following:

(1)   That the contractor disclose each subject invention to the Federal agency within a reasonable time after it becomes known to contractor personnel responsible for the administration of patent matters, and that the Federal Government may receive title to any subject invention not disclosed to it within such time.

(2)   That the contractor make a written election within two years after disclosure to the Federal agency (or such additional time as may be approved by the Federal agency) whether the contractor will retain title to a subject invention: *Provided*, That in any case where publication, on sale, or public use, has initiated the one year statutory period in which valid patent protection can still be obtained in the United States, the period for election may be shortened by the Federal agency to a date that is not more than sixty days prior to the end of the statutory period: And *provided further*, That the Federal Government may receive title to any subject invention in which the contractor does not elect to retain rights or fails to elect rights within such times.

(3)   That a contractor electing rights in a subject invention agrees to file a patent application prior to any statutory bar date that may occur under this title due to publication, on sale, or public use, and shall thereafter file corresponding patent applications in other countries in which it wishes to retain title within reasonable times, and that the Federal Government may receive title to any subject inventions in the United States or other countries in which the contractor has not filed patent applications on the subject invention within such times.

(4)   With respect to any invention in which the contractor elects rights, the Federal agency shall have a nonexclusive, nontransferable, irrevocable, paid-up license to practice or have practiced for or on behalf of the United States any subject invention throughout the world: *Provided*, That the funding agreement may provide for such additional rights; including the right to assign or have assigned foreign patent rights in the subject invention, as are determined by the agency as necessary for meeting the obligations of the United States under any treaty, international agreement, arrangement of cooperation, memorandum of understanding, or similar arrangement, including

military agreements relating to weapons development and production.

(5)   The right of the Federal agency to require periodic reporting on the utilization or efforts at obtaining utilization that are being made by the contractor or his licensees or assignees: *Provided*, That any such information, as well as any information on utilization or efforts at obtaining utilization obtained as part of a proceeding under section 203 of this chapter shall be treated by the Federal agency as commercial and financial information obtained from a person and privileged and confidential and not subject to disclosure under section 552 of title 5 of the United States Code.

(6)   An obligation on the part of the contractor, in the event a United States patent application is filed by or on its behalf or by any assignee of the contractor, to include within the specification of such application and any patent issuing thereon, a statement specifying that the invention was made with Government support and that the Government has certain rights in the invention.

(7)   In the case of a nonprofit organization, (A) a prohibition upon the assignment of rights to a subject invention in the United States without the approval of the Federal agency, except where such assignment is made to an organization which has as one of its primary functions the management of inventions (provided that such assignee shall be subject to the same provisions as the contractor); (B) a requirement that the contractor share royalties with the inventor; (C) except with respect to a funding agreement for the operation of a Government-owned-contractor-operated facility, a requirement that the balance of any royalties or income earned by the contractor with respect to subject inventions, after payment of expenses (including payments to inventors) incidental to the administration of subject inventions, be utilized for the support of scientific research, or education; (D) a requirement that, except where it proves infeasible after a reasonable inquiry, in the licensing of subject inventions shall be given to small business firms; and (E) with respect to a funding agreement for the operation of a Government-owned-contractor-operator facility, requirements (i) that after payment of patenting costs, licensing costs, payments to inventors, and other expenses incidental to the administration of subject inventions, 100 percent of the balance of any royalties or income earned and retained by the contractor during any fiscal year, up to an amount equal to 5 percent of the annual budget of the facility, shall be used by the contractor for scientific research, development, and education consistent with the research and development mission and objectives of the facility, including activities that increase the licensing potential of other inventions of the facility provided that if said balance exceeds 5 percent of the annual budget of the

MANUAL OF PATENT EXAMINING PROCEDURE

facility, that 75 percent of such excess shall be paid to the Treasury of the United States and the remaining 25 percent shall be used for the same purposes as described above in this clause (D); and (ii) that, to the extent it provides the most effective technology transfer, the licensing of subject inventions shall be administered by contractor employees on location at the facility.

(8)   The requirements of sections 203 and 204 of this chapter.

(d)   If a contractor does not elect to retain title to a subject invention in cases subject to this section, the Federal agency may consider and after consultation with the contractor grant requests for retention of rights by the inventor subject to the provisions of this Act and regulations promulgated hereunder.

(e)   In any case when a Federal employee is a coinventor of any invention made under a funding agreement with a nonprofit organization or small business firm, the Federal agency employing such coinventor is authorized to transfer or assign whatever rights it may acquire in the subject invention from its employee to the contractor subject to the conditions set forth in this chapter.

(f)(1)   No funding agreement with a small business firm or nonprofit organization shall contain a provision allowing a Federal agency to require the licensing to third parties of inventions owned by the contractor that are not subject inventions unless such provision has been approved by the head of the agency and a written justification has been signed by the head of the agency. Any such provision shall clearly state whether the licensing may be required in connection with the practice of a subject invention, a specifically identified work object, or both. The head of the agency may not delegate the authority to approve provisions or sign justifications required by this paragraph.

(2)   A Federal agency shall not require the licensing of third parties under any such provision unless the head of the agency determines that the use of the invention by others is necessary for the practice of a subject invention or for the use of a work object of the funding agreement and that such action is necessary to achieve the practical application of the subject invention or work object. Any such determination shall be on the record after an opportunity for an agency hearing. Any action commenced for judicial review of such determination shall be brought within sixty days after notification of such determination.

(Subsection (f)(2) added Dec. 12, 1980, Public Law 96-517, sec. 6(a), 94 Stat. 3020.)

(Subsection (a) amended Nov. 8, 1984, Public Law 98-620, sec. 501(3), 98 Stat. 3364.)

(Subsection (b)(1) and (b)(2) amended Nov. 8, 1984, Public Law 98-620, sec. 501(4), 98 Stat. 3365.)

(Subsection (b)(4) added Nov. 8, 1984, Public Law 98-620, sec. 501(4A), 98 Stat. 3365.)

(Subsection (c)(4) amended Nov. 8, 1984, Public Law 98-620, sec. 501(5), 98 Stat. 3365.)

(Subsection (c)(5) amended Nov. 8, 1984, Public Law 98-620, sec. 501(6), 98 Stat. 3365.)

(Subsection (c)(7) amended Nov. 8, 1984, Public Law 98-620, sec. 501(7), (8), 98 Stat. 3366.)

(Subsection (b)(3) amended Dec. 10, 1991, Public Law 102-204, sec. 10, 105 Stat. 1641.)

35 U.S.C. 203   March-in rights.

(1)   With respect to any subject invention in which a small business firm or nonprofit organization has acquired title under this chapter, the Federal agency under whose funding agreement the subject invention was made shall have the right, in accordance with such procedures as are provided in regulations promulgated hereunder, to require the contractor, an assignee, or exclusive licensee of a subject invention to grant a nonexclusive, partially exclusive, or exclusive license in any field of use to a responsible applicant or applicants, upon terms that are reasonable under the circumstances, and if the contractor, assignee, or exclusive licensee refuses such request, to grant such a license itself, if the Federal agency determines that such —

(a)   action is necessary because the contractor or assignee has not taken, or is not expected to take within a reasonable time, effective steps to achieve practical application of the subject invention in such field of use;

(b)   action is necessary to alleviate health or safety needs which are not reasonably satisfied by the contractor, assignee, or their licensees;

(c)   action is necessary to meet requirements for public use specified by Federal regulations and such requirements are not reasonably satisfied by the contractor, assignee, or licensees; or

(d)   action is necessary because the agreement required by section 204 has not been obtained or waived or because a licensee of the exclusive right to use or sell any subject invention in the United States is in breach of its agreement obtained pursuant to section 204.

(2)   A determination pursuant to this section or section 202(b)(4) shall not be subject to the Contract Disputes Act (41 U.S.C. § 601 et seq.). An administrative appeals procedure shall be established by regulations promulgated in accordance with section 206. Additionally, any contractor, inventor, assignee, or exclusive licensee adversely affected by a determination under this section may, at any time within sixty days after the determination is issued, file a petition in the United States Court of Federal Claims, which shall have jurisdiction to determine the appeal on the record and to affirm, reverse, remand or modify, as appro-

PATENT LAWS

priate, the determination of the Federal agency. In cases described in paragraphs (a) and (c), the agency's determination shall be held in abeyance pending the exhaustion of appeals or petitions filed under the preceding sentence.

(Added Dec. 12, 1980, Public Law 96-517, sec. 6(a), 94 Stat. 3022; amended Nov. 8, 1984, Public Law 98-620, sec. 501(9), 98 Stat. 3367; Oct. 29, 1992, Public Law 102-572, sec. 902(b)(1), 106 Stat. 4516.)

35 U.S.C. 204   Preference for United States industry.

Notwithstanding any other provision of this chapter, no small business firm or nonprofit organization which receives title to any subject invention and no assignee of any such small business firm or nonprofit organization shall grant to any person the exclusive right to use or sell any subject invention in the United States unless such person agrees that any products embodying the subject invention or produced through the use of the subject invention will be manufactured substantially in the United States. However, in individual cases, the requirement for such an agreement may be waived by the Federal agency under whose funding agreement the invention was made upon a showing by the small business firm, nonprofit organization, or assignee that reasonable but unsuccessful efforts have been made to grant licenses on similar terms to potential licensees that would be likely to manufacture substantially in the United States or that under the circumstances domestic manufacture is not commercially feasible.

(Added Dec. 12, 1980, Public Law 96-517, sec. 6(a), 94 Stat. 3023.)

35 U.S.C. 205   Confidentiality.

Federal agencies are authorized to withhold from disclosure to the public information disclosing any invention in which the Federal Government owns or may own a right, title, or interest (including a nonexclusive license) for a reasonable time in order for a patent application to be filed. Furthermore, Federal agencies shall not be required to release copies of any document which is part of an application for patent filed with the United States Patent and Trademark Office or with any foreign patent office.

(Added Dec. 12, 1980, Public Law 96-517, sec. 6(a), 94 Stat. 3023.)

35 U.S.C. 206   Uniform clauses and regulations.

The Secretary of Commerce may issue regulations which may be made applicable to Federal agencies implementing the provisions of sections 202 through 204 of this chapter and shall establish standard funding agreement provisions required under this chapter. The regulations and the standard funding agreement shall be subject to public comment before their issuance.

(Added Dec. 12, 1980, Public Law 96-517, sec. 6(a), 94 Stat. 3023; amended Nov. 8, 1984, Public Law 98-620, sec. 501(10), 98 Stat. 3367.)

35 U.S.C. 207   Domestic and foreign protection of federally owned inventions.

(a)   Each Federal agency is authorized to —

(1)   apply for, obtain, and maintain patents or other forms of protection in the United States and in foreign countries on inventions in which the Federal Government owns a right, title, or interest;

(2)   grant nonexclusive, exclusive, or partially exclusive licenses under federally owned patent applications, patents, or other forms of protection obtained, royalty-free or for royalties or other consideration, and on such terms and conditions, including the grant to the licensee of the right of enforcement pursuant to the provisions of chapter 29 of this title as determined appropriate in the public interest;

(3)   undertake all other suitable and necessary steps to protect and administer rights to federally owned inventions on behalf of the Federal Government either directly or through contract; and

(4)   transfer custody and administration, in whole or in part, to another Federal agency, of the right, title, or interest in any federally owned invention.

(b)   For the purpose of assuring the effective management of Government-owned inventions, the Secretary of Commerce authorized to -

(1)   assist Federal agency efforts to promote the licensing and utilization of Government-owned inventions;

(2)   assist Federal agencies in seeking protection and maintaining inventions in foreign countries, including the payment of fees and costs connected therewith; and

(3)   consult with and advise Federal agencies as to areas of science and technology research and development with potential for commercial utilization.

(Added Dec. 12, 1980, Public Law 96-517, sec. 6(a), 94 Stat. 3023; amended Nov. 8, 1984, Public Law 98-620, sec. 501(11), 98 Stat. 3367.)

35 U.S.C. 208   Regulations governing Federal licensing.

The Secretary of Commerce is authorized to promulgate regulations specifying the terms and conditions upon which any federally owned invention, other than inventions owned by the Tennessee Valley Authority, may be licensed on a nonexclusive, partially exclusive, or exclusive basis.

(Added Dec. 12, 1980, Public Law 96-517, sec. 6(a), 94 Stat. 3024; amended Nov. 8, 1984, Public Law 98-620, sec. 501(12), 98 Stat. 3367.)

35 U.S.C. 209   Restrictions on licensing of federally owned inventions.

MANUAL OF PATENT EXAMINING PROCEDURE

(a)   No Federal agency shall grant any license under a patent or patent application on a federally owned invention unless the person requesting the license has supplied the agency with a plan for development and/or marketing of the invention, except that any such plan may be treated by the Federal agency as commercial and financial information obtained from a person and privileged and confidential and not subject to disclosure under section 552 of title 5 of the United States Code.

(b)   A Federal agency shall normally grant the right to use or sell any federally owned invention in the United States only to a licensee that agrees that any products embodying the invention or produced through the use of the invention will be manufactured substantially in the United States.

(c)(1) Each Federal agency may grant exclusive or partially exclusive licenses in any invention covered by a federally owned domestic patent or patent application only if, after public notice and opportunity for filing written objections, it is determined that —

(A)   the interests of the Federal Government and the public will best be served by the proposed license, in view of the applicant's intentions, plans, and ability to bring the invention to practical application or otherwise promote the invention's utilization by the public;

(B)   the desired practical application has not been achieved, or is not likely expeditiously to be achieved, under any nonexclusive license which has been granted, or which may be granted, on the invention;

(C)   exclusive or partially exclusive licensing is a reasonable and necessary incentive to call forth the investment of risk capital and expenditures to bring the invention to practical application or otherwise promote the invention's utilization by the public; and

(D)   the proposed terms and scope of exclusivity are not greater than reasonably necessary to provide the incentive for bringing the invention to practical application or otherwise promote the invention's utilization by the public.

(2)   A Federal agency shall not grant such exclusive or partially exclusive license under paragraph (1) of this subsection if it determines that the grant of such license will tend substantially to lessen competition or result in undue concentration in any section of the country in any line of commerce to which the technology to be licensed relates, or to create or maintain other situations inconsistent with the antitrust laws.

(3)   First preference in the exclusive or partially exclusive licensing of federally owned inventions shall go to small business firms submitting plans that are determined by the agency to be within the capabilities of the firms and equally likely, if executed, to bring the invention

to practical application as any plans submitted by applicants that are not small business firms.

(d)   After consideration of whether the interests of the Federal Government or United States industry in foreign commerce will be enhanced, any Federal agency may grant exclusive or partially exclusive licenses in any invention covered by a foreign patent application or patent, after public notice and opportunity for filing written objections, except that a Federal agency shall not grant such exclusive or partially exclusive license if it determines that the grant of such license will tend substantially to lessen competition or result in undue concentration in any section of the United States in any line of commerce to which the technology to be licensed relates, or to create or maintain other situations inconsistent with antitrust laws.

(e)   The Federal agency shall maintain a record of determinations to grant exclusive or partially exclusive licenses.

(f)   Any grant of a license shall contain such terms and conditions as the Federal agency determines appropriate for the protection of the interests of the Federal Government and the public, including provisions for the following:

(1)   periodic reporting on the utilization or efforts at obtaining utilization that are being made by the licensee with particular reference to the plan submitted: *Provided,* That any such information may be treated by the Federal agency as commercial and financial information obtained from a person and privileged and confidential and not subject to disclosure under section 552 of title 5 of the United States Code;

(2)   the right of the Federal agency to terminate such license in whole or in part if it determines that the licensee is not executing the plan submitted with its request for a license and the licensee cannot otherwise demonstrate to the satisfaction of the Federal agency that it has taken or can be expected to take within a reasonable time, effective steps to achieve practical application of the invention;

(3)   the right of the Federal agency to terminate such license in whole or in part if the licensee is in breach of an agreement obtained pursuant to paragraph (b) of this section; and

(4)   the right of the Federal agency to terminate the license in whole or in part if the agency determines that such action is necessary to meet requirements for public use specified by Federal regulations issued after the date of the license and such requirements are not reasonably satisfied by the licensee.

(Added Dec. 12, 1980, Public Law 96-517, sec. 6(a), 94 Stat. 3024.)

35 U.S.C. 210   Precedence of chapter.

(a)   This chapter shall take precedence over any other Act which would require a disposition of rights in

PATENT LAWS

subject inventions of small business firms or nonprofit organizations contractors in a manner that is inconsistent with this chapter, including but not necessarily limited to the following:

(1) section 10(a) of the Act of June 29, 1935, as added by title I of the Act of August 14, 1946 (7 U.S.C. 427i(a); 60 Stat. 1085);

(2) section 205(a) of the Act of August 14, 1946 (7 U.S.C. 1624(a); 60 Stat. 1090);

(3) section 501(c) of the Federal Mine Safety and Health Act of 1977 (30 U.S.C. 951(c); 83 Stat. 742);

(4) section 30168(e) of title 49;

(5) section 12 of the National Science Foundation Act of 1950 (42 U.S.C. 1871(a); 82 Stat. 360);

(6) section 152 of the Atomic Energy Act of 1954 (42 U.S.C. 2182; 68 Stat. 943);

(7) section 305 of the National Aeronautics and Space Act of 1958 (42 U.S.C. 2457);

(8) section 6 of the Coal Research Development Act of 1960 (30 U.S.C. 666; 74 Stat. 337);

(9) section 4 of the Helium Act Amendments of 1960 (50 U.S.C. 167b; 74 Stat. 920);

(10) section 32 of the Arms Control and Disarmament Act of 1961 (22 U.S.C. 2572; 75 Stat. 634);

(11) subsection (e) of section 302 of the Appalachian Regional Development Act of 1965 (40 U.S.C. App. 302(e); 79 Stat. 5);

(12) section 9 of the Federal Nonnuclear Energy Research and Development Act of 1974 (42 U.S.C. 5901; 88 Stat. 1878);

(13) section 5(d) of the Consumer Product Safety Act (15 U.S.C. 2054(d); 86 Stat. 1211);

(14) section 3 of the Act of April 5, 1944 (30 U.S.C. 323; 58 Stat. 191);

(15) section 8001(c)(3) of the Solid Waste Disposal Act (42 U.S.C. 6981(c); 90 Stat. 2829);

(16) section 219 of the Foreign Assistance Act of 1961 (22 U.S.C. 2179; 83 Stat. 806);

(17) section 427(b) of the Federal Mine Health and Safety Act of 1977 (30 U.S.C. 937(b); 86 Stat. 155);

(18) section 306(d) of the Surface Mining and Reclamation Act of 1977 (30 U.S.C. 1226(d); 91 Stat. 455);

(19) section 21(d) of the Federal Fire Prevention and Control Act of 1974 (15 U.S.C. 2218(d); 88 Stat. 1548);

(20) section 6(b) of the Solar Photovoltaic Energy Research Development and Demonstration Act of 1978 (42 U.S.C. 5585(b); 92 Stat. 2516);

(21) section 12 of the Native Latex Commer cialization and Economic Development Act of 1978 (7 U.S.C. 178(j); 92 Stat. 2533); and

(22) section 408 of the Water Resources and Development Act of 1978 (42 U.S.C. 7879; 92 Stat. 1360).

The Act creating this chapter shall be construed to take precedence over any future Act unless that Act specifically cites this Act and provides that it shall take precedence over this Act.

(b) Nothing in this chapter is intended to alter the effect of the laws cited in paragraph (a) of this section or any other laws with respect to the disposition of rights in inventions made in the performance of funding agreements with persons other than nonprofit organizations or small business firms.

(c) Nothing in this chapter is intended to limit the authority of agencies to agree to the disposition of rights in inventions made in the performance of funding agreements with persons other than nonprofit organizations or small business firms in accordance with the Statement of Government Patent Policy issued on February 18, 1983, agency regulations, or other applicable regulations or to otherwise limit the authority of agencies to allow such persons to retain ownership of inventions, except that all funding agreements, including those with other than small business firms and nonprofit organizations, shall include the requirements established in paragraph 202(c)(4) and section 203 of this title. Any disposition of rights in inventions made in accordance with the Statement or implementing regulations, including any disposition occurring before enactment of this section, are hereby authorized.

(d) Nothing in this chapter shall be construed to require the disclosure of intelligence sources or methods or to otherwise affect the authority granted to the Director of Central Intelligence by statute or Executive order for the protection of intelligence sources or methods.

(e) The provisions of the Stevenson-Wydler Technology Innovation Act of 1980 shall take precedence over the provisions of this chapter to the extent that they permit or require a disposition of rights in subject inventions which is inconsistent with this chapter.

(Added Dec. 12, 1980, Public Law 96-517, sec. 6(a), 94 Stat. 3026.)

(Subsection (c) amended Nov. 8, 1984, Public Law 98-620, sec. 501(13), 98 Stat. 3367.)

(Subsection (e) added Oct. 20, 1986, Public Law 99-502, sec. 9(c), 100 Stat. 1796.)

(Subsection (a)(4) amended July 5, 1994, Public Law 103-272, sec. 5(j), 108 Stat. 1375.)

(Subsection (e) amended Mar. 7, 1996, Public Law 104-113, sec. 7, 110 Stat. 779.)

35 U.S.C. 211   Relationship to antitrust laws.

MANUAL OF PATENT EXAMINING PROCEDURE

Nothing in this chapter shall be deemed to convey to any person immunity from civil or criminal liability, or to create any defenses to actions, under any antitrust law.

(Added Dec.12, 1980, Public Law 96-517, sec. 6(a), 94 Stat. 3027.)

35 U.S.C. 212   Disposition of rights in educational awards.

No scholarship, fellowship, training grant, or other funding agreement made by a Federal agency primarily to an awardee for educational purposes will contain any provision giving the Federal agency any rights to inventions made by the awardee.

(Added Nov. 8, 1984, Public Law 98-620, sec. 501(14), 98 Stat. 3368.)

PART III — PATENTS AND PROTECTION OF PATENT RIGHTS

CHAPTER 25 — AMENDMENT AND CORRECTION OF PATENTS

35 U.S.C. 251   Reissue of defective patents.

Whenever any patent is, through error without any deceptive intention, deemed wholly or partly inoperative or invalid, by reason of a defective specification or drawing, or by reason of the patentee claiming more or less then he had a right to claim in the patent, the Commissioner shall, on the surrender of such patent and the payment of the fee required by law, reissue the patent for the invention disclosed in the original patent, and in accordance with a new and amended application, for the unexpired part of the term of the original patent. No new matter shall be introduced into the application for reissue.

The Commissioner may issue several reissued patents for distinct and separate parts of the thing patented, upon demand of the applicant, and upon payment of the required fee for a reissue for each of such reissued patents.

The provisions of this title relating to applications for patent shall be applicable to applications for reissue of a patent, except that application for reissue may be made and sworn to by the assignee of the entire interest if the application does not seek to enlarge the scope of the claims of the original patent.

No reissued patent shall be granted enlarging the scope of the claims of the original patent unless applied for within two years from the grant of the original patent.

35 U.S.C. 252   Effect of reissue.

The surrender of the original patent shall take effect upon the issue of the reissued patent, and every reissued patent shall have the same effect and operation in law, on the trial of actions for causes thereafter arising, as if the same had been originally granted in such amended form, but in so far as the claims of the original and reissued patents are identical, such surrender shall not affect any action then pending nor abate any cause of action then existing, and the reissued patent, to the extent that its claims are identical with the original patent, shall constitute a continuation thereof and have effect continuously from the date of the original patent.

A reissued patent shall not abridge or affect the right of any person or that person's successors in business who, prior to the grant of a reissue, made, purchased, offered to sell, or used within the United States, or imported into the United States, anything patented by the reissued patent, to continue the use of, to offer to sell, or to sell to others to be used, offered for sale, or sold, the specific thing so made, purchased, offered for sale, used, or imported unless the making, using, offering for sale, or selling of such thing infringes a valid claim of the reissued patent which was in the original patent. The court before which such matter is in question may provide for the continued manufacture, use, offer for sale, or sale of the thing made, purchased, offered for sale, used, or imported as specified, or for the manufacture, use, offer for sale, or sale in the United States of which substantial preparation was made before the grant of the reissue, and the court may also provide for the continued practice of any process patented by the reissue that is practiced, or for the practice of which substantial preparation was made, before the grant of the reissue, to the extent and under such terms as the court deems equitable for the protection of investments made or business commenced before the grant of the reissue.

(Amended Dec. 8, 1994, Public Law 103-465, sec. 533(b)(2), 108 Stat. 4989.)

35 U.S.C. 253   Disclaimer.

Whenever, without any deceptive intention, a claim of a patent is invalid the remaining claims shall not thereby be rendered invalid. A patentee, whether of the whole or any sectional interest therein, may, on payment of the fee required by law, make disclaimer of any complete claim, stating therein the extent of his interest in such patent. Such disclaimer shall be in writing and recorded in the Patent and Trademark Office, and it shall thereafter be considered as part of the original patent to the extent of the interest

PATENT LAWS

possessed by the disclaimant and by those claiming under him.

In like manner any patentee or applicant may disclaim or dedicate to the public the entire term, or any terminal part of the term, of the patent granted or to be granted.

(Amended Jan. 2, 1975, Public Law 93-596, sec. 1, 88 Stat. 1949.)

35 U.S.C. 254   Certificate of correction of Patent and Trademark Office mistake.

Whenever a mistake in a patent, incurred through the fault of the Patent and Trademark Office, is clearly disclosed by the records of the Office, the Commissioner may issue a certificate of correction stating the fact and nature of such mistake, under seal, without charge, to be recorded in the records of patents. A printed copy thereof shall be attached to each printed copy of the patent, and such certificate shall be considered as part of the original patent. Every such patent, together with such certificate, shall have the same effect and operation in law on the trial of actions for causes thereafter arising as if the same had been originally issued in such corrected form. The Commissioner may issue a corrected patent without charge in lieu of and with like effect as a certificate of correction.

(Amended Jan. 2, 1975, Public Law 93-596, sec. 1, 88 Stat. 1949.)

35 U.S.C. 255   Certificate of correction of applicant's mistake.

Whenever a mistake of a clerical or typographical nature, or of minor character, which was not the fault of the Patent and Trademark Office, appears in a patent and a showing has been made that such mistake occurred in good faith, the Commissioner may, upon payment of the required fee, issue a certificate of correction, if the correction does not involve such changes in the patent as would constitute new matter or would require reexamination. Such patent, together with the certificate, shall have the same effect and operation in law on the trial of actions for causes thereafter arising as if the same had been originally issued in such corrected form.

(Amended Jan. 2, 1975, Public Law 93-596, sec. 1, 88 Stat. 1949.)

35 U.S.C. 256   Correction of named inventor.

Whenever through error a person is named in an issued patent as the inventor, or through error an inventor is not named in an issued patent and such error arose without any deceptive intention on his part, the Commissioner may, on application of all the parties and assignees, with proof of the facts and such other requirements as may be imposed, issue a certificate correcting such error.

The error of omitting inventors or naming persons who are not inventors shall not invalidate the patent in which such error occurred if it can be corrected as provided in this section. The court before which such matter is called in question may order correction of the patent on notice and hearing of all parties concerned and the Commissioner shall issue a certificate accordingly.

(Amended Aug. 27, 1982, Public Law 97-247, sec. 6(b), 96 Stat. 320.)

CHAPTER 26 — OWNERSHIP AND ASSIGNMENT

Sec.
261   Ownership; assignment.
262   Joint owners.

35 U.S.C. 261   Ownership; assignment.

Subject to the provisions of this title, patents shall have the attributes of personal property.

Applications for patent, patents, or any interest therein, shall be assignable in law by an instrument in writing. The applicant, patentee, or his assigns or legal representatives may in like manner grant and convey an exclusive right under his application for patent, or patents, to the whole or any specified part of the United States.

A certificate of acknowledgment under the hand and official seal of a person authorized to administer oaths within the United States, or, in a foreign country, of a diplomatic or consular officer of the United States or an officer authorized to administer oaths whose authority is proved by a certificate of a diplomatic or consular officer of the United States, or apostille of an official designated by a foreign country which, by treaty or convention, accords like effect to apostilles of designated officials in the United States, shall be *prima facie* evidence of the execution of an assignment, grant, or conveyance of a patent or application for patent.

An assignment, grant, or conveyance shall be void as against any subsequent purchaser or mortgagee for a valuable consideration, without notice, unless it is recorded in the Patent and Trademark Office within three months from its date or prior to the date of such subsequent purchase or mortgage.

(Amended Jan. 2, 1975, Public Law 93-596, sec. 1, 88 Stat. 1949; Aug. 27, 1982, Public Law 97-247, sec. 14(b), 96 Stat. 321.)

35 U.S.C. 262   Joint owners.

In the absence of any agreement to the contrary, each of the joint owners of a patent may make, use, offer to sell, or sell the patented invention within the United States, or import the patented invention into the United States, with-

MANUAL OF PATENT EXAMINING PROCEDURE

out the consent of and without accounting to the other owners.

(Amended Dec. 8, 1994, Public Law 103-465 sec. 533(b)(3), 108 Stat. 4989.)

CHAPTER 27 — GOVERNMENT INTERESTS IN PATENTS

Sec.
266 [Repealed.]
267 Time for taking action in Government applications.

35 U.S.C. 266 [Repealed.]

(Repealed July 24, 1965, Public Law 89-83, sec. 8, 79 Stat. 261.)

35 U.S.C. 267 Time for taking action in Government applications.

Notwithstanding the provisions of sections 133 and 151 of this title, the Commissioner may extend the time for taking any action to three years, when an application has become the property of the United States and the head of the appropriate department or agency of the Government has certified to the Commissioner that the invention disclosed therein is important to the armament or defense of the United States.

CHAPTER 28 — INFRINGEMENT OF PATENTS

Sec.
271 Infringement of patent.
272 Temporary presence in the United States.
273 Defense to infringement based on earlier inventor.

35 U.S.C. 271 Infringement of patent.

(a) Except as otherwise provided in this title, whoever without authority makes, uses, offers to sell, or sells any patented invention, within the United States, or imports into the United States any patented invention during the term of the patent therefor, infringes the patent.

(b) Whoever actively induces infringement of a patent shall be liable as an infringer.

(c) Whoever offers to sell or sells within the United States or imports into the United States a component of a patented machine, manufacture, combination, or composition, or a material or apparatus for use in practicing a patented process, constituting a material part of the invention, knowing the same to be especially made or especially adapted for use in an infringement of such patent, and not a staple article or commodity of commerce suitable for substantial noninfringing use, shall be liable as a contributory infringer.

(d) No patent owner otherwise entitled to relief for infringement or contributory infringement of a patent shall be denied relief or deemed guilty of misuse or illegal exten-

sion of the patent right by reason of his having done one or more of the following: (1) derived revenue from acts which if performed by another without his consent would constitute contributory infringement of the patent; (2) licensed or authorized another to perform acts which if performed without his consent would constitute contributory infringement of the patent; (3) sought to enforce his patent rights against infringement or contributory infringement; (4) refused to license or use any rights to the patent; or (5) conditioned the license of any rights to the patent or the sale of the patented product on the acquisition of a license to rights in another patent or purchase of a separate product, unless, in view of the circumstances, the patent owner has market power in the relevant market for the patent or patented product on which the license or sale is conditioned.

(e)(1) It shall not be an act of infringement to make, use, offer to sell, or sell within the United States or import into the United States a patented invention (other than a new animal drug or veterinary biological product (as those terms are used in the Federal Food, Drug, and Cosmetic Act and the Act of March 4, 1913) which is primarily manufactured using recombinant DNA, recombinant RNA, hybridoma technology, or other processes involving site specific genetic manipulation techniques) solely for uses reasonably related to the development and submission of information under a Federal law which regulates the manufacture, use, or sale of drugs or veterinary biological products.

(2) It shall be an act of infringement to submit -

(A) an application under section 505(j) of the Federal Food, Drug, and Cosmetic Act or described in section 505(b)(2) of such Act for a drug claimed in a patent or the use of which is claimed in a patent, or

(B) an application under section 512 of such Act or under the Act of March 4, 1913 (21 U.S.C. 151 - 158) for a drug or veterinary biological product which is not primarily manufactured using recombinant DNA, recombinant RNA, hybridoma technology, or other processes involving site specific genetic manipulation techniques and which is claimed in a patent or the use of which is claimed in a patent, if the purpose of such submission is to obtain approval under such Act to engage in the commercial manufacture, use, or sale of a drug or veterinary biological product claimed in a patent or the use of which is claimed in a patent before the expiration of such patent.

(3) In any action for patent infringement brought under this section, no injunctive or other relief may be granted which would prohibit the making, using, offering to sell, or selling within the United States or importing into the United States of a patented invention under paragraph (1).

PATENT LAWS

(4) For an act of infringement described in paragraph (2)—

(A) the court shall order the effective date of any approval of the drug or veterinary biological product involved in the infringement to be a date which is not earlier than the date of the expiration of the patent which has been infringed,

(B) injunctive relief may be granted against an infringer to prevent the commercial manufacture, use, offer to sell, or sale within the United States or importation into the United States of an approved drug or veterinary biological product, and

(C) damages or other monetary relief may be awarded against an infringer only if there has been commercial manufacture, use, offer to sell, or sale within the United States or importation into the United States of an approved drug or veterinary biological product.

The remedies prescribed by subparagraphs (A), (B), and (C) are the only remedies which may be granted by a court for an act of infringement described in paragraph (2), except that a court may award attorney fees under section 285.

(f)(1) Whoever without authority supplies or causes to be supplied in or from the United States all or a substantial portion of the components of a patented invention, where such components are uncombined in whole or in part, in such manner as to actively induce the combination of such components outside of the United States in a manner that would infringe the patent if such combination occurred within the United States, shall be liable as an infringer.

(2) Whoever without authority supplies or causes to be supplied in or from the United States any component of a patented invention that is especially made or especially adapted for use in the invention and not a staple article or commodity of commerce suitable for substantial noninfringing use, where such component is uncombined in whole or in part, knowing that such component is so made or adapted and intending that such component will be combined outside of the United States in a manner that would infringe the patent if such combination occurred within the United States, shall be liable as an infringer.

(g) Whoever without authority imports into the United States or offers to sell, sells, or uses within the United States a product which is made by a process patented in the United States shall be liable as an infringer, if the importation, offer to sell, sale, or use of the product occurs during the term of such process patent. In an action for infringement of a process patent, no remedy may be granted for infringement on account of the noncommercial use or retail sale of a product unless there is no adequate remedy under this title for infringement on account of the importation or other use, offer to sell, or sale of that product. A product which is made by a patented process will, for purposes of this title, not be considered to be so made after —

(1) it is materially changed by subsequent processes; or

(2) it becomes a trivial and nonessential component of another product.

(h) As used in this section, the term "whoever" includes any State, any instrumentality of a State, any officer or employee of a State or instrumentality of a State acting in his official capacity. Any State, and any such instrumentality, officer, or employee, shall be subject to the provisions of this title in the same manner and to the same extent as any nongovernmental entity.

(i) As used in this section, an "offer for sale" or an "offer to sell" by a person other than the patentee or any assignee of the patentee, is that in which the sale will occur before the expiration of the term of the patent.

(Subsection (e) added Sept. 24, 1984, Public Law 98-417, sec. 202, 98 Stat. 1603.)

(Subsection (f) added Nov. 8, 1984, Public Law 98-622, sec. 101(a), 98 Stat. 3383.)

(Subsection (g) added Aug. 23, 1988, Public Law 100-418, sec. 9003, 102 Stat. 1564.)

(Subsection (e) amended Nov. 16, 1988, Public Law 100-670, sec. 201(i), 102 Stat. 3988.)

(Subsection (d) amended Nov. 19, 1988, Public Law 100-703, sec. 201, 102 Stat. 4676.)

(Subsection (h) added Oct. 28, 1992, Public Law 102-560, sec. 2(a)(1), 106 Stat. 4230.)

(Subsections (a), (c), (e), and (g) amended Dec. 8, 1994, Public Law 103-465, sec. 533(a), 108 Stat. 4988.)

(Subsection (i) added Dec. 8, 1994, Public Law 103-465, sec. 533(a), 108 Stat. 4988.)

35 U.S.C. 272   Temporary presence in the United States.

The use of any invention in any vessel, aircraft or vehicle of any country which affords similar privileges to vessels, aircraft, or vehicles of the United States, entering the United States temporarily or accidentally, shall not constitute infringement of any patent, if the invention is used exclusively for the needs of the vessel, aircraft, or vehicle and is not offered for sale or sold in or used for the manufacture of anything to be sold in or exported from the United States.

(Amended Dec. 8, 1994, Public Law 103-465, sec. 533(b)(4), 108 Stat. 4989.)

35 U.S.C. 273   Defense to infringement based on earlier inventor.

MANUAL OF PATENT EXAMINING PROCEDURE

(a) DEFINITIONS.— For purposes of this section—

(1) the terms "commercially used" and "commercial use" mean use of a method in the United States, so long as such use is in connection with an internal commercial use or an actual arm's-length sale or other arm's-length commercial transfer of a useful end result, whether or not the subject matter at issue is accessible to or otherwise known to the public, except that the subject matter for which commercial marketing or use is subject to a premarketing regulatory review period during which the safety or efficacy of the subject matter is established, including any period specified in section 156(g), shall be deemed " commercially used" and in " commercial use" during such regulatory review period;

(2) in the case of activities performed by a nonprofit research laboratory, or nonprofit entity such as a university, research center, or hospital, a use for which the public is the intended beneficiary shall be considered to be a use described in paragraph (1), except that the use—

(A) may be asserted as a defense under this section only for continued use by and in the laboratory or nonprofit entity; and

(B) may not be asserted as a defense with respect to any subsequent commercialization or use outside such laboratory or nonprofit entity;

(3) the term "method" means a method of doing or conducting business; and

(4) the "effective filing date" of a patent is the earlier of the actual filing date of the application for the patent or the filing date of any earlier United States, foreign, or international application to which the subject matter at issue is entitled under section 119, 120, or 365 of this title.

(b) DEFENSE TO INFRINGEMENT.—

(1) IN GENERAL.— It shall be a defense to an action for infringement under section 271 of this title with respect to any subject matter that would otherwise infringe one or more claims for a method in the patent being asserted against a person, if such person had, acting in good faith, actually reduced the subject matter to practice at least 1 year before the effective filing date of such patent, and commercially used the subject matter before the effective filing date of such patent.

(2) EXHAUSTION OF RIGHT.— The sale or other disposition of a useful end product produced by a patented method, by a person entitled to assert a defense under this section with respect to that useful end result shall exhaust the patent owner's rights under the patent to the extent such rights would have been exhausted had such sale or other disposition been made by the patent owner.

(3) LIMITATIONS AND QUALIFICATIONS OF DEFENSE.— The defense to infringement under this section is subject to the following:

(A) PATENT.— A person may not assert the defense under this section unless the invention for which the defense is asserted is for a method.

(B) DERIVATION.— A person may not assert the defense under this section if the subject matter on which the defense is based was derived from the patentee or persons in privity with the patentee.

(C) NOT A GENERAL LICENSE.— The defense asserted by a person under this section is not a general license under all claims of the patent at issue, but extends only to the specific subject matter claimed in the patent with respect to which the person can assert a defense under this chapter, except that the defense shall also extend to variations in the quantity or volume of use of the claimed subject matter, and to improvements in the claimed subject matter that do not infringe additional specifically claimed subject matter of the patent.

(4) BURDEN OF PROOF.— A person asserting the defense under this section shall have the burden of establishing the defense by clear and convincing evidence.

(5) ABANDONMENT OF USE.— A person who has abandoned commercial use of subject matter may not rely on activities performed before the date of such abandonment in establishing a defense under this section with respect to actions taken after the date of such abandonment.

(6) PERSONAL DEFENSE.— The defense under this section may be asserted only by the person who performed the acts necessary to establish the defense and, except for any transfer to the patent owner, the right to assert the defense shall not be licensed or assigned or transferred to another person except as an ancillary and subordinate part of a good faith assignment or transfer for other reasons of the entire enterprise or line of business to which the defense relates.

(7) LIMITATION ON SITES.— A defense under this section, when acquired as part of a good faith assignment or transfer of an entire enterprise or line of business to which the defense relates, may only be asserted for uses at sites where the subject matter that would otherwise infringe one or more of the claims is in use before the later of the effective filing date of the patent or the date of the assignment or transfer of such enterprise or line of business.

(8) UNSUCCESSFUL ASSERTION OF DEFENSE.— If the defense under this section is pleaded by a person who is found to infringe the patent and who subsequently fails to demonstrate a reasonable basis for asserting the defense, the court shall find the case excep-

PATENT LAWS

tional for the purpose of awarding attorney fees under section 285 of this title.

(9) INVALIDITY.— A patent shall not be deemed to be invalid under section 102 or 103 of this title solely because a defense is raised or established under this section.

(Added Nov. 29, 1999, Public Law 106-113, sec. 1000(a)(9), S. 1948 sec. 4302(a), 113 Stat. 1501.)

CHAPTER 29 — REMEDIES FOR INFRINGEMENT OF PATENT, AND OTHER ACTIONS

35 U.S.C. 281 Remedy for infringement of patent.

A patentee shall have remedy by civil action for infringement of his patent.

35 U.S.C. 282 Presumption of validity; defenses.

A patent shall be presumed valid. Each claim of a patent (whether in independent, dependent, or multiple dependent form) shall be presumed valid independently of the validity of other claims; dependent or multiple dependent claims shall be presumed valid even though dependent upon an invalid claim. Notwithstanding the preceding sentence, if a claim to a composition of matter is held invalid and that claim was the basis of a determination of nonobviousness under section 103(b)(1), the process shall no longer be considered nonobvious solely on the basis of section 103(b)(1). The burden of establishing invalidity of a patent or any claim thereof shall rest on the party asserting such invalidity.

The following shall be defenses in any action involving the validity or infringement of a patent and shall be pleaded:

(1) Noninfringement, absence of liability for infringement, or unenforceability,

(2) Invalidity of the patent or any claim in suit on any ground specified in part II of this title as a condition for patentability,

(3) Invalidity of the patent or any claim in suit for failure to comply with any requirement of sections 112 or 251 of this title,

(4) Any other fact or act made a defense by this title.

In actions involving the validity or infringement of a patent the party asserting invalidity or noninfringement shall give notice in the pleadings or otherwise in writing to the adverse party at least thirty days before the trial, of the country, number, date, and name of the patentee of any patent, the title, date, and page numbers of any publication to be relied upon as anticipation of the patent in suit or, except in actions in the United States Court of Federal Claims, as showing the state of the art, and the name and address of any person who may be relied upon as the prior inventor or as having prior knowledge of or as having previously used or offered for sale the invention of the patent in suit. In the absence of such notice proof of the said matters may not be made at the trial except on such terms as the court requires.

Invalidity of the extension of a patent term or any portion thereof under section 156 of this title because of the material failure—

(1) by the applicant for the extension, or

(2) by the Commissioner,

to comply with the requirements of such section shall be a defense in any action involving the infringement of a patent during the period of the extension of its term and shall be pleaded. A due diligence determination under section 156(d)(2) is not subject to review in such an action.

(Amended July 24, 1965, Public Law 89-83, sec. 10, 79 Stat. 261; Nov. 14, 1975, Public Law 94-131, sec. 10, 89 Stat. 692; Apr. 2, 1982, Public Law 97-164, sec. 161(7), 96 Stat. 49; Sept. 24, 1984, Public Law 98-417, sec. 203, 98 Stat. 1603; Oct. 29, 1992, Public Law 102-572, sec. 902 (b)(1), 106 Stat. 4516; Nov. 1, 1995, Public Law 104-41, sec. 2, 109 Stat. 352.)

35 U.S.C. 283 Injunction.

The several courts having jurisdiction of cases under this title may grant injunctions in accordance with the principles of equity to prevent the violation of any right secured by patent, on such terms as the court deems reasonable.

35 U.S.C. 284 Damages.

Upon finding for the claimant the court shall award the claimant damages adequate to compensate for the infringe-

MANUAL OF PATENT EXAMINING PROCEDURE

ment but in no event less that a reasonable royalty for the use made of the invention by the infringer, together with interest and costs as fixed by the court.

When the damages are not found by a jury, the court shall assess them. In either event the court may increase the damages up to three times the amount found or assessed.

The court may receive expert testimony as an aid to the determination of damages or of what royalty would be reasonable under the circumstances.

35 U.S.C. 285   Attorney fees.

The court in exceptional cases may award reasonable attorney fees to the prevailing party.

35 U.S.C. 286   Time limitation on damages.

Except as otherwise provided by law, no recovery shall be had for any infringement committed more than six years prior to the filing of the complaint or counterclaim for infringement in the action.

In the case of claims against the United States Government for use of a patented invention, the period before bringing suit, up to six years, between the date of receipt of a written claim for compensation by the department or agency of the Government having authority to settle such claim, and the date of mailing by the Government of a notice to the claimant that his claim has been denied shall not be counted as a part of the period referred to in the preceding paragraph.

35 U.S.C. 287   Limitation on damages and other remedies; marking and notice.

(a)   Patentees, and persons making, offering for sale, or selling within the United States any patented article for or under them, or importing any patented article into the United States, may give notice to the public that the same is patented, either by fixing thereon the word "patent" or the abbreviation "pat.", together with the number of the patent, or when, from the character of the article, this cannot be done, by fixing to it, or to the package wherein one or more of them is contained, a label containing a like notice. In the event of failure so to mark, no damages shall be recovered by the patentee in any action for infringement, except on proof that the infringer was notified of the infringement and continued to infringe thereafter, in which event damages may be recovered only for infringement occurring after such notice. Filing of an action for infringement shall constitute such notice.

(b)(1) An infringer under section 271(g) shall be subject to all the provisions of this title relating to damages and injunctions except to the extent those remedies are modified by this subsection or section 9006 of the Process Patent Amendments Act of 1988. The modifications of remedies provided in this subsection shall not be available to any person who —

(A)   practiced the patented process;

(B)   owns or controls, or is owned or controlled by, the person who practiced the patented process; or

(C)   had knowledge before the infringement that a patented process was used to make the product the importation, use, offer for sale, or sale of which constitutes the infringement.

(2)   No remedies for infringement under section 271(g) of this title shall be available with respect to any product in the possession of, or in transit to, the person subject to liability under such section before that person had notice of infringement with respect to that product. The person subject to liability shall bear the burden of proving any such possession or transit.

(3)(A)In making a determination with respect to the remedy in an action brought for infringement under section 271(g), the court shall consider—

(i)   the good faith demonstrated by the defendant with respect to a request for disclosure;

(ii)   the good faith demonstrated by the plaintiff with respect to a request for disclosure, and

(iii)   the need to restore the exclusive rights secured by the patent.

(B)   For purposes of subparagraph (A), the following are evidence of good faith:

(i)   a request for disclosure made by the defendant;

(ii)   a response within a reasonable time by the person receiving the request for disclosure; and

(iii)   the submission of the response by the defendant to the manufacturer, or if the manufacturer is not known, to the supplier, of the product to be purchased by the defendant, together with a request for a written statement that the process claimed in any patent disclosed in the response is not used to produce such product.

The failure to perform any acts described in the preceding sentence is evidence of absence of good faith unless there are mitigating circumstances. Mitigating circumstances include the case in which, due to the nature of the product, the number of sources for the product, or like commercial circumstances, a request for disclosure is not necessary or practicable to avoid infringement.

(4)(A)For purposes of this subsection, a "request for disclosure" means a written request made to a person then engaged in the manufacture of a product to identify all process patents owned by or licensed to that person, as of the time of the request, that the person then reasonably believes could be asserted to be infringed under section 271(g) if that product were imported into, or sold, offered for sale, or used in, the United States by an unauthorized person. A request for disclosure is further limited to a request —

PATENT LAWS

(i)   which is made by a person regularly engaged in the United States in the sale of the type of products as those manufactured by the person to whom the request is directed, or which includes facts showing that the person making the request plans to engage in the sale of such products in the United States;

(ii)   which is made by such person before the person's first importation, use, offer for sale, or sale of units of the product produced by an infringing process and before the person had notice of infringement with respect to the product; and

(iii)   which includes a representation by the person making the request that such person will promptly submit the patents identified pursuant to the request to the manufacturer, or if the manufacturer is not known, to the supplier, of the product to be purchased by the person making the request, and will request from that manufacturer or supplier a written statement that none of the processes claimed in those patents is used in the manufacture of the product.

(B)   In the case of a request for disclosure received by a person to whom a patent is licensed, that person shall either identify the patent or promptly notify the licensor of the request for disclosure.

(C)   A person who has marked, in the manner prescribed by subsection (a), the number of the process patent on all products made by the patented process which have been offered for sale or sold by that person in the United States, or imported by the person into the United States, before a request for disclosure is received is not required to respond to the request for disclosure. For purposes of the preceding sentence, the term "all products" does not include products made before the effective date of the Process Patent Amendments Act of 1988.

(5)(A)For purposes of this subsection, notice of infringement means actual knowledge, or receipt by a person of a written notification, or a combination thereof, of information sufficient to persuade a reasonable person that it is likely that a product was made by a process patented in the United States.

(B)   A written notification from the patent holder charging a person with infringement shall specify the patented process alleged to have been used and the reasons for a good faith belief that such process was used. The patent holder shall include in the notification such information as is reasonably necessary to explain fairly the patent holder's belief, except that the patent holder is not required to disclose any trade secret information.

(C)   A person who receives a written notification described in subparagraph (B) or a written response to a request for disclosure described in paragraph (4) shall be deemed to have notice of infringement with respect to any patent referred to in such written notification or response unless that person, absent mitigating circumstances—

(i)   promptly transmits the written notification or response to the manufacturer or, if the manufacturer is not known, to the supplier, of the product purchased or to be purchased by that person; and

(ii)   receives a written statement from the manufacturer or supplier which on its face sets forth a well grounded factual basis for a belief that the identified patents are not infringed.

(D)   For purposes of this subsection, a person who obtains a product made by a process patented in the United States in a quantity which is abnormally large in relation to the volume of business of such person or an efficient inventory level shall be rebuttably presumed to have actual knowledge that the product was made by such patented process.

(6)   A person who receives a response to a request for disclosure under this subsection shall pay to the person to whom the request was made a reasonable fee to cover actual costs incurred in complying with the request, which may not exceed the cost of a commercially available automated patent search of the matter involved, but in no case more than $500.

(c)(1) With respect to a medical practitioner's performance of a medical activity that constitutes an infringement under section 271(a) or (b) of this title, the provisions of sections 281, 283, 284, and 285 of this title shall not apply against the medical practitioner or against a related health care entity with respect to such medical activity.

(2)   For the purposes of this subsection:

(A)   the term "medical activity" means the performance of a medical or surgical procedure on a body, but shall not include (i) the use of a patented machine, manufacture, or composition of matter in violation of such patent, (ii) the practice of a patented use of a composition of matter in violation of such patent, or (iii) the practice of a process in violation of a biotechnology patent.

(B)   the term "medical practitioner" means any natural person who is licensed by a State to provide the medical activity described in subsection (c)(1) or who is acting under the direction of such person in the performance of the medical activity.

(C)   the term "related health care entity" shall mean an entity with which a medical practitioner has a professional affiliation under which the medical practitioner performs the medical activity, including but not limited to a nursing home, hospital, university, medical school, health maintenance organization, group medical practice, or a medical clinic.

(D)   the term "professional affiliation" shall mean staff privileges, medical staff membership, employ-

MANUAL OF PATENT EXAMINING PROCEDURE

ment or contractual relationship, partnership or ownership interest, academic appointment, or other affiliation under which a medical practitioner provides the medical activity on behalf of, or in association with, the health care entity.

(E) the term "body" shall mean a human body, organ or cadaver, or a nonhuman animal used in medical research or instruction directly relating to the treatment of humans.

(F) the term "patented use of a composition of matter" does not include a claim for a method of performing a medical or surgical procedure on a body that recites the use of a composition of matter where the use of that composition of matter does not directly contribute to achievement of the objective of the claimed method.

(G) the term "State" shall mean any state or territory of the United States, the District of Columbia, and the Commonwealth of Puerto Rico.

(3) This subsection does not apply to the activities of any person, or employee or agent of such person (regardless of whether such person is a tax exempt organization under section 501(c) of the Internal Revenue Code), who is engaged in the commercial development, manufacture, sale, importation, or distribution of a machine, manufacture, or composition of matter or the provision of pharmacy or clinical laboratory services (other than clinical laboratory services provided in a physician's office), where such activities are:

(A) directly related to the commercial development, manufacture, sale, importation, or distribution of a machine, manufacture, or composition of matter or the provision of pharmacy or clinical laboratory services (other than clinical laboratory services provided in a physician's office), and

(B) regulated under the Federal Food, Drug, and Cosmetic Act, the Public Health Service Act, or the Clinical Laboratories Improvement Act.

(4) This subsection shall not apply to any patent issued based on an application the earliest effective filing date of which is prior to September 30, 1996.

(Amended Aug. 23, 1988, Public Law 100-418, sec. 9004(a), 102 Stat. 1564; Dec. 8, 1994, Public Law 103-465, sec. 533(b)(5), 108 Stat. 4989.)

(Subsection (c) added Sept. 30, 1996, Public Law 104-208, sec. 616, 110 Stat. 3009; amended Nov. 29, 1999, Public Law 106-113, sec. 1000(a)(9), S. 1948 sec. 4803, 113 Stat. 1501.)

35 U.S.C. 288   Action for infringement of a patent containing an invalid claim.

Whenever, without deceptive intention, a claim of a patent is invalid, an action may be maintained for the infringement of a claim of the patent which may be valid. The patentee shall recover no costs unless a disclaimer of

the invalid claim has been entered at the Patent and Trademark Office before the commencement of the suit.

(Amended Jan. 2, 1975, Public Law 93-596, sec. 1, 88 Stat. 1949.)

35 U.S.C. 289   Additional remedy for infringement of design patent.

Whoever during the term of a patent for a design, without license of the owner, (1) applies the patented design, or any colorable imitation thereof, to any article of manufacture for the purpose of sale, or (2) sells or exposes for sale any article of manufacture to which such design or colorable imitation has been applied shall be liable to the owner to the extent of his total profit, but not less than $250, recoverable in any United States district court having jurisdiction of the parties.

Nothing in this section shall prevent, lessen, or impeach any other remedy which an owner of an infringed patent has under the provisions of this title, but he shall not twice recover the profit made from the infringement.

35 U.S.C. 290   Notice of patent suits.

The clerks of the courts of the United States, within one month after the filing of an action under this title, shall give notice thereof in writing to the Commissioner, setting forth so far as known the names and addresses of the parties, name of the inventor, and the designating number of the patent upon which the action has been brought. If any other patent is subsequently included in the action he shall give like notice thereof. Within one month after the decision is rendered or a judgment issued the clerk of the court shall give notice thereof to the Commissioner. The Commissioner shall, on receipt of such notices, enter the same in the file of such patent.

35 U.S.C. 291   Interfering patents.

The owner of an interfering patent may have relief against the owner of another by civil action, and the court may adjudge the question of validity of any of the interfering patents, in whole or in part. The provisions of the second paragraph of section 146 of this title shall apply to actions brought under this section.

35 U.S.C. 292   False marking.

(a) Whoever, without the consent of the patentee, marks upon, or affixes to, or uses in advertising in connection with anything made, used, offered for sale, or sold by same person within the United States, or imported by the person into the United States, the name or any imitation of the name of the patentee, the patent number, or the words "patent," "patentee," or the like, with the intent of counterfeiting or imitating the mark of the patentee, or of deceiving the public and inducing them to believe that the thing was made, offered for sale, sold, or imported into the United States by or with the consent of the patentee; or

Whoever marks upon, or affixes to, or uses in advertising in connection with any unpatented article the word "patent" or any word or number importing the same is patented, for the purpose of deceiving the public; or

Whoever marks upon, or affixes to, or uses in advertising in connection with any article the words "patent applied for," "patent pending," or any word importing that an application for patent has been made, when no application for patent has been made, or if made, is not pending, for the purpose of deceiving the public —

Shall be fined not more than $500 for every such offense.

(b)   Any person may sue for the penalty, in which event one-half shall go to the person suing and the other to the use of the United States.

(Subsection (a) amended Dec. 8, 1994, Public Law 103-465, sec. 533(b)(6), 108 Stat. 4990.)

35 U.S.C. 293   Nonresident patentee; service and notice.

Every patentee not residing in the United States may file in the Patent and Trademark Office a written designation stating the name and address of a person residing within the United States on whom may be served process or notice of proceedings affecting the patent or rights thereunder. If the person designated cannot be found at the address given in the last designation, or if no person has been designated, the United States District Court for the District of Columbia shall have jurisdiction and summons s all be served by publication or otherwise as the court directs. The court shall have the same jurisdiction to take any action respecting the patent or rights thereunder that it would have if the patentee were personally within the jurisdiction of the court.

(Amended Jan. 2, 1975, Public Law 93-596, sec. 1, 88 Stat. 1949.)

35 U.S.C. 294   Voluntary arbitration.

(a)   A contract involving a patent or any right under a patent may contain a provision requiring arbitration of any dispute relating to patent validity or infringement arising under the contract. In the absence of such a provision, the parties to an existing patent validity or infringement dispute may agree in writing to settle such dispute by arbitration. Any such provision or agreement shall be valid, irrevocable, and enforceable, except for any grounds that exist at law or in equity for revocation of a contract.

(b)   Arbitration of such disputes, awards by arbitrators, and confirmation of awards shall be governed by title 9, United States Code, to the extent such title is not inconsistent with this section. In any such arbitration proceeding, the defenses provided for under section 282 of this title

shall be considered by the arbitrator if raised by any party to the proceeding.

(c)   An award by an arbitrator shall be final and binding between the parties to the arbitration but shall have no force or effect on any other person. The parties to an arbitration may agree that in the event a patent which is the subject matter of an award is subsequently determined to be invalid or unenforceable in a judgment rendered by a court to competent jurisdiction from which no appeal can or has been taken, such award may be modified by any court of competent jurisdiction upon application by any party to the arbitration. Any such modification shall govern the rights and obligations between such parties from the date of such modification.

(d)   When an award is made by an arbitrator, the patentee, his assignee or licensee shall give notice thereof in writing to the Commissioner. There shall be a separate notice prepared for each patent involved in such proceeding. Such notice shall set forth the names and addresses of the parties, the name of the inventor, and the name of the patent owner, shall designate the number of the patent, and shall contain a copy of the award. If an award is modified by a court, the party requesting such modification shall give notice of such modification to the Commissioner. The Commissioner shall, upon receipt of either notice, enter the same in the record of the prosecution of such patent. If the required notice is not filed with the Commissioner, any party to the proceeding may provide such notice to the Commissioner.

(e)   The award shall be unenforceable until the notice required by subsection (d) is received by the Commissioner.

(Added Aug. 27, 1982, Public Law 97-247, sec. 17(b)(1), 96 Stat. 322.)

35 U.S.C. 295   Presumption: Product made by patented process.

In actions alleging infringement of a process patent based on the importation, sale, offered for sale, or use of a product which is made from a process patented in the United States, if the court finds—

(1)   that a substantial likelihood exists that the product was made by the patented process, and

(2)   that the plaintiff has made a reasonable effort to determine the process actually used in the production of the product and was unable so to determine, the product shall be presumed to have been so made, and the burden of establishing that the product was not made by the process shall be on the party asserting that it was not so made.

(Added Aug. 23, 1988, Public Law 100-418, sec. 9005(a), 102 Stat. 1566; amended Dec. 8, 1994, Public Law 103-465, sec. 533(b)(7), 108 Stat. 4990.)

MANUAL OF PATENT EXAMINING PROCEDURE

35 U.S.C. 296   Liability of States, instrumentalities of States, and State officials for infringement of patents.

(a)   IN GENERAL. - Any State, any instrumentality of a State, and any officer or employee of a State or instrumentality of a State, acting in his official capacity, shall not be immune, under the eleventh amendment of the Constitution of the United States or under any other doctrine of sovereign immunity, from suit in Federal court by any person, including any governmental or nongovernmental entity, for infringement of a patent under section 271, or for any other violation under this title.

(b)   REMEDIES. - In a suit described in subsection (a) for a violation described in that subsection, remedies (including remedies both at law and in equity) are available for the violation to the same extent as such remedies are available for such a violation in a suit against any private entity. Such remedies include damages, interest, costs, and treble damages under section 284, attorney fees under section 285, and the additional remedy for infringement of design patents under section 289.

(Added Oct. 28, 1992, Public Law 102-560, sec.2(a)(2), 106 Stat. 4230.)

35 U.S.C. 297   Improper and deceptive invention promotion.

(a)   IN GENERAL.— An invention promoter shall have a duty to disclose the following information to a customer in writing, prior to entering into a contract for invention promotion services:

(1)   the total number of inventions evaluated by the invention promoter for commercial potential in the past 5 years, as well as the number of those inventions that received positive evaluations, and the number of those inventions that received negative evaluations;

(2)   the total number of customers who have contracted with the invention promoter in the past 5 years, not including customers who have purchased trade show services, research, advertising, or other nonmarketing services from the invention promoter, or who have defaulted in their payment to the invention promoter;

(3)   the total number of customers known by the invention promoter to have received a net financial profit as a direct result of the invention promotion services provided by such invention promoter;

(4)   the total number of customers known by the invention promoter to have received license agreements for their inventions as a direct result of the invention promotion services provided by such invention promoter; and

(5)   the names and addresses of all previous invention promotion companies with which the invention promoter or its officers have collectively or individually been affiliated in the previous 10 years.

(b)   CIVIL ACTION.—

(1)   Any customer who enters into a contract with an invention promoter and who is found by a court to have been injured by any material false or fraudulent statement or representation, or any omission of material fact, by that invention promoter (or any agent, employee, director, officer, partner, or independent contractor of such invention promoter), or by the failure of that invention promoter to disclose such information as required under subsection (a), may recover in a civil action against the invention promoter (or the officers, directors, or partners of such invention promoter), in addition to reasonable costs and attorneys' fees--

(A)   the amount of actual damages incurred by the customer; or

(B)   at the election of the customer at any time before final judgment is rendered, statutory damages in a sum of not more than $5,000, as the court considers just.

(2)   Notwithstanding paragraph (1), in a case where the customer sustains the burden of proof, and the court finds, that the invention promoter intentionally misrepresented or omitted a material fact to such customer, or willfully failed to disclose such information as required under subsection (a), with the purpose of deceiving that customer, the court may increase damages to not more than three times the amount awarded, taking into account past complaints made against the invention promoter that resulted in regulatory sanctions or other corrective actions based on those records compiled by the Commissioner of Patents under subsection (d).

(c)   DEFINITIONS.— For purposes of this section—

(1)   a "contract for invention promotion services" means a contract by which an invention promoter undertakes invention promotion services for a customer;

(2)   a "customer" is any individual who enters into a contract with an invention promoter for invention promotion services;

(3)   the term "invention promoter" means any person, firm, partnership, corporation, or other entity who offers to perform or performs invention promotion services for, or on behalf of, a customer, and who holds itself out through advertising in any mass media as providing such services, but does not include—

(A)   any department or agency of the Federal Government or of a State or local government;

(B)   any nonprofit, charitable, scientific, or educational organization, qualified under applicable State law or described under section 170(b)(1)(A) of the Internal Revenue Code of 1986;

(C)   any person or entity involved in the evaluation to determine commercial potential of, or offering to license or sell, a utility patent or a previously filed nonprovisional utility patent application;

(D) any party participating in a transaction involving the sale of the stock or assets of a business; or

(E) any party who directly engages in the business of retail sales of products or the distribution of products; and

(4) the term "invention promotion services" means the procurement or attempted procurement for a customer of a firm, corporation, or other entity to develop and market products or services that include the invention of the customer.

(d) RECORDS OF COMPLAINTS.—

(1) RELEASE OF COMPLAINTS.— The Commissioner of Patents shall make all complaints received by the Patent and Trademark Office involving invention promoters publicly available, together with any response of the invention promoters. The Commissioner of Patents shall notify the invention promoter of a complaint and provide a reasonable opportunity to reply prior to making such complaint publicly available.

(2) REQUEST FOR COMPLAINTS.— The Commissioner of Patents may request complaints relating to invention promotion services from any Federal or State agency and include such complaints in the records maintained under paragraph (1), together with any response of the invention promoters.

(Added Nov. 29, 1999, Public Law 106-113, sec. 1000(a)(9), S. 1948 sec. 4102(a), 113 Stat. 1501.)

CHAPTER 30 — PRIOR ART CITATIONS TO OFFICE AND EX PARTE REEXAMINATION OF PATENTS

35 U.S.C. 301   Citation of prior art.

Any person at any time may cite to the Office in writing prior art consisting of patents or printed publications which that person believes to have a bearing on the patentability of any claim of a particular patent. If the person explains in writing the pertinency and manner of applying such prior art to at least one claim of the patent, the citation of such prior art and the explanation thereof will become a part of the official file of the patent. At the written request of the person citing the prior art, his or her identity will be excluded from the patent file and kept confidential.

(Added Dec. 12, 1980, Public Law 96-517, sec. 1, 94 Stat. 3015.)

35 U.S.C. 302   Request for reexamination.

Any person at any time may file a request for reexamination by the Office of any claim of a patent on the basis of any prior art cited under the provisions of section 301 of this title. The request must be in writing and must be accompanied by payment of a reexamination fee established by the Commissioner of Patents pursuant to the provisions of section 41 of this title. The request must set forth the pertinency and manner of applying cited prior art to every claim for which reexamination is requested. Unless the requesting person is the owner of the patent, the Commissioner promptly will send a copy of the request to the owner of record of the patent.

(Added Dec. 12, 1980, Public Law 96-517, sec. 1, 94 Stat. 3015.)

35 U.S.C. 303   Determination of issue by Commissioner.

(a) Within three months following the filing of a request for reexamination under the provisions of section 302 of this title, the Commissioner will determine whether a substantial new question of patentability affecting any claim of the patent concerned is raised by the request, with or without consideration of other patents or printed publications. On his own initiative, and any time, the Commissioner may determine whether a substantial new question of patentability is raised by patents and publications discovered by him or cited under the provisions of section 301 of this title.

(b) A record of the Commissioner's determination under subsection (a) of this section will be placed in the official file of the patent, and a copy promptly will be given or mailed to the owner of record of the patent and to the person requesting reexamination, if any.

(c) A determination by the Commissioner pursuant to subsection (a) of this section that no substantial new question of patentability has been raised will be final and nonappealable. Upon such a determination, the Commissioner may refund a portion of the reexamination fee required under section 302 of this title.

(Added Dec. 12, 1980, Public Law 96-517, sec. 1, 94 Stat. 3015.)

35 U.S.C. 304   Reexamination order by Commissioner.

If, in a determination made under the provisions of subsection 303(a) of this title, the Commissioner finds that a substantial new question of patentability affecting any claim of a patent is raised, the determination will include an

MANUAL OF PATENT EXAMINING PROCEDURE

order for reexamination of the patent for resolution of the question. The patent owner will be given a reasonable period, not less than two months from the date a copy of the determination is given or mailed to him, within which he may file a statement on such question, including any amendment to his patent and new claim or claims he may wish to propose, for consideration in the reexamination. If the patent owner files such a statement, he promptly will serve a copy of it on the person who has requested reexamination under the provisions of section 302 of this title. Within a period of two months from the date of service, that person may file and have considered in the reexamination a reply to any statement filed by the patent owner. That person promptly will serve on the patent owner a copy of any reply filed.

(Added Dec. 12, 1980, Public Law 96-517, sec. 1, 94 Stat. 3016.)

35 U.S.C. 305   Conduct of reexamination proceedings.

After the times for filing the statement and reply provided for by section 304 of this title have expired, reexamination will be conducted according to the procedures established for initial examination under the provisions of sections 132 and 133 of this title. In any reexamination proceeding under this chapter, the patent owner will be permitted to propose any amendment to his patent and a new claim or claims thereto, in order to distinguish the invention as claimed from the prior art cited under the provisions of section 301 of this title, or in response to a decision adverse to the patentability of a claim of a patent. No proposed amended or new claim enlarging the scope of a claim of the patent will be permitted in a reexamination proceeding under this chapter. All reexamination proceedings under this section, including any appeal to the Board of Patent Appeals and Interferences, will be conducted with special dispatch within the Office.

(Added Dec. 12, 1980, Public Law 96-517, sec. 1, 94 Stat. 3016; amended Nov. 8, 1984, Public Law 98-622, sec. 204(c), 98 Stat. 3388.)

35 U.S.C. 306   Appeal.

The patent owner involved in a reexamination proceeding under this chapter may appeal under the provisions of section 134 of this title, and may seek court review under the provisions of sections 141 to 145 of this title, with respect to any decision adverse to the patentability of any original or proposed amended or new claim of the patent.

(Added Dec. 12, 1980, Public Law 96-517, sec. 1, 94 Stat. 3016.)

35 U.S.C. 307   Certificate of patentability, unpatentability, and claim cancellation.

(a)   In a reexamination proceeding under this chapter, when the time for appeal has expired or any appeal pro-

ceeding has terminated, the Commissioner will issue and publish a certificate canceling any claim of the patent finally determined to be unpatentable, confirming any claim of the patent determined to be patentable, and incorporating in the patent any proposed amended or new claim determined to be patentable.

(b)   Any proposed amended or new claim determined to be patentable and incorporated into a patent following a reexamination proceeding will have the same effect as that specified in section 252 of this title for reissued patents on the right of any person who made, purchased, or used within the United States, or imported into the United States, anything patented by such proposed amended or new claim, or who made substantial preparation for the same, prior to issuance of a certificate under the provisions of subsection (a) of this section.

(Added Dec. 12, 1980, Public Law 96-517, sec. 1, 94 Stat. 3016; amended Dec. 8, 1994, Public Law 103-465, sec. 533(b)(8), 108 Stat. 4990.)

CHAPTER 31 — OPTIONAL INTER PARTES REEXAMINATION PROCEDURES

35 U.S.C. 311   Request for inter partes reexamination

(a)   IN GENERAL.— Any person at any time may file a request for inter partes reexamination by the Office of a patent on the basis of any prior art cited under the provisions of section 301.

(b)   REQUIREMENTS.— The request shall—

(1)   be in writing, include the identity of the real party in interest, and be accompanied by payment of an inter partes reexamination fee established by the Director under section 41; and

(2)   set forth the pertinency and manner of applying cited prior art to every claim for which reexamination is requested.

(c)   COPY.— Unless the requesting person is the owner of the patent, the Director promptly shall send a copy of the request to the owner of record of the patent.

(Added Nov. 29, 1999, Public Law 106-113, sec. 1000(a)(9), S. 1948 sec. 4604(a), 113 Stat. 1501.)

PATENT LAWS

35 U.S.C. 312   Determination of issue by Director

(a)   REEXAMINATION.— Not later than 3 months after the filing of a request for inter partes reexamination under section 311, the Director shall determine whether a substantial new question of patentability affecting any claim of the patent concerned is raised by the request, with or without consideration of other patents or printed publications. On the Director's initiative, and at any time, the Director may determine whether a substantial new question of patentability is raised by patents and publications.

(b)   RECORD.— A record of the Director's determination under subsection (a) shall be placed in the official file of the patent, and a copy shall be promptly given or mailed to the owner of record of the patent and to the third-party requester, if any.

(c)   FINAL DECISION.— A determination by the Director under subsection (a) shall be final and non-appealable. Upon a determination that no substantial new question of patentability has been raised, the Director may refund a portion of the inter partes reexamination fee required under section 311.

(Added Nov. 29, 1999, Public Law 106-113, sec. 1000(a)(9), S. 1948 sec. 4604(a), 113 Stat. 1501.)

35 U.S.C. 313   Inter partes reexamination order by Director

If, in a determination made under section 312(a), the Director finds that a substantial new question of patentability affecting a claim of a patent is raised, the determination shall include an order for inter partes reexamination of the patent for resolution of the question. The order may be accompanied by the initial action of the Patent and Trademark Office on the merits of the inter partes reexamination conducted in accordance with section 314.

(Added Nov. 29, 1999, Public Law 106-113, sec. 1000(a)(9), S. 1948 sec. 4604(a), 113 Stat. 1501.)

35 U.S.C. 314   Conduct of inter partes reexamination proceedings

(a)   IN GENERAL.— Except as otherwise provided in this section, reexamination shall be conducted according to the procedures established for initial examination under the provisions of sections 132 and 133. In any inter partes reexamination proceeding under this chapter, the patent owner shall be permitted to propose any amendment to the patent and a new claim or claims, except that no proposed amended or new claim enlarging the scope of the claims of the patent shall be permitted.

(b)   RESPONSE.—

(1)   This subsection shall apply to any inter partes reexamination proceeding in which the order for inter partes reexamination is based upon a request by a third-party requester.

(2)   With the exception of the inter partes reexamination request, any document filed by either the patent owner or the third-party requester shall be served on the other party. In addition, the third-party requester shall receive a copy of any communication sent by the Office to the patent owner concerning the patent subject to the inter partes reexamination proceeding.

(3)   Each time that the patent owner files a response to an action on the merits from the Patent and Trademark Office, the third-party requester shall have one opportunity to file written comments addressing issues raised by the action of the Office or the patent owner's response thereto, if those written comments are received by the Office within 30 days after the date of service of the patent owner's response.

(c)   SPECIAL DISPATCH.— Unless otherwise provided by the Director for good cause, all inter partes reexamination proceedings under this section, including any appeal to the Board of Patent Appeals and Interferences, shall be conducted with special dispatch within the Office.

(Added Nov. 29, 1999, Public Law 106-113, sec. 1000(a)(9), S. 1948 sec. 4604(a), 113 Stat. 1501.)

35 U.S.C. 315   Appeal

(a)   PATENT OWNER.— The patent owner involved in an inter partes reexamination proceeding under this chapter—

(1)   may appeal under the provisions of section 134 and may appeal under the provisions of sections 141 through 144, with respect to any decision adverse to the patentability of any original or proposed amended or new claim of the patent; and

(2)   may be a party to any appeal taken by a third-party requester under subsection (b).

(b)   THIRD-PARTY REQUESTER.— A third-party requester may—

(1)   appeal under the provisions of section 134 with respect to any final decision favorable to the patentability of any original or proposed amended or new claim of the patent; or

(2)   be a party to any appeal taken by the patent owner under the provisions of section 134, subject to subsection (c).

(c)   CIVIL ACTION.— A third-party requester whose request for an inter partes reexamination results in an order under section 313 is estopped from asserting at a later time, in any civil action arising in whole or in part under section 1338 of title 28, United States Code, the invalidity of any claim finally determined to be valid and patentable on any ground which the third-party requester raised or could have raised during the inter partes reexamination proceedings. This subsection does not prevent the assertion of invalidity based on newly discovered prior art

MANUAL OF PATENT EXAMINING PROCEDURE

unavailable to the third-party requester and the Patent and Trademark Office at the time of the inter partes reexamination proceedings.

(Added Nov. 29, 1999, Public Law 106-113, sec. 1000(a)(9), S. 1948 sec. 4604(a), 113 Stat. 1501.)

35 U.S.C. 316   Certificate of patentability, unpatentability and claim cancellation

(a)   IN GENERAL.— In an inter partes reexamination proceeding under this chapter, when the time for appeal has expired or any appeal proceeding has terminated, the Director shall issue and publish a certificate canceling any claim of the patent finally determined to be unpatentable, confirming any claim of the patent determined to be patentable, and incorporating in the patent any proposed amended or new claim determined to be patentable.

(b)   AMENDED OR NEW CLAIM.— Any proposed amended or new claim determined to be patentable and incorporated into a patent following an inter partes reexamination proceeding shall have the same effect as that specified in section 252 of this title for reissued patents on the right of any person who made, purchased, or used within the United States, or imported into the United States, anything patented by such proposed amended or new claim, or who made substantial preparation therefor, prior to issuance of a certificate under the provisions of subsection (a) of this section.

(Added Nov. 29, 1999, Public Law 106-113, sec. 1000(a)(9), S. 1948 sec. 4604(a), 113 Stat. 1501.)

35 U.S.C. 317   Inter partes reexamination prohibited

(a)   ORDER FOR REEXAMINATION.— Notwithstanding any provision of this chapter, once an order for inter partes reexamination of a patent has been issued under section 313, neither the patent owner nor the third-party requester, if any, nor privies of either, may file a subsequent request for inter partes reexamination of the patent until an inter partes reexamination certificate is issued and published under section 316, unless authorized by the Director.

(b)   FINAL DECISION.— Once a final decision has been entered against a party in a civil action arising in whole or in part under section 1338 of title 28, United States Code, that the party has not sustained its burden of proving the invalidity of any patent claim in suit or if a final decision in an inter partes reexamination proceeding instituted by a third-party requester is favorable to the patentability of any original or proposed amended or new claim of the patent, then neither that party nor its privies may thereafter request an inter partes reexamination of any such patent claim on the basis of issues which that party or its privies raised or could have raised in such civil action or inter partes reexamination proceeding, and an inter partes

reexamination requested by that party or its privies on the basis of such issues may not thereafter be maintained by the Office, notwithstanding any other provision of this chapter. This subsection does not prevent the assertion of invalidity based on newly discovered prior art unavailable to the third-party requester and the Patent and Trademark Office at the time of the inter partes reexamination proceedings.

(Added Nov. 29, 1999, Public Law 106-113, sec. 1000(a)(9), S. 1948 sec. 4604(a), 113 Stat. 1501.)

35 U.S.C. 318   Stay of litigation

Once an order for inter partes reexamination of a patent has been issued under section 313, the patent owner may obtain a stay of any pending litigation which involves an issue of patentability of any claims of the patent which are the subject of the inter partes reexamination order, unless the court before which such litigation is pending determines that a stay would not serve the interests of justice.

(Added Nov. 29, 1999, Public Law 106-113, sec. 1000(a)(9), S. 1948 sec. 4604(a), 113 Stat. 1501.)

PART IV — PATENT COOPERATION TREATY

CHAPTER 35 — DEFINITIONS

Sec.
351   Definitions.

35 U.S.C. 351   Definitions.

When used in this part unless the context otherwise indicates—

(a)   The term "treaty" means the Patent Cooperation Treaty done at Washington, on June 19, 1970.

(b)   The term "Regulations," when capitalized, means the Regulations under the treaty, done at Washington on the same date as the treaty. The term "regulations," when not capitalized, means the regulations established by the Commissioner under this title.

(c)   The term "international application" means an application filed under the treaty.

(d)   The term "international application originating in the United States" means an international application filed in the Patent and Trademark Office when it is acting as a Receiving Office under the treaty, irrespective of whether or not the United States has been designated in that international application.

(e)   The term "international application designating the United States" means an international application specifying the United States as a country in which a patent is sought, regardless where such international application is filed.

(f)   The term "Receiving Office" means a national patent office or intergovernmental organization which receives and processes international applications as prescribed by the treaty and the Regulations.

(g)   The terms "International Searching Authority" and "International Preliminary Examining Authority" mean a national patent office or intergovernmental organization as appointed under the treaty which processes international applications as prescribed by the treaty and the Regulations.

(h)   The term "International Bureau" means the inter national intergovernmental organization which is recognized as the coordinating body under the treaty and the Regulations.

(i)   Terms and expressions not defined in this part are to be taken in the sense indicated by the treaty and the Regulations.

(Added Nov. 14, 1975, Public Law 94-131, sec. 1, 89 Stat. 685; amended Nov. 8, 1984, Public Law 98-622, sec. 403(a), 98 Stat. 3392; Nov. 6, 1986, Public Law 99-616, sec. 2 (a)-(c), 100 Stat. 3485.)

CHAPTER 36 — INTERNATIONAL STAGE

Sec.
361   Receiving Office.
362   International Searching Authority and International Preliminary Examining Authority.
363   International application designating the United States: Effect.
364   International stage: Procedure.
365   Right of priority; benefit of the filing date of a prior application.
366   Withdrawn international application.
367   Actions of other authorities: Review.
368   Secrecy of certain inventions; filing international applications in foreign countries.

35 U.S.C. 361   Receiving Office.

(a)   The Patent and Trademark Office shall act as a Receiving Office for international applications filed by nationals or residents of the United States. In accordance with any agreement made between the United States and another country, the Patent and Trademark Office may also act as a Receiving Office for international applications filed by residents or nationals of such country who are entitled to file international applications.

(b)   The Patent and Trademark Office shall perform all acts connected with the discharge of duties required of a Receiving Office, including the collection of international fees and their transmittal to the International Bureau.

(c)   International applications filed in the Patent and Trademark Office shall be in the English language.

(d)   The international fee, and the transmittal and search fees prescribed under section 376(a) of this part, shall either be paid on filing of an international application

or within such later time as may be fixed by the Commissioner.

(Added Nov. 14, 1975, Public Law 94-131, sec. 1, 89 Stat. 686; amended Nov. 8, 1984, Public Law 98-622, sec. 401(a), 98 Stat. 3391; Nov. 6, 1986, Public Law 99-616, sec. 2 (d), 100 Stat. 3485.)

35 U.S.C. 362   International Searching Authority and International Preliminary Examining Authority.

(a)   The Patent and Trademark Office may act as an International Searching Authority and International Preliminary Examining Authority with respect to international applications in accordance with the terms and conditions of an agreement which may be concluded with the International Bureau, and may discharge all duties required of such Authorities, including the collection of handling fees and their transmittal to the International Bureau.

(b)   The handling fee, preliminary examination fee, and any additional fees due for international preliminary examination shall be paid within such time as may be fixed by the Commissioner.

(Added Nov. 14, 1975, Public Law 94-131, sec. 1, 89 Stat. 686; amended Nov. 8, 1984, Public Law 98-622, sec. 403 (a), 98 Stat. 3392; Nov. 6, 1986, Public Law 99-616, sec. 4, 100 Stat. 3485.)

35 U.S.C. 363   International application designating the United States: Effect.

An international application designating the United States shall have the effect, from its international filing date under article 11 of the treaty, of a national application for patent regularly filed in the Patent and Trademark Office except as otherwise provided in section 102(e) of this title.

(Added Nov. 14, 1975, Public Law 94-131, sec. 1, 89 Stat. 686; amended Nov. 8, 1984, Public Law 98-622, sec. 403(a), 98 Stat. 3392.)

35 U.S.C. 364   International stage: Procedure.

(a)   International applications shall be processed by the Patent and Trademark Office when acting as a Receiving Office, International Searching Authority, or International Preliminary Examining Authority, in accordance with the applicable provisions of the treaty, the Regulations, and this title.

(b)   An applicant's failure to act within prescribed time limits in connection with requirements pertaining to a pending international application may be excused upon a showing satisfactory to the Commissioner of unavoidable delay, to the extent not precluded by the treaty and the Regulations, and provided the conditions imposed by the treaty and the Regulations regarding the excuse of such failure to act are complied with.

MANUAL OF PATENT EXAMINING PROCEDURE

(Added Nov. 14, 1975, Public Law 94-131, sec. 1, 89 Stat. 686; amended Nov. 8, 1984, Public Law 98-622, sec. 403(a), 98 Stat. 3392.)

(Subsection (a) amended Nov. 6, 1986, Public Law 99-616, sec. 5, 100 Stat. 3485.)

35 U.S.C. 365   Right of priority; benefit of the filing date of a prior application.

(a)   In accordance with the conditions and requirements of subsections (a) through (d) of section 119 of this title, a national application shall be entitled to the right of priority based on a prior filed international application which designated at least one country other than the United States.

(b)   In accordance with the conditions and requirements of section 119(a) of this title and the treaty and the Regulations, an international application designating the United States shall be entitled to the right of priority based on a prior foreign application, or a prior international application designating at least one country other than the United States.

(c)   In accordance with the conditions and requirements of section 120 of this title, an international application designating the United States shall be entitled to the benefit of the filing date of a prior national application or a prior international application designating the United States, and a national application shall be entitled to the benefit of the filing date of a prior international application designating the United States. If any claim for the benefit of an earlier filing date is based on a prior international application which designated but did not originate in the United States, the Commissioner may require the filing in the Patent and Trademark Office of a certified copy of such application together with a translation thereof into the English language, if it was filed in another language.

(Added Nov. 14, 1975, Public Law 94-131, sec. 1, 89 Stat. 686; amended Nov. 8, 1984, Public Law 98-622, sec. 403(a), 98 Stat. 3392; Dec. 8, 1994, Public Law 103-465, sec. 532(c)(4), 108 Stat. 4987.)

35 U.S.C. 366   Withdrawn international application.

Subject to section 367 of this part, if an international application designating the United States is withdrawn or considered withdrawn, either generally or as to the United States, under the conditions of the treaty and the Regulations, before the applicant has complied with the applicable requirements prescribed by section 371(c) of this part, the designation of the United States shall have no effect after the date of withdrawal and shall be considered as not having been made, unless a claim for benefit of a prior filing date under section 365(c) of this section was made in a national application, or an international application desig-

nating the United States, filed before the date of such withdrawal. However, such withdrawn international application may serve as the basis for a claim of priority under section 365 (a) and (b) of this part, if it designated a country other than the United States.

(Added Nov. 14, 1975, Public Law 94-131, sec. 1, 89 Stat. 687; amended Nov. 8, 1984, Public Law 98-622, sec. 401(b), 98 Stat. 3391.)

35 U.S.C. 367   Actions of other authorities: Review.

(a)   Where a Receiving Office other than the Patent and Trademark Office has refused to accord an international filing date to an international application designating the United States or where it has held such application to be withdrawn either generally or as to the United States, the applicant may request review of the matter by the Commissioner, on compliance with the requirements of and within the time limits specified by the treaty and the Regulations. Such review may result in a determination that such application be considered as pending in the national stage.

(b)   The review under subsection (a) of this section, subject to the same requirements and conditions, may also be requested in those instances where an international application designating the United States is considered withdrawn due to a finding by the International Bureau under article 12 (3) of the treaty.

(Added Nov. 14, 1975, Public Law 94-131, sec. 1, 89 Stat. 687; amended Nov. 8, 1984, Public Law 98-622, sec. 403(a), 98 Stat 3392.)

35 U.S.C. 368   Secrecy of certain inventions; filing international applications in foreign countries.

(a)   International applications filed in the Patent and Trademark Office shall be subject to the provisions of chapter 17 of this title.

(b)   In accordance with article 27 (8) of the treaty, the filing of an international application in a country other than the United States on the invention made in this country shall be considered the filing of an application in a foreign country within the meaning of chapter 17 of this title, whether or not the United States is designated in that international application.

(c)   If a license to file in a foreign country is refused or if an international application is ordered to be kept secret and a permit refused, the Patent and Trademark Office when acting as a Receiving Office, International Searching Authority, or International Preliminary Examining Authority, may not disclose the contents of such application to anyone not authorized to receive such disclosure.

PATENT LAWS

(Added Nov. 14, 1975, Public Law 94-131, sec. 1, 89 Stat. 687; amended Nov. 8, 1984, Public Law 98-622, sec. 403(a), 98 Stat. 3392; Nov. 6, 1986, Public Law 99-616, sec. 6, 100 Stat. 3486.)

CHAPTER 37 — NATIONAL STAGE

Sec.

371   National stage: Commencement.

372   National stage: Requirements and procedure.

373   Improper applicant.

374   Publication of international application: Effect.

375   Patent issued on international application: Effect.

376   Fees.

35 U.S.C. 371   National stage: Commencement.

(a)   Receipt from the International Bureau of copies of international applications with any amendments to the claims, international search reports, and international preliminary examination reports including any annexes thereto may be required in the case of international applications designating or electing the United States.

(b)   Subject to subsection (f) of this section, the national stage shall commence with the expiration of the applicable time limit under article 22 (1) or (2), or under article 39 (1)(a) of the treaty.

(c)   The applicant shall file in the Patent and Trademark Office —

(1)   the national fee provided in section 41(a) of this title;

(2)   a copy of the international application, unless not required under subsection (a) of this section or already communicated by the International Bureau, and a translation into the English language of the international application, if it was filed in another language;

(3)   amendments, if any, to the claims in the international application, made under article 19 of the treaty, unless such amendments have been communicated to the Patent and Trademark Office by the International Bureau, and a translation into the English language if such amendments were made in another language;

(4)   an oath or declaration of the inventor (or other person authorized under chapter 11 of this title) complying with the requirements of section 115 of this title and with regulations prescribed for oaths or declarations of applicants;

(5)   a translation into the English language of any annexes to the international preliminary examination report, if such annexes were made in another language.

(d)   The requirement with respect to the national fee referred to in subsection (c)(1), the translation referred to in subsection (c)(2), and the oath or declaration referred to in subsection (c)(4) of this section shall be complied with by the date of the commencement of the national stage or by such later time as may be fixed by the Commissioner. The copy of the international application referred to in subsection (c)(2) shall be submitted by the date of the commencement of the national stage. Failure to comply with these requirements shall be regarded as abandonment of the application by the parties thereof, unless it be shown to the satisfaction of the Commissioner that such failure to comply was unavoidable. The payment of a surcharge may be required as a condition of accepting the national fee referred to in subsection (c)(1) or the oath or declaration referred to in subsection (c)(4) of this section if these requirements are not met by the date of the commencement of the national stage. The requirements of subsection (c)(3) of this section shall be complied with by the date of the commencement of the national stage, and failure to do so shall be regarded as a cancellation of the amendments to the claims in the international application made under article 19 of the treaty. The requirement of subsection (c)(5) shall be complied with at such time as may be fixed by the Commissioner and failure to do so shall be regarded as cancellation of the amendments made under article 34 (2)(b) of the treaty.

(e)   After an international application has entered the national stage, no patent may be granted or refused thereon before the expiration of the applicable time limit under article 28 or article 41 of the treaty, except with the express consent of the applicant. The applicant may present amendments to the specification, claims, and drawings of the application after the national stage has commenced.

(f)   At the express request of the applicant, the national stage of processing may be commenced at any time at which the application is in order for such purpose and the applicable requirements of subsection (c) of this section have been complied with.

(Added Nov. 14, 1975, Public Law 94-131, sec. 1, 89 Stat. 688; amended Nov. 8, 1984, Public Law 98-622, sec. 402(a)-(d), 403(a), 98 Stat. 3391, 3392.)

MANUAL OF PATENT EXAMINING PROCEDURE

(Subsections (a), (b), (c), (d), and (e) amended Nov. 6, 1986, Public Law, 99-616, sec. 7, 100 Stat. 3486.)

(Subsection (c)(1) amended Dec. 10, 1991, Public Law 102-204, sec. 5(g)(2), 105 Stat. 1641.)

35 U.S.C. 372   National stage: Requirements and procedure.

(a)   All questions of substance and, within the scope of the requirements of the treaty and Regulations, procedure in an international application designating the United States shall be determined as in the case of national applications regularly filed in the Patent and Trademark Office.

(b)   In case of international applications designating but not originating in, the United States -

(1)   the Commissioner may cause to be reexamined questions relating to form and contents of the application in accordance with the requirements of the treaty and the Regulations;

(2)   the Commissioner may cause the question of unity of invention to be reexamined under section 121 of this title, within the scope of the requirements of the treaty and the Regulations; and

(3)   the Commissioner may require a verification of the translation of the international application or any other document pertaining to the application if the application or other document was filed in a language other than English.

(Added Nov. 14, 1975, Public Law 94-131, sec. 1, 89 Stat. 689; amended Nov. 8, 1984, Public Law 98-622, sec. 402(e), (f), 403(a), 98 Stat. 3392.)

35 U.S.C. 373   Improper applicant.

An international application designating the United States, shall not be accepted by the Patent and Trademark Office for the national stage if it was filed by anyone not qualified under chapter 11 of this title to be an applicant for the purpose of filing a national application in the United States. Such international applications shall not serve as the basis for the benefit of an earlier filing date under section 120 of this title in a subsequently filed application, but may serve as the basis for a claim of the right of priority under subsections (a) through (d) of section 119 of this title, if the United States was not the sole country designated in such international application.

(Added Nov. 14, 1975, Public Law 94-131, sec. 1, 89 Stat. 689; amended Nov. 8, 1984, Public Law 98-622, sec. 403(a), 98 Stat. 3392; Dec. 8, 1994, Public Law 103-465, sec. 532(c)(5), 108 Stat. 4987.)

35 U.S.C. 374   Publication of international application: Effect.

The publication under the treaty of an international application shall confer no rights and shall have no effect under this title other than that of a printed publication.

(Added Nov. 14, 1975, Public Law 94-131, sec. 1, 89 Stat. 689.)

35 U.S.C. 375   Patent issued on international application: Effect.

(a)   A patent may be issued by the Commissioner based on an international application designating the United States, in accordance with the provisions of this title. Subject to section 102(e) of this title, such patent shall have the force and effect of a patent issued on a national application filed under the provisions of chapter 11 of this title.

(b)   Where due to an incorrect translation the scope of a patent granted on an international application designating the United States, which was not originally filed in the English language, exceeds the scope of the international application in its original language, a court of competent jurisdiction may retroactively limit the scope of the patent, by declaring it unenforceable to the extent that it exceeds the scope of the international application in its original language.

(Added Nov. 14, 1975, Public Law 94-131, sec. 1, 89 Stat. 689.)

35 U.S.C. 376   Fees.

(a)   The required payment of the international fee and the handling fee, which amounts are specified in the Regulations, shall be paid in United States currency. The Patent and Trademark Office shall charge a national fee as provided in section 41(a), and may also charge the following fees:

(1)   A transmittal fee (see section 361(d));

(2)   A search fee (see section 361(d));

(3)   A supplemental search fee (to be paid when required);

(4)   A preliminary examination fee and any additional fees (see section 362(b)).

(5)   Such other fees as established by the Commissioner.

(b)   The amounts of fees specified in subsection (a) of this section, except the international fee and the handling fee, shall be prescribed by the Commissioner. He may refund any sum paid by mistake or in excess of the fees so specified, or if required under the treaty and the Regulations. The Commissioner may also refund any part of the search fee, the national fee, the preliminary examination fee and any additional fees, where he determines such refund to be warranted.

PATENT LAWS

(Added Nov. 14, 1975, Public Law 94-131, sec. 1, 89 Stat. 690, amended Nov. 8, 1984, Public Law 98-622, sec. 402(g), 403(a), 98 Stat. 3392; Nov. 6, 1986, Public Law 99-616, sec. 8(a) & (b), 100 Stat. 3486; Dec. 10, 1991, Public Law 102-204, sec. 5(g)(1), 105 Stat. 1640.)

●●●●●●●●●●●●●●●●●●●●●●●●●●●●●●●●●●●●

LAWS NOT IN TITLE 35, UNITED STATES CODE

18 U.S.C. 1001 Statements or entries generally.

Whoever, in any matter within the jurisdiction of any department or agency of the United States knowingly and willfully falsifies, conceals, or covers up by any trick, scheme, or device a material fact, or makes any false, fictitious or fraudulent statements or representations, or makes or uses any false writing or document knowing the same to contain any false, fictitious or fraudulent statement or entry, shall be fined under this title or imprisoned not more than five years, or both.

(Amended Sept. 13, 1994, Public Law 103-322, sec. 330016(1)(L), 108 Stat. 2147.)

18 U.S.C. 2071 Concealment, removal, or mutilation generally.

(a)   Whoever willfully and unlawfully conceals, removes, mutilates, obliterates, or destroys, or attempts to do so, or, with intent to do so takes and carries away any record, proceeding, map, book, paper, document, or other thing, filed or deposited with any clerk or officer of any court of the United States, or in any public office, or with any judicial or public officer of the United States, shall be fined under this title or imprisoned not more than three years, or both.

(b)   Whoever, having the custody of any such record, proceeding, map, book, document, paper, or other thing, willfully and unlawfully conceals, removes, mutilates, obliterates, falsifies, or destroys the same, shall be fined under this title or imprisoned not more than three years, or both; and shall forfeit his office and be disqualified from holding any office under the United States. As used in this subsection, the term "office" does not include the office held by any person as a retired officer of the Armed Forces of the United States.

(Amended Nov. 5, 1990, Public Law 101-510, sec. 552(a), 104 Stat. 1566; Sept. 13, 1994, Public Law 103-322, sec. 330016(1)(I), 108 Stat. 2147.)

Index